THEOLOGICAL
ETHICS
OF THE NEW
TESTAMENT

THEOLOGICAL
ETHICS
OF THE NEW
TESTAMENT

EDUARD LOHSE

Translated by
M. Eugene Boring

Fortress Press   Minneapolis

Translated by M. Eugene Boring from the German *Theologische Ethik des Neuen Testaments*. Copyright © W. Kohlhammer, Stuttgart 1988.

English Translation Copyright © 1991 by Augsburg Fortress

Scripture quotations, unless otherwise noted, are from the New Revised Standard Version of the Bible, copyright © 1989 by the Division of Christian Education of the National Council of Churches of Christ in the United States of America.

Library of Congress Cataloging-in-Publication Data

Lohse, Eduard, 1924–
    [Theologische Ethik des Neuen Testaments. English]
    Theological Ethics of the New Testament / Eduard Lohse :
  translated by M. Eugene Boring.
      p.   cm.
    Translation of: Theologische Ethik des Neuen Testaments.
    Includes index.
    ISBN 0-8006-2506-4 (alk. paper)
    1. Ethics in the Bible. 2. Bible. N.T.–Criticism,
  interpretation, etc. I. Title.
  BS2545.E8L6413 1991
  241–dc20   91-19232
                                            CIP

Manufactured in the U.S.A.   AF 1-2506

95   94   93   92   91   1   2   3   4   5   6   7   8   9   10

CONTENTS

Contents

Preface

In view of the increasing significance being attributed to ethical problems both in ecclesiastical discussions, and in society at large, the proclamation of the Christian message must be careful to reflect on contemporary ethical decisions in the light of the biblical witness. Christians of every time and place are charged with the responsibility of living their life "in a manner worthy of the gospel of Christ" (Phil. 1:27). The writings of the New Testament are a choir of witnesses that address us with a variety of voices. What they have to say needs to be understood first within the context of its own time and then, with considered judgment, translated into our time.

Providing the orientation necessary for this interpretive process is the goal of this basic outline. It is offered only as a survey, and concentrates on the essential points of contact without making any claim to touch every base. More detailed discussions pertaining to the historical development of the New Testament writings as well as their lines of theological thought may be found in other volumes originally published in this same German series, now available in English as Eduard Lohse, *The Formation of the New Testament* (translated by M. Eugene Boring, Nashville: Abingdon, 1981) and Eduard Lohse, *Grundriss der neutestamentlichen Theologie* (Stuttgart: Kohlhammer, 1984³).

—*Eduard Lohse*

Translator's Preface

I have mostly adopted the NRSV for English translations of the Bible, but have occasionally adopted other translations or rendered the Greek text into English in such a way as to correspond to the German translation made or used by Lohse, in order to bring out the nuance called for by his discussion.

I hereby express my heartful gratitude to Edward J. McMahon for able research assistance, including locating and checking English translations of ancient texts and for help in expanding the bibliographies; to Lana N. Byrd for superb secretarial work, including adjusting the biblical quotations to the NRSV text; and to James A. Farrar who gave the manuscript a "test reading" for his ethics classes, and made valuable suggestions regarding style and bibliography.

—*M. Eugene Boring*

THEOLOGICAL
ETHICS
OF THE NEW
TESTAMENT

NEW TESTAMENT ETHICS

Task and Method

The task of a theological ethic of the New Testament is to make clear the implications of confessing faith in Jesus as the crucified and resurrected Christ for the life and actions of the community of faith. Just as Christians are resolute in their hope that they live in the beginning of God's new world, they are aware that faith and love are to be expressed in the way they structure their lives. They are filled with the conviction that salvation is not to be obtained by their own doing and achievement, but as God's gracious gift for the sake of Christ, given to those who place their trust in him. Those who are poor and suffering, those who are sick and despairing, know themselves to be comforted through the message of God's mercy, a message that they experience not only as a gift, but as a challenge to lead their lives henceforth by harkening to this word of God.

Faith therefore understands itself in a positive way to be relieved of the compulsion of attempting to establish itself before God through pious conduct or by the accumulation of good works. It rather knows itself to be called into the liberty of the children of God. For Christians, however, implications for the conduct of life necessarily arise from this confidence. What sort of implications are we talking about?

The concept "ethics" (ἡ ἠθική) is not of Christian origin, but was coined in Greek philosophy, where it received its form, content, and connotations. Aristotle relates it to ἔθος (usage, custom), because "it is clear that none of the moral virtues is engendered in us by nature," for "the virtues are engendered in us neither by nature nor yet in violation of nature; nature gives us the capacity to receive them, and this capacity is brought to maturity by habit" (*Nic. Eth.* 1103a). Ethics is thus a discussion of the formation of human conduct. Since Aristotle, philosophical reflection, which aims at conceptually clear statements, has been concerned to set forth in detail how responsible human beings capable of critical judgment should live. It does this through reflection on fundamental issues and descriptions of concrete cases.

The New Testament does not know the term "ethics," but does know the task of reflecting on the nature of the moral life, and sometimes indicates what corresponding action should be. Thus the apostle Paul, in the oldest extant document from early Christianity (First Thessalonians, probably written in 50 C.E.), urges the congregation to strive constantly to live a life more and more pleasing to God. These Christians in a church founded only a short time previously by Paul had already received instructions in Christian living on how they "ought to live and to please God" (1 Thess. 4:1). "For," the apostle continues, "you know what instructions we gave you through the Lord Jesus" (v. 2). To this general instruction there is added a series of individual exhortations, which are then in turn strengthened by the reminder "to aspire to live quietly, to mind your own affairs, and to work with your hands, as we directed you, so that you may behave properly toward outsiders" (vv. 11–12). These statements include references to tradition and to specific commandments, and to that which is generally accepted as right conduct. The confession of Jesus as Lord is to be validated to "outsiders" by the credible conduct of Christians. If a positive evaluation of Christians by "outsiders" is expected, this means that the rules that govern good moral conduct in general are also to be observed by Christians. To live in accordance with the instructions given through the Lord Jesus (v. 2)—in this expression, the content of Christian ethics is briefly summarized. It refers to conduct of the individual (=personal ethics) as well as to the common life in the community (=social ethics), without separating either from the other. The commanding authority of the Lord applies to all realms of the life of believers.

All the writings of the New Testament are directed to a specific situation within the early Christian congregations, and are not systematic essays or tractates devoted to specific themes. Ethical instruction always occurs as exhortation to concrete action—also in those passages that do not have actual problems in view, but where catechetical instruction is developed as general Christian tradition in order to remind the community of that teaching intended as a description of a manner of life appropriate to the gospel in all circumstances.

Christian ethics appears in the New Testament in the mode of preaching and teaching. The particular sense in which ethics is represented by the modes of address and instruction must be inferred from the contexts of preaching and teaching that are presented in the writings of the New Testament as the elaboration of the one gospel. Thus on the one hand, ethical instruction can appear as the response to specific questions from the churches, or as criticism of particular events that have occurred in them—as for example in First Corinthians. On the other hand, ethical instruction is often given in established complexes of tradition that have been handed on orally in more or less fixed form—as for example in the twelfth and thirteenth chapters of Romans. Only when the *Sitz im Leben* (setting in life) that the individual units had in the context of early Christian exhortation is taken into consideration can their ethical instruction be appropriately determined.

Ethical statements are found primarily in the hortatory parts of the New Testament letters, but are also found in sections of the Gospels and in the Apocalypse, as well as in the Acts' depictions of early Christian life. The formal structure of ethical instruction can be very different from case to case. Instructions give the directions that responsible Christian life must follow; prohibitions show the boundaries that must not be transgressed. A series of proverbs and rules of wisdom gives a standard in relation to which one can orient one's own judgment. In catalogues of virtues and vices, lists of positive and negative terms

are ranged together in order that one can see what is to be done
and what is to be avoided. Parables and metaphorical expressions, which have been handed on principally in the tradition
of Jesus' sayings, can often be provided with a short application
that has proper moral conduct in view. Reports and narratives
not infrequently end with an application that makes the application concrete.

The multiplicity of forms in which ethical instruction
occurs in the writings of the New Testament points to the fact
that its content did not assume the formulation of a fixed legal
code, but was set forth in a living variety that corresponded to
the situations in which the Christian life had to find its way. The
fundamental and lasting characteristics of early Christian ethics
are to be distilled from these different forms in which moral
instruction was expressed. These fundamental characteristics —
with some divergence in detail — can be summarized in a relatively consistent sequence of ideas (see below, pp. 210–14).

While all the writings of the New Testament seek to
address the churches with the Christian gospel and to communicate the compelling call to commitment inherent in it, the contents of the ethical instruction contained in these documents
mostly have a long previous history. Their traditions are rooted
both in the Old Testament–Jewish tradition and in the world of
Greek philosophy and the ways of thinking current in popular
philosophy. This broad stream of traditions has incorporated
the experiences, reflection, and teaching of many generations
that have striven for right knowledge. But what is the connection
between this rich treasury of traditional ethical instruction and
the commanding authority of the Lord? How are traditional
rules for living to be related to a grounding for conduct that is
authentically Christian? And what is the distinctive character of
the Christian life when seen in the context of the understandings of the ancient world? One of the tasks of a New Testament
ethics is to indicate how traditional content not only received a
new grounding by being related to the gospel, but in essential
parts also had its intrinsic meaning apprehended in a new way.

It has been customary in formulating outlines of the subject of New Testament ethics to proceed in historical order — that
is, to begin with the preaching of Jesus or the kerygma of the

early church, then to advance to the great theological figures of the New Testament—Paul, the synoptic Gospels, and the Johannine writings—and to conclude with the so-called later writings: the Deutero-Paulines, the Catholic Letters, and the Apocalypse. Organizing the materials along these lines has a certain justification, in that it follows the chronology of events and can pursue the theological course of development of that period. A disadvantage inherent in this structure, however, is the difficulty of pointing out clearly enough the extensive common character of early Christian instruction and the systematic motifs that determined the development of that ethical content guided by the gospel that was considered valid and binding by all the New Testament witnesses. In addition, a delineation oriented strictly to chronology can allow the misunderstanding to slip in that the course of early Christian history represented a decline, in which the writings that originated later in the New Testament no longer attained the high level of theological power of expression found in the earlier witnesses. Although such a judgment may be appropriate in a few cases, we still cannot speak simply of a monodirectional development.

On the other hand, if one attempts to ignore the particular historical settings of the individual New Testament documents in constructing an outline of early Christian ethics, and to organize it in a strictly thematic manner, the result of such a construction is that the distinctive contours of the individual early Christian witnesses slip into the background or disappear altogether. This would produce an inappropriate impression of a homogenized early Christian ethic in which the distinctive traits in the different theological constructions of the New Testament writings could no longer be recognized.

I have attempted to avoid the disadvantages of each way of proceeding by choosing a middle way. The fundamental orientation is set forth by documenting the history-of-religions presuppositions and the principal systematic motifs, while the distinctive features of each witness are worked into the description of the ethical thought structures of each document. Since catechetical instruction in which ethical teaching is elaborated is determined to a large extent by tradition, we may assume that despite the different emphases there were constituent elements of early Christian ethics common to them all. These common elements are of course not so extensive that one can speak of an early Christian catechism presupposed by the different groupings of New Testament documents—at least not one that we can reconstruct (see below, p. 215). But it is probable that in the ethical instruction of early Christianity convictions came to expression that were generally shared. These basic affirmations were the common foundation of the ethical instructions found in the different witnesses of the New Testament. In the different contexts of their argumentation, each provided them with applications and emphases relevant to their particular situations. We now turn to the task of tracing out more precisely how these presuppositions and procedures for applying them were worked out in practice.

Suggestions for Further Reading

Childress, J. F. "Scripture and Christian Ethics." *Interpretation* 34 (1980): 371–80.

Curran, C., and R. McCormick, eds. *The Use of Scripture in Moral Theology: Readings in Moral Theology, No. 4.* New York/Ramsey: Paulist Press, 1984.

Daly, R., ed. *Christian Biblical Ethics.* New York/Ramsey: Paulist Press, 1984.

Gerhardsson, B. *The Ethos of the Bible.* Philadelphia: Fortress Press, 1981.

Hauerwas, S. "The Moral Authority of Scripture." *Interpretation* 34 (1980): 356–70.

Houlden, J. L. *Ethics and the New Testament.* New York: Oxford University Press, 1979.

Meeks, W. A. "Understanding Early Christian Ethics." *Journal of Biblical Literature* 105 (1986): 3–11.

Osborn, E. *Ethical Patterns in Early Christian Thought.* Cambridge: Cambridge University Press, 1976.

Sanders, J. T. *Ethics in the New Testament.* Philadelphia: Fortress Press, 1975.

Schnackenburg, R. *The Moral Teaching of the New Testament.* New York: Seabury, 1979 (reprint).

Schrage, W. *The Ethics of the New Testament.* Philadelphia: Fortress Press, 1988.

Chapter One

ETHICAL TRADITIONS IN THE CONTEXT OF THE NEW TESTAMENT

Old Testament and Judaism

The Old Testament writings know neither the concept of "ethics" nor a systematic development of moral prescriptions. To be sure, from the earliest days of Israel, Yahweh's command and will was proclaimed as binding regulation for the life of his people. If Israel's legal regulations and ethical rules are often closely related to the world of the ancient Near East from which they derive, still the sovereignty of the holy God, to the exclusion of all other gods as objects of worship and prayer, is the sole authority whose commanding word gives directions for all realms of life. A sufficient grounding for all moral instruction is therefore provided by the affirmation "I am Yahweh your God." Whether in the time of the patriarchs, or in the process of conquest and settlement of the land, or during the rule of judges and kings, or the exile or the postexilic new beginning, irrespective of the course of historical conditions, Israel was constantly bound to the commanding holiness of its God, which determined both personal ethical conduct and the social life of the community. God makes sure that his law is not despised but obediently followed, and punishes both its transgression and its misuse.

How human life and business is to be conducted under the commanding holiness of the only God was the constant subject of the preaching of the prophets, as they confronted Israel in the various situations of the course of their life through the centuries. Over against superficial trafficking with Yahweh's commands and injustice perpetrated with no consideration of the rights of others, Amos announced God's judgment and called to repentance: "Seek me and live" (5:4). Unless a radical change occurs in Israel's life at the last moment, there will be no escape from the deserved judgment of God.

What comprises the will of God in detail cannot yet be documented in the prophetic preaching by referring to a formulated law, since the fixation of the legal sections of the Old Testament was not achieved until a later time. Still, the admonishing and demanding instruction of the God of Israel (the Torah) is everywhere presupposed. The people know of the holiness of its God. It therefore knows that this holiness must be respected, and that one must conduct oneself accordingly.

Micah 6:8 is formulated as a virtual summarizing rule of ethical instruction: "He has showed you, O mortal, what is good; and what does the Lord require of you, but to do justice, and to love kindness, and to walk humbly with your God?" Just as the distinction between good and evil is the point of orientation for all ethical thinking and doing since time immemorial, so no one can get by with the excuse that they did not know what to do or refrain from doing. The people of Israel have received this in a clear and explicit revelation from their God.

The moral demands directed to the people by the commanding will of God are summarized in the law. Prior to the process of written formulation of the law lay a long time of oral instruction and formation of traditions. The rigid regulations of the commandments were introduced by the expression "you shall" or "you shall not" and grounded in the sovereignty of the holy God who brought his people out of Egypt, out of slavery. The obligatory demands of the holy God were often summarized in compact series, and were expressed in concentrated form in the Decalogue. Israel shall have no other gods besides its God and Lord, shall make no image or likeness of God, shall neither bow down to nor serve them. "For I the Lord your God am a jealous God, punishing children for the iniquity of parents to the third and fourth generation of those who reject me, but showing steadfast love to the thousandth generation of those who love me and keep my commandments" (Exod. 20:5-6). The name of the God of Israel must not be misused, the Sabbath must be kept holy, parents must be honored. God's law forbids killing, adultery, stealing, speaking false witness against one's neighbor, and coveting the neighbor's house, wife, servant, maid, ox, donkey, or anything else (Exod. 20:7-17).

These declarations were proclaimed by priests at holy places, and repeated from generation to generation. They were explained, interpreted, and applied to the multicolored variety of individual cases that occur in the fullness of life. In view of the many-sided problems and experiences of everyday life, people carried on fundamental discussions attempting to clarify which cases constituted a transgression of the commandment and the conditions under which one remained within the boundaries set by the law. Israel was convinced that God had given his law to his people to show them the way of life. Whoever follows it will enjoy God's good pleasure. It was therefore advisable to build a fence around the prohibitions, in order that one would be warned in time, before coming into the danger zone, that forbidden area to be avoided at all costs. Just as the blessing of God is promised to those who fulfill the commandments, so the one is cursed "who does not confirm the words of this law by doing them" (RSV) (Deut. 27:26).

Alongside the unambiguous regulatory command expressed in the apodictic form of a clear "you shall" or "you shalt not," ancient Israel also knew legal stipulations formulated casuistically, what was to be done under this or that condition: "Whoever kidnaps a person, whether that person has been sold or is still held in possession, shall be put to death. Whoever curses father or mother shall be put to death" (Exod. 21:16-17). "When a slaveowner strikes the eye of a male or female slave, destroying it, the owner shall let the slave go a free person to compensate for the eye" (Exod. 21:26). In these and other similarly formulated legal stipulations, we find the deposit of legal decisions as they had been worked out in the time-tested practice of the ancient Near East. Within the circle of the gatherings of the experienced men of the community, traditional rules were discussed and applied in view of new cases that had arisen, and in this manner the legal tradition was developed further. It was on this basis that one could then decide how to pronounce judgment as to right and wrong when particular cases called for it.

These traditions, repeated, expanded, and constantly rethought in the light of new cases through the centuries, were finally written down in different textual collections, the latest of which is represented by the so-called priestly strand of the law. The prescriptions and traditions bound together in the Pentateuch attained general acknowledgment as the first part of the developing canon of holy Scripture. Only by a conscientious following of the law can Israel fulfill the will of its God and live worthily of his calling.

Alongside collections of laws and commandments there was a broad stream of insights from the wisdom tradition, which had been discussed and tested through the generations. In this process, too, many rules from the surrounding culture of the ancient Near East had been adopted and added to the treasure of wisdom instruction gathered under the rubric "the fear of the Lord is the beginning of knowledge" (Prov. 1:7).

From the collection of wisdom sayings, young people were supposed to learn how one rightly lives. As Proverbs say:

> My child, if you accept my words
>   and treasure up my commandments within you,
> making your ear attentive to wisdom
>   and inclining your heart to understanding;
> if you cry out for insight,
>   and raise your voice for understanding,
> if you seek it like silver,
>   and search for it as for hidden treasures—
> then you will understand the fear of the Lord
>   and find the knowledge of God.

For the LORD gives wisdom;
>from his mouth come knowledge and understanding.
>>(Prov. 2:1–6)

Reason and insight know how to evaluate the appropriate way to live, when judged by the standards of traditional common sense. They teach one not to withhold help from the needy, when it is in one's power to do good (Prov. 3:27). They urge one not to plan evil against the neighbor (Prov. 3:29), or to associate with the godless and scornful. They lead to authentic wisdom and show the way to right knowledge. They warn against sloth, laziness, or violating the rules of fair play, against harlotry or adultery, and admonish one not to forsake the way of life marked out by God's command. "In Israel, there are certain things that are simply not done"–this rule provides an unambiguous norm (Gen. 34:7; Judg. 20:6, 10; 2 Sam. 13:12).

The multiplicity of commandments stands under the commanding sovereignty of Yahweh. God makes sure that transgressions do not go unpunished, and confers his blessing on those who live according to his law. Human community life, which must provide for the welfare of both the individual and the society as a whole, can only flourish if it is oriented to the God who is the creator and preserver of heaven and earth, and is determined by God's will and commandment not only in worship, but in everyday life. The command to love one's neighbor as oneself (Lev. 19:18) also provides a criterion by which insight can determine both what is good and the corresponding action that it requires. To the liturgical question, "Who may dwell on your [God's] holy hill?" the answer is given:

Those who walk blamelessly, and do what is right,
>and speak truth from their heart;
who do not slander with their tongue,
>and do no evil to their friends,
>>nor take up a reproach against their neighbors;
in whose eyes the wicked are despised,
>but who honor those who fear the LORD;
who stand by their oath even to their hurt;

> who do not lend money at interest,
>   and do not take a bribe against the innocent.
> Those who do these things shall never be moved.
>   (Ps. 15:2–5)

The ancient Near Eastern world was acquainted with comparable lists, like the one found in the Egyptian Book of the Dead. There a long confessional statement, to be presented before the judges of the dead, reads:

> I have committed no injustice against my fellow human
>   beings,
> I have not blasphemed the gods,
> I have not oppressed the poor,
> I have not violated the tabu of a god,
> I have not blackened the name of any servant to his
>   superior,
> I have not caused people to be sick,
> I have not made people cry,
> I have not killed,
> I have not told others to kill,
> I have not caused anybody's suffering,
> I have not falsified measures, either the bushel or
>   acreage,
> I have not taken over anyone's field,
> I have not tampered with the scales, etc. (Saying 125)

As in a guide for the examination of one's conscience prior to confession, the list of possible infractions is examined point by point, in order to assure oneself that one has not incurred guilt by having committed any of the listed transgressions. In ancient Egypt, a magical idea was associated with the recitation of this list. Whoever brings this list to consciousness and recites it responsibly is separated from their transgressions. By bringing before one's eyes the kind of questioning to which one will be subject in the last judgment, one becomes aware of what is to be done and avoided in daily life here and now (see below, p. 123).

In the same way, worshipers in ancient Israel clarify for themselves what must be done and avoided in order to be permitted to walk in the holy courts of God's temple. Psalm 24 declares who is permitted to stand in the holy place:

> those who have clean hands and pure hearts,
> who do not lift up their souls to what is false,
> and do not swear deceitfully. (v. 4)

In postbiblical Judaism it was the law as inscribed in the Pentateuch and interpreted in the tradition that was regarded as the valid direction that determined all of life. In obedience to the divine law Israel becomes aware of its election and assigned task. The Torah was not only honored as revered material taken over from the past, it was followed as the valid instruction for the people of God in the present. What was to be considered and executed as God's will was explored and decided in the detailed and comprehensive discussions of the scribes. The binding authority of legal prescriptions, refined in ever more precise ways, and later written down in the Mishnah and Talmud had in each case to be established by basing them on the Pentateuch or attempting to derive them from it exegetically. The tradition thereby attained to the same authority as the written law, since both—the Torah of oral tradition and the Torah preserved in writing—were traced back to the Sinai event where both were given to Moses, so that the one will of God sounded forth from both.

Since the God of Israel has made known the divine will in the law, the relation of human beings to God can be found and ordered only by their relation to the law. The law simply regulates everything that must occur, prescribes the way in which not only prayer and worship but daily tasks must be done, and leaves no possible case that might arise out of consideration. In a carefully nuanced casuistry, carried on in constantly more refined ramifications, prescriptions for every situation in life are given. The process always presupposes that the law can in fact be fulfilled and that people can in fact keep its commandments. The use of the patriarchs as models—especially Abraham and Moses—shows that the righteous are in fact capable of keeping the law in all respects. As a result they receive the divine reward; on the last day they will be raised from the dead and enter into the life of the future world.

The law is a gift, the proof of God's love for Israel. By this means God opened up the possibility for his people to accomplish good works, earn merit, and attain righteousness. The law therefore means life, and without the law there is no life. It is only through the Torah that human beings can attain fellowship with God and preserve it in the daily business of life. For "when two sit together and discuss words of Torah, the Shekinah (that is, God) is present with them" (Aboth III, 2).

Since in practice many Jews did not follow the law rigorously enough, groups of religious believers formed smaller groups in order to observe the law with strictness. Thus the Pharisees separated themselves from the rest of the people, who did not sufficiently know the law (cf. John 7:49), and took upon themselves the obligations of keeping not only the Ten Commandments, but the purity regulations observed by the priests as well. By their obedience to the law they sought to represent the true people of God, in hope for the arrival of the messianic age. The rigorous understanding of the law held by the Essenes, the Qumran community, went substantially beyond even that of the Pharisees. It was demanded of each member of the community that *all* commands of the Torah—the whole law, not just the Decalogue—be kept. The one will of God, to which persons must give undivided obedience, was contained in the multiplicity of commands. On the basis of catalogues that delineate both good and evil conduct, they can derive a clear orientation as to the kind of instruction given by the law.

Basically all the commands and ordinances of the law have the same significance and the same rank; none of them may be carelessly violated. Since scribal expositions had elaborated the divine will in 613 positive and negative rules, a compelling need must have been felt for some kind of summary of all the laws amid this maze of commandments. This issue was discussed by various rabbis in different ways, and answered by R. Hillel (ca. 20 B.C.E.) with the brief statement "What is hateful to you, do not do to your neighbor. That is the whole Torah; while the rest is the commentary thereof" (Sabb. 31a). And

Rabbi Akiba (d. ca. 135 C.E.) said: "You shall love your neighbor as yourself. That is a great and comprehensive principle in the Torah" (Sipra Rab. Lev. 19:18). To relate to one's fellow human beings as one who expects good from them as well—this tried and true rule, which could serve as the primary guideline for one's own conduct, circulated as the advice of experienced teachers (*Letter of Aristeas* 207).

The Old Testament is, on the one hand, imbued with the view that humanity owes a debt of love to the one and only God (Deut. 6:5), and on the other hand, teaches the love of neighbor as oneself (Lev. 19:18). In the Old Testament, however, these two commands are not related to each other. It was first in the kind of reflections that were taking place in the Jewish discussions of the time of Jesus that people began to connect these two commands. Thus we find in the *Testament of the Twelve Patriarchs:* "Love the Lord and your neighbor, be compassionate toward poverty and sickness" (Test. Issachar 5:2; cf. 7:6). Or it was said: "Fear the Lord and love your neighbor" (Test. Benjamin 3:2) and "Throughout all your life love the Lord, and one another with a pure heart" (Test. Dan 5:3; cf. also Test. Zebulon 5:1–2). These statements show that the loving fear of God and the helping deed shown to the neighbor are inherently related to each other. All the same, the scribal discussion of the profusion of commandments was not able to isolate one as the greatest that summarized and determined all the others. God's will was encountered in each of the many commandments; God's will was respected and done by the careful observance of them individually. To be sure, the reflections on how one knows the divine will raised the question of the commandment that includes all others within itself. But the answers given to this question remain stuck in the conviction that all the commandments stand side by side in the same rank.

Suggestions for Further Reading

Alt, A. "The Origins of Israelite Law." In *Essays on Old Testament History and Religion*, pp. 79–132. Oxford: Basil Blackwell, 1966.
Buber, M. *On the Bible.* Nahum N. Glatzer, ed. New York: Schocken, 1968.

Charlesworth, J., ed. *The Old Testament Pseudepigrapha,* 2 vols. Garden City: Doubleday, 1983, 1985.

Collins, J. J. *Between Athens and Jerusalem.* New York: Crossroad, 1983.

Crenshaw, J. L. *Old Testament Wisdom.* Atlanta: John Knox Press, 1981.

Falk, Z. W. *Introduction to Jewish Law of the Second Commonwealth,* 2 parts. Leiden: E. J. Brill, 1972, 1978.

Kaiser, W. C. *Toward Old Testament Ethics.* Grand Rapids: Zondervan, 1983.

Knierim, R. "The Problem of Ancient Israel's Prescriptive Legal Traditions." *Semeia* 45 (1989): 7–27.

Koch, K. *The Prophets.* 2 vols. Philadelphia: Fortress Press, 1982, 1984.

Neusner, J. *Judaism: The Evidence of the Mishnah.* 2nd ed. Atlanta: Scholars Press, 1988.

———. *Vanquished Nation, Broken Spirit. The Virtues of the Heart in Formative Judaism.* Cambridge: Cambridge University Press, 1987.

Rad, G. von. *Old Testament Theology. I. The Theology of Israel's Historical Traditions,* Edinburgh and London: Oliver & Boyd, 1962.

Schiffman, L. *Sectarian Law in the Dead Sea Scrolls.* Brown Judaic Studies 33. Chico: Scholars Press, 1983.

Greek-Hellenistic World

In continual debate with the sophists, who claimed to be able to direct people along the paths that lead to a successful life, Socrates repeatedly raised the question of what is truly good, and thereby pointed to the basis of all responsible conduct. The *Dialogues,* in which Plato described his teacher's works, illustrate Socrates' ability to bring his conversation partners to insights from within themselves. He believed that through critical reflection and incorruptible pursuit after knowledge of the true good, the path to a morally responsible life can be found. This teaching is guided by the conviction that rational insight must result in a virtuous life consistent with it. From the knowledge of the good, a corresponding virtuous life is supposed to result. Thus Socrates always relates the discussion to everyday life and its decisive questions, and thereby laid the foundations of a philosophically reflective ethic.

By taking up and developing the ideas of Socrates and Plato, Aristotle elaborated the issue of the knowledge of the good into an academic discipline that renders a methodological account of the judgments it makes. In this process he gives up Socrates' confidence that the knowledge of the good must necessarily lead to corresponding conduct. Rather, he considers the important factor in ethical orientation to be the formation of habits, the right kind of training as well as to the right kind of insight. Ethical reflection is focused on knowledge of virtue (ἀρετή), which alone can lead to true happiness (εὐδαιμονία). "But human goodness" — as he defines ἀρετή — "means in our view excellence of soul, not excellence of body; also our definition of happiness is an activity of the soul" (*Nic. Eth.* 1102a). The happiness that is striven for does not in itself provide any satisfying blessedness, but a life in circumstances and conditions that by poise and measured response facilitate a distinctive manner of life (1099b).

Excess on either extreme would be detrimental to happiness. That applies on the one hand to burdens, losses, and disappointments that are too severe, but on the other hand it also applies to having too many material goods or to excess in food or drink. If these are just as damaging to health as is poverty or malnutrition, "temperance (σωφροσύνη) and courage (ἀνδρεία) are destroyed by excess and deficiency, and preserved by the observance of the mean" (1104a). Ethical reflection must therefore seek a balance between extreme positions, which are to be avoided. This golden mean between cowardice and recklessness is defined as courage (ἀνδρεία) (1107b). The mean between being too sensitive to pleasure and pain and not being sensitive enough is called temperance (σωφροσύνη), the mean between lusting after money and wanting to give it all away is called generosity, the mean between the vanity that seeks excessive honor and the smallness of soul that is not interested in it at all can be called "greatness of soul." There is also a virtuous middle ground between fits of temper and apathy (1107b/1108a). It is no easy task to maintain one's balance between the possible extremes of conduct; the center of a circle can be determined not by just anyone, but only by those skilled in geometry (1109a).

A morally responsible life will give attention to determining the available possibilities, and conduct itself accordingly (1131a). Even so, the right is still considered to be the balance between extremes, just as in business the right is the mean between loss and excess profit (1132a). A happy life will therefore be directed toward virtue (1177a), and moral conduct will be oriented to laws that serve the common welfare, whether they are written or unwritten. The logical outcome of ethics is thus politics. Since human beings are by nature social, political beings (φύσει πολιτικός 1097b), who experience their happiness in right conduct and dealings with each other, ethics receives its ultimate determination in political action, and human happiness finds its fulfillment not in an individualistic life, "but also [with] one's parents and children and wife, and one's friends and fellow citizens in general." Such a life can be called self-sufficient in the most authentic sense. Happiness represented by the Ideal Good is "something final and self-sufficient, is the End at which all actions aim" (ibid.).

Discussions within the philosophical schools of the Hellenistic world manifested considerable interest in practical problems. Ethics was thus a major theme, since it attempted to answer the question of the highest good and the goal of life.

The teaching of Epicurus (ca. 342–270 B.C.E.) was oriented in a decidedly individualistic direction. He advised people to withdraw from public life and to remain in the tranquility of a private existence, since there is no higher good than to simply enjoy life. By "enjoyment" one should understand that state of human well-being attained by one who has found true wisdom and thus knows how to find and do the right in every situation. Since excessive desire could disturb this condition of equilibrium, it is a matter of clever reflection to figure out what should be chosen and what should be avoided, and to clear all obstacles out of the way that could disrupt a tranquil inner life. The fulfillment of the meaning of life is not given to the human soul in some transcendent world; it is experienced in this world or not at all. Since a balanced, harmonious life can only be found on an individual basis, every person has the right to seek such a life without taking the community into consideration.

The teaching of the Stoics can be clearly distinguished from that of the Epicureans. To be sure, they too were concerned to respond to the individual's question about the meaning of life, but they attempted to develop criteria for a way of life that was related to the common welfare. By means of this orientation the Stoic philosophy achieved extraordinary significance for the Hellenistic-Roman world. The Stoic doctrine could be applied by the practical common sense of the Romans, who sought for philosophically grounded directions for a statecraft and administrative practice for their far-flung empire that was both grounded in philosophy and adequately just. Such an ethic could be used by members of other national groups in the different parts of the empire who were concerned to formulate a cosmopolitan consciousness. The Stoic philosophers knew how to carry on such discussions not only in small groups of educated people, but also how to converse seriously with people in the street and gatherings in the marketplace. In statement and counterstatement, in the normal course of question and answer, a compact train of thought was developed that could persuade the hearers and offer concrete help for the conduct of their practical life.

A characteristic example of such instruction developed in oral dialogue is provided by the discourses (diatribes) of Epictetus, who taught at the end of the first and beginning of the second century c.e. They were written down not by himself, but by his students, so that his writings reflect the lively speech of oral discourse. The teaching of Epictetus directed to a wide spectrum of hearers was summarized in a brief handbook (*Enchiridion*), which presents his understanding of the most important basic ideas of Stoic doctrine. This booklet can therefore serve as an exemplary witness of the popular philosophical teaching in the period of the early development of Christianity.

According to the *Enchiridion*, the most important principle is to differentiate between those things that we can do something about and those things not at our disposal. If one knows how to distinguish what can be molded and changed by our own decision, and what we must simply accept as given, then it is possible to walk with tranquil heart into the face of the unavoidable, but to act justly in the realm where we can make responsible decisions. "You must" — so Epictetus taught his disciples — "be one person, either good or bad; you must labour to improve either your own governing principle or externals; you must work hard either on the inner man, or on things outside; that is, play either the role of a philosopher or else that of a layman [ἰδιώτης, cf. 1 Cor. 14:16]" (*Ench.* 29). Philosophers will relate to their fellow human beings in a studied, deliberate, and therefore superior attitude. Has your brother done you wrong? "Very well then, maintain the relation that you have toward him; and do not consider what he is doing, but what you will have to do, if your moral purpose will be in harmony with nature" (*Ench.* 30). Right judgment will be oriented to the laws of nature (φύσις) and will strive to be in harmony with them. Whoever proceeds according to this rule will know how to discover his or her duty (τὸ καθῆκον) to the closest relative, to the neighbor, to fellow citizens, or to those in authority. It is always a matter of distinguishing between that which is in our hands to do something about, and that which is not, and to refer to "good" and "bad" in our conduct purely in terms of what we can influence and what we cannot.

In things that pertain to the body, the following advice is given: "Take only as much as your bare need requires, I mean such things as food, drink, clothing, shelter, and household slaves; but cut down everything that is for outward show or luxury" (*Ench.* 33). In summary, Epictetus says:

> Signs of one who is making progress are: He censures no one, praises no one, blames no one, finds fault with no one, says nothing about himself as though he were somebody or knew something. When he is hampered or prevented, he blames himself. And if anyone compliments him, he smiles to himself at the person complimenting; while if any one censures him, he makes no defense. . . . In a word, he keeps guard against himself as though he were his own enemy lying in wait (*Ench.* 48).

He therefore gives as the rule of life:

> Make up your mind, therefore, before it is too late, that the fitting thing for you to do is to live as a mature man who is making progress, and let everything that seems to you to be best be for you a law that must not be transgressed. . . . This is the

way Socrates [his model was always held in high esteem among the Stoics] became what he was, by paying attention to nothing but his reason (λόγος) in everything that he encountered. And even if you are not yet a Socrates, still you ought to live as one who wishes to be a Socrates (*Ench.* 51).

Thoughtful, deliberate conduct, guided by the insight of reason into the cosmic order, wants neither to live a life formed purely by individualism nor to pay too much attention to what others think (*Ench.* 47). It should rather contribute to people's living together in harmony within a just order, with all serving the common good according to their competence and possibilities.

By its alignment with practical concerns, Stoic ethics, which taught people how to perceive their life's task in agreement with natural law, experienced wide dissemination in the world of late antiquity. Limited by the boundaries of neither city nor nation, it manifested points of contact with the Cynic view that human beings should be content and live modestly. Cynic and Stoic teachings were united into a Cynic-Stoic popular philosophy that was offered by itinerant teachers as practical help for living. They pointed out human failings, in order to call people to reflect on them and offer them a solid moral teaching by means of which they could order their lives. This doctrine was elaborated in lively discussions and discourses, in order to compel unsophisticated hearers to follow the argument and to convince them of its persuasiveness.

The doctrine of the law based on the Jewish Scriptures was combined in the Hellenistic synagogue with this popular philosophical ethic to form a Jewish doctrine of virtue that preserved its Israelite heritage, but at the same time made its legal piety understandable to the surrounding Greek culture. The Jewish communities that had emerged everywhere in the Mediterranean world made extensive use of the Greek language, and often lost their knowledge of Hebrew or Aramaic. They not only read the books of their law in Greek, but also had to think in Greek concepts and to attempt with their help to explain what constituted the ground and content of their faith. Above all, however, they had to render account to themselves as to how they could hold fast to the faith of their ancestors amid a strange new world. Their teachers worked at finding and exhibiting the points of contact and agreement between the traditional law by which Israel lived and the knowledge obtained by the philosophers, especially their moral instruction. They were concerned to demonstrate that the Greek thinkers were ultimately disciples of Moses. The Torah was supposed to be not only of an earlier origin, but to have a higher rank, and thus was to be honored as the fount of all wisdom and knowledge.

Complicated exegetical techniques applied to Scripture, which often made use of artful allegorizing, was intended to document in detail that philosophical insights were not only in harmony with the moral commands of the law, but were dependent on and had been determined by their content. This theory enabled the members of the Jewish community to respond to emerging feelings of inferiority, and replace them with pride and self-confidence. They need not be ashamed of their peculiarities, but on the contrary could make the claim that they were following the oldest and most important teaching in existence and shaping their lives according to its instruction.

The literature of Hellenistic Judaism had extensive branches, the influence of some of them being felt even in the synagogues of Palestine. Only a fraction of this voluminous literature has been preserved; most works have unfortunately been lost. Alongside the writings of the religious philosopher Philo of Alexandria, who stands out as the striking individual from the circle of contemporaneous authors and whose works exercised a strong effect on the formation of theological doctrine in early Christianity, there are also many fragments and smaller texts that document the ways the intellectual orientation of the Hellenistic synagogue was constructed. A characteristic example of the views disseminated in the Judaism of that time is presented by the *Sentences of Pseudo-Phocylides*. The 230 lines of this document are transmitted as verses composed in Greek in the name of Phocylides, a Greek author of the sixth century B.C.E. An anonymous author, who apparently composed these verses about the time of the birth of Christ, placed these sentences in the mouth of a Greek thinker who lived centuries earlier in order to show that already in ancient times the wisdom of the Greeks was influenced by the spirit of Moses, with the result that Jewish Torah and Greek ethic were thoroughly in agreement. In this process, the ceremonial parts of the law were ignored, and the interest of the author is directed exclusively to the issue of how one should so lead one's life that it pleases God and receives God's blessing.

The first part of this didactic poem makes unmistakable allusions to the Decalogue. There are versions of the prohibition of adultery and murder, as well as the commandment not to enrich oneself by unjust means, not to lie, and to always speak the truth (3–8). These instructions are, however, joined with the exhortation to "be content with what you have" (6), reminiscent of the oft-repeated advice of the Stoics. On the one hand, Old Testament tradition is brought over into Greek verse. Thus we find: "If you judge evilly, subsequently God will judge you" (11), or "Give to the poor man at once, and do not tell him to come tomorrow" (22). On the other hand, sentences from the popular philosophy are united to Old Testament-Jewish wisdom: "The love of money is the mother of all evil. Gold and silver are always a lure for human beings. Gold, originator of evil, destroyer of life, crushing all things, would that you were not a desirable calamity to mortals!" (42–45).

One God stands over all—in the confession to the one God, Israel's faith is expressed and then explained with the following predicates: "The only God is wise and mighty and at the same time rich in blessings" (54). People who confess faith in this God should fashion their manner of life in association with those with whom they share their lives. Thus counsel is given against remaining unmarried, so that one will not some-day die nameless, but will hand on life to the next generation (175–76). In contrast to the widespread attitude and practice, abortion is strictly forbidden, as is the killing of newborns (184–86). One should not deal harshly with children, but treat them gently (207). In everything, care should be taken to preserve good customs. "If a child is a boy, do not let locks grow on his head. Do not braid his crown nor the cross knots at the top of his head. Long hair is not fit for boys, but for voluptuous women" (210–12). One should be considerate not only in relation to children, but also in dealing with slaves: "Provide your slave with the tribute he owes his stomach. Apportion to a slave what is appointed so that he will do as you wish" (223–24). The conclusion promises that whoever lives by these and other instructions contained in Phocylides' *Sentences* will "live out (your) life well, . . . up to the threshold of old age" (230).

This didactic poem can illustrate how Old Testament–Jewish wisdom, based on God's command, has entered into a close bond with Hellenistic popular philosophy. This union could be made all the more easily since both realms of thought were concerned with the formulation of a righteous life in conscious responsibility for others. Such ethical instruction, in the forms it had already attained in the Hellenistic synagogue and beyond, was present to all who were interested as a rich resource of ethical traditions for early Christianity, from which it in turn could both learn and further develop.

Suggestions for Further Reading

Burkert, W. *Greek Religion.* Cambridge: Harvard University Press, 1985.

Fiore, B. *The Function of Personal Example in the Socratic and Pastoral Epistles,* pp. 26–164. Rome: Biblical Institute Press, 1986.

Fitzgerald, J. T. *Cracks in an Earthen Vessel. An Examination of the Catalogues of Hardships in the Corinthian Correspondence,* pp. 47–116. Atlanta: Scholars Press, 1988.

Hengel, M. *Judaism and Hellenism.* Philadelphia: Fortress Press, 1981.

MacMullen, R. *Paganism in the Roman Empire.* New Haven: Yale University Press, 1981.

Malherbe, A. J. "Greco-Roman Religion and Philosophy and the New Testament." In *The New Testament and Its Modern Interpreters,* E. J. Epp and G. W. MacRae, eds., pp. 3–26. Philadelphia: Fortress Press, 1989; Atlanta: Scholars Press, 1989.

———. *Moral Exhortation, a Greco-Roman Sourcebook.* Philadelphia: Westminster Press, 1986.

Martin, L. *Hellenistic Religions.* New York: Oxford University Press, 1987.

Reale, G. *A History of Ancient Philosophy. III. The Systems of the Hellenistic Age.* Albany: SUNY, 1985.

Rudolph, K. *Gnosis: The Nature and History of Gnosticism,* pp. 204–73. San Francisco: Harper & Row, 1984.

van der Horst, P. W. *The Sentences of Pseudo-Phocylides.* Leiden: E. J. Brill, 1978.

Chapter Two

THE CHRISTOLOGICAL GROUNDING OF EARLY CHRISTIAN ETHICS

Words of the Lord

The early Christian community confessed its faith in the crucified Christ as the resurrected Lord. The content of this confession, "Jesus is Lord," corresponds to the faith that "God raised him from the dead" (Rom. 10:9). This means that whoever believes in the crucified Christ confesses him as the living Lord, and conversely that only those can confess Christ as Lord who have accepted the proclamation of his resurrection from the dead. Affirming the message that Jesus was raised from the dead includes the affirmation that he is the Lord. His lordship is determinative for every area of the life of the believer.

Jesus' words were conceived as the present address of the Lord to his own. Because Jesus of Nazareth was proclaimed and confessed as the living Lord, his words were understood as the encouraging voice of the risen Christ sounding forth in the here and now, whose call to discipleship must be met by faith and obedient response.

Whenever a word of the Lord was drawn from the oral tradition that circulated in the Christian community and introduced into preaching, it communicated binding authority. This does not mean that in every case it could be proven that the saying in fact could be traced back to the historical Jesus. Rather, the word of the Lord demonstrated its obligatory force by the power of truth with which it addressed the situation.

Binding authority was also claimed for those words of the Lord that were spoken by Christian prophets speaking in the name of the Lord. By making use of the biblical expression "thus says the Lord," they mediated to the community the message of the risen Lord Jesus that was valid and appropriate for the present. In the Apocalypse each of the seven churches in Asia Minor is addressed with a prophetic message appropriate to its situation and called to obedience to the exalted Lord by a word spoken with authority (Rev. 2–3). Whether prophetic directives presented in the name of the Lord could be legitimately accepted as authentically from (the risen) Jesus was an issue that had to be decided from case to case by the churches, by means of the gift of distinguishing the spirits. Not everyone who said "Lord, Lord" could legitimately appeal to his authority (Matt. 7:21–22). By their fruits – good or bad – the church could identify whether it was a true prophet who spoke, or a false one.

Sayings of Jesus were used especially in the context of ethical exhortations. Sometimes moral instruction alluded to words of the Lord without explicitly quoting them as such. It was thoroughly appropriate to the character of individual sayings that they were worked into the mesh of Christian instruction having to do with right conduct. Thus in the section Romans 12:14–21 are found several clear echoes of sayings of Jesus that are also transmitted in the Gospels "Bless those who persecute you; bless and do not curse them" (v. 14=Luke 6:28); "Do not repay anyone evil for evil" (v. 17a=Luke 6:29; Matt. 5:39b–41); "live peaceably with all" (v. 18=Mark 9:50; Matt. 5:9); "Beloved, never avenge yourselves, but leave room for the wrath of God" (v. 19=Luke 6:27a, 35; Matt. 5:44a). The repeated appeal to the love commandment (Gal. 5:14; Rom. 13:8–10) alludes to the saying of Jesus without making it explicit.

The ethical instruction of the Letter of James also contains many statements that contain echoes and allusions of words of the Lord. Although there is never an explicit quotation formula or use of the name of Jesus, the points of contact are clearly discernable. Both forbid oaths and command the disciple to say a simple yes or no (James 5:12=Matt. 5:34–37). Positive assurance that God hears prayer is found in the words of Jesus (Matt. 7:7) and in James 1:5. Jesus' summons to obey his word (Matt. 7:24–27) corresponds to the challenge to be doers of the word and not hearers only (James 1:22). Both Jesus and James give the strictest prohibitions against judging the brother or sister (Matt. 7:1–2; James 4:11–12).

These examples, to which more could be added, are sufficient evidence that words of Jesus could be incorporated into catechetical contexts without explicit indications. They were presented as a part of the ethical teaching of the community as instruction that provides an unambiguous point of orientation for the Christian life.

Where words of the Lord are clearly identified by an introductory formula, their binding authority with regard to their ethical content is emphasized. They are thereby consistently couched in such a way that they address the present situation of the community. Thus in Acts the responsibility of attending to the needs of the weaker members of the community is made more pointed by appealing to a saying of Jesus: "It is more blessed to give than to receive" (Acts 20:35). In the context of correcting the eschatological ideas of the community, Paul first refers to the common Christian confession: "since we believe that Jesus died and rose again, even so, through Jesus, God will bring with him those who have died" (1 Thess. 4:14). Alongside this appeal to the kerygma, he then places a "word of the Lord" as having equal weight. The saying of Jesus, intended to strengthen the encouragement derived from the kerygma, affirms "that we who are alive, who are left until the coming of the Lord, will by no means precede those who have died" (v. 15).

The we-form, which binds the apostle and the community together, is to be attributed to the hand of Paul. The original form of this word of the Lord might likely have declared that those still alive at the parousia would have no advantage. This saying would then have been elaborated by the addition of a piece of apocalyptic tradition that dealt with the appearing of the Lord, the resurrection of the dead, and the reunion of the Lord with his own (vv. 16–17). Although Paul ascribes compelling power to this word of the Lord, and regards it as settling the argument, he saw nothing to prevent him from changing the wording and so formulating it from his perspective so that it gave a direct answer to the question troubling the community.

In 1 Corinthians 7:10 Paul appeals to a word of the Lord that declares that a woman should not separate from her husband. The apostle explains, however, that in view of the problems that could arise in a gentile Christian congregation, it is conceivable that a marriage might end in divorce in certain circumstances over which the Christian partner has no control— namely, "if the unbelieving partner separates" (v. 15). In this case, the Christian partner should not refuse a divorce, but agree to the dissolution of the marriage, for "it is to peace that God has called you" (v. 15). The concrete application of the traditional word of the Lord must therefore be understood and interpreted from the basic general perspective of the gospel of peace.

In 1 Corinthians 9:14 the right of a preacher to be supported by the congregation is grounded on a word of the Lord that says "those who proclaim the gospel should get their living by the gospel." This word of the Lord is understood in such a way that it can be applied as a rule for the conduct of the life of the early church, for the "gospel" terminology reflects the vocabulary of the early Christian mission, not the setting of the life of the historical Jesus (cf. 1 Cor. 15:3–5). Thus here too we have a traditional "word of the Lord" appropriately reinterpreted in the situation of the Christian community.

As a final example, we see an ethical application of a word of the Lord in the context of the Lord's Supper tradition presented by Paul (1 Cor. 11:23–25). In this case, the apostle has allowed both the praxis of the Christian congregation founded by him, as well as his own theological interpretation, to influence the wording of the saying. The bread-saying receives special emphasis through the expression "body, that is for you" (1 Cor. 11:24). This means that in the elements of the Lord's Supper believers receive the body of Christ given for them and thereby participate as members in the one body of Christ, the church, being joined to each other and made responsible for each other (see below, p. 121).

The oral tradition of the sayings of Jesus was heavily influenced by its use in parenesis, that preaching and teaching of the community devoted to teaching and exhorting to right conduct. Many sayings and parables could be directly applied, without being supplemented—as in the case of the warning not to strive for Mammon or to yield oneself to anxiety (Matt. 6:24–34). The same is true of the parable of the unforgiving servant, which warns of the necessity of forgiving one's Christian brother or sister (Matt. 18:21–35).

Other sayings had to be provided with an appended explanation, or changed in content, before they could find a place in the context of ethical instruction. Thus it is repeatedly the case that statements originally made in debates with Pharisees and scribes were applied secondarily to disciples, in order to draw lessons from these sayings for the conduct of Christians. Originally the parable of the lost sheep was directed against the objection of Jesus' opponents who were scandalized at his fellowship with publicans and sinners. Just as the return of the lost sheep brings joy to the family, so God rejoices over a sinner who repents (Luke 15:1–7). In the context of community instruction, the accent is shifted by Matthew's Gospel so that the emphasis is placed on the persistent seeking that finally finds the lost. In the same way, a disciple should seek out and accept a straying brother or sister (Matt. 18:10–14).

Many parables that had originally been charged with imminent eschatological expectation were, by giving them ethical applications, later incorporated into the complex of materials used for instruction of the disciples, in order to encourage them to patient endurance and faithful alertness (Mark 13:33–37 par). The collection and editing of the tradition of Jesus sayings took place under the dominant perspective of their ethical application, as for example in the context of Mark 10:1–31, which in its present form presents a series of dominical sayings on marriage, relation to children, and attitude to possessions. A similar example is offered by the collection of sayings in which Jesus' message is summarized as the Sermon on the Plain or Sermon on the Mount (see below, p. 61).

The ethical application of Jesus' aphorisms and parables often led to an alteration of their scope. The parable of the four kinds of soil (Mark 4:3-9 par.) first describes three kinds of sowing that have no results—the seed is eaten by birds, the young plants are scorched by the sun, or strangled by weeds. To these failures, there is juxtaposed an incredibly rich harvest: some falls on good soil and brings forth fruit that increases to thirty, sixty, and one hundred times what was sown. The numbers mentioned in the parable considerably exceed the usual expectation, in which an increase of seven to twelve times was considered a good harvest. The emphasis lies on the contrast: on the one side the threefold failure, on the other side the fabulously rich result. This contrast points to the creative work of God. In the wonder of the harvest that God brings to fruition without human aid one can see the promise of God's coming kingdom, which will arrive without human activity (cf. Mark 4:26-29).

To this parable a secondary interpretation has been added (Mark 4:13-20 par.). In this interpretation, the emphasis is no longer on the contrast created by the unexpected miraculous harvest, but offers an urgent admonition. The word of God that is spread abroad in the world must not be neglected. The fruitless sowings are applied to various types of hearers. Some allow themselves to be robbed of the word by Satan. Others, after an initial period of enthusiasm, again fall away. Still others do indeed hear the word, but allow the cares of the world, greed, or the deceitfulness of riches to suffocate it, and thus remain without fruit. The hearer is thereby warned not to respond like the bad types of soil, but to follow the good example of those who hear the word, accept it, and bring forth a rich harvest. "Let anyone with ears to hear listen!"

The parable of the unjust steward (Luke 16:1-13) is reevaluated as parenetic instruction in another manner. In this case no extensive interpretation is added, but the tradition has undertaken to understand the troublesome example of the unjust administrator's conduct by appending a series of aphorisms in order to make it usable for ethical instruction (vv. 8b-13). Beginning with the final addition, these are: (v. 13) no one can serve two masters (Matt. 6:24), so one must decide between earthly

wealth and God. Verses 10–12 attempt to find a way to understand the story as a warning example: whoever mishandles
earthly property cannot be trusted to handle the true riches of
heaven. In v. 9 the accent is placed still differently: the steward
has shown how one might use money in a clever way, the lesson
being that one should use one's money in order to win lasting
friends. And v. 8b expresses the proverbial wisdom that the
children of this world—such as the unjust steward—are more
clever than the "children of light" (who are oriented to different
values).

None of these appended sayings, which are intended to
make the parable useful for ethical application, corresponds to
the original viewpoint of the parable. Each of these bits of
proverbial wisdom, though containing an insightful thought in
and of itself, is related to the parable's own inherent message.
It is clear that Jesus is not using this provocative story to communicate ethical maxims; the conduct of the "hero" of the story
rules that out. Rather, the scandalous story is intended to
illustrate the meaning of prudent conduct: in the critical moment
to discern one's situation and decisively do the one thing that
is necessary in order to win the future (cf. Matt. 7:24–27).

The earliest Christian community gathered, preserved,
handed on, and interpreted the preaching of Jesus under the
guidance of the leading question of the relevance of this
message for Christian conduct. By so doing, they sought to
provide a christological foundation for ethical instruction.
Through the word of Jesus, burdened people were enabled to
stand erect, the sick were filled with hope, the suffering were
given encouragement, and the poor were filled with the confidence that all was not lost. People for whom society had little
regard, who were disdained and discriminated against, received
the testimony of God's compassionate nearness. The heartening
and comforting words of the Lord assured them all that they
were not abandoned by God, but were accepted by his grace as
children of the heavenly Father. But to be accepted by him
meant henceforth to stand under the regulatory power of his
word. Thus when believers hear the word of Jesus, think
through its message, and interpret its instructions in their proclaimed message of challenge and encouragement, they know

themselves to be placed under the claim of his commandments that contain concrete affirmations as to how the Christian life is to attain its proper shape as the words of the Lord find realization in their deeds.

Suggestions for Further Reading

Boring, M. E. *The Continuing Voice of Jesus.* Louisville: Westminster/John Knox, 1991.

Bultmann, R. *The History of the Synoptic Tradition.* New York: Harper & Row, 1963.

Crossan, J. D. *In Fragments. The Aphorisms of Jesus.* San Francisco: Harper & Row, 1983.

Donahue, J. R. *The Gospel in Parable.* Philadelphia: Fortress Press, 1988.

Dungan, D. L. *The Sayings of Jesus in the Churches of Paul: The Use of the Synoptic Tradition in the Regulation of Early Church Life.* Philadelphia: Fortress Press, 1971.

Jeremias, J. *The Parables of Jesus,* 3rd ed. New York: Scribner's, 1972.

Kelber, W. *The Oral and Written Gospel.* Philadelphia: Fortress Press, 1983.

Kloppenborg, J. *The Formation of Q.* Philadelphia: Fortress Press, 1987.

Sanders, E. P. *Jewish Law from Jesus to the Mishnah.* Philadelphia: Trinity Press International, 1990.

Scott, B. B. *Hear Then the Parable.* Minneapolis: Fortress Press, 1989.

Life in the Lord

The confession of Christ as Lord brings with it the obligation for Christians to live out their vocation in a way appropriate to their confession. When the hearing and acceptance of the gospel message is experienced as God's call, the response to this call is to be realized in the lives of those who believe. The apostle Paul's understanding of Christian existence receives pregnant expression in his formula "in Christ." The new life of believers no longer stands under the fateful sign of Adam's disobedience, but is subject to the lordship of the crucified and risen Christ (1 Cor. 15:22). Whoever still stands on Adam's side is subjected to sin, law, and death. That person lives "in the flesh" (e.g., Gal. 2:20, Rom. 8:8–9) or "in the law" that dominates one as long as one lives (Rom. 7:1). But whoever belongs to Christ stands in the freedom of the children of God, those who are obedient to the Lord.

As the pre-Pauline hymn confesses, Christ has humbled himself even to death, but has been exalted by God and installed as Lord of all that is (Phil. 2:5-11). Whoever has been consigned to this Lord henceforth has every thought and wish determined by the Christ event (Phil. 2:5). By baptism εἰς Χριστόν (into Christ) (Rom. 6:3) that person is incorporated into the body of Christ and, as a member of the people of God, is delivered from the violent power of sin, law, and death. A real change of lord-ships takes place in baptism, a change that transforms and renews all of life from the ground up. What has happened in the past no longer has any valid claim on one's life. That means, however, that the saints, those who belong to God, may no longer live their lives according to their own will, but walk in the newness of life, that life filled with the righteousness of God (1 Cor. 6:9-11). If anyone is in Christ, he or she is a new creature (2 Cor. 5:17), so that henceforth the old "I" no longer has the authority, but Christ as Lord lives in him or her.

Alongside the expression "in Christ," found not only in the authentic Pauline letters but also in the Deutero-Pauline and post-Pauline literature such as 1 Peter, is found the similar phrase "in the Lord" (ἐν κυρίῳ), which means exactly the same thing (e.g., 1 Thess. 3:8; 1 Cor. 7:39; Rom. 16:2; Phil. 4:2). It is found primarily in parenetic contexts, in order to ground ethical instruction in the authority of the Lord. If the kingly status of the exalted Lord is still hidden from the eyes of the world, still all who call on the name of the Lord know that the resurrected Lord has called his own through the gospel, and holds them responsible to walk in his ways.

"Walk" or "way" is a characteristic term for the whole conduct of one's life in both the environment determined by the Old Testament and Judaism, and the environment determined by Hellenistic ways of thinking. In Jewish thought walking in the right way (=halakah) describes obedience to the law as the will of God made known to Israel; in the Cynic-Stoic popular philosophy, a manner of life guided by reason and insight is considered the right way of life. The members of the community are admonished by the early Christian ethical instruction to live their lives as "walking" in the "way" of the Lord, and that means to "lead a life worthy of God," who has called them into God's own kingdom and glory (1 Thess. 2:12). The repeated use of the term "worthy" in this connection indicates that a fundamental point of orientation for the living of one's life must be given: worthy of the Lord (Col. 1:10), worthy of the gospel (Phil. 1:27), worthy of one's calling (Eph. 4:1). Thus believers should walk on their life's way as "children of light" (Eph. 5:8). To live a life "worthy of the Lord" cannot then mean that one is bound to a new legalism. Christians who belong to the exalted Lord are established in the freedom of Christ, in which they are delivered from the domination of the principalities and powers, which they no longer must serve at all. The freedom of Christ can be preserved only by binding oneself to Christ, which gives to the "walk" and "way" of the believers' life its ground, direction, and goal.

Life in the Lord is also described as life in the Spirit. To be "in Christ" means to be "in the Spirit" (Rom. 8:9). Thus in Romans 8:9-11 Paul can use the series of expressions without any difference in meaning "Spirit of God" (v. 9), "Spirit of Christ" (v. 9), "Christ in you" (v. 10), "the Spirit of him who raised Jesus from the dead" (v. 11). Especially to be "in the Spirit" — as spelled out in Pauline theology—does not mean to be in an ecstatic state (as in Rev. 1:10) in which one is temporarily lifted out of the reality of the conditions of everyday earthly life. It is rather the case that life "in the Spirit" means that the exalted Lord deals with his own through the Spirit, who proves the reality of his living presence in the proclaimed word and in the variety of "working" within the members of the community. But where the Spirit is at work, there is freedom (2 Cor. 3:17), a freedom that is the very opposite of arbitrariness and can exist only by being bound to the Lord. That is why the New Testament consistently makes the connection: "If we live by the Spirit, let us also be guided by the Spirit" (Gal. 5:25).

The power to determine the life of the believers that issues forth from the exalted and present Lord can also be indicated by the preposition κατά (according to, corresponding to), which gives the norm to which the life of the Christian is to be oriented. Those who live "in Christ" must orient their thinking and acting "in accordance with Christ Jesus" (κατὰ Χριστὸν Ἰησοῦν) (Rom. 15:5). Their speaking must be ordered "with the Lord's authority" (κατὰ κύριον) (2 Cor. 11:17). They must "walk not according to the flesh but according to the Spirit" (Rom. 8:4). If "flesh" (σάρξ) indicates the independent power of human beings who think they can manage their own lives without God, then the concept "Spirit" (πνεῦμα) points to the activity of God through Christ in the present that is the basis for the new life of believers. They have received the Spirit, who gives them the power, ability, and obligation to be led by him. They must struggle in the battle against the flesh, a battle they are enabled to win by the grace of God they have received.

A critical probing of the transmitted ethical traditions allows us to define more precisely how "leading a life worthy of the Lord" is to take concrete shape. Christians are obligated to attend carefully and considerately to conventional teaching about how the good is to be understood, what constitutes just interactions of people, and the responsibilities that come with citizenship. Of course, the fundamental orientation of their lives, that they are to lead a life worthy of the Lord, gives them the principle that helps them distinguish what is valid for the life "in Christ" and what is not. A Christian ethic can advocate neither a mere common religiosity nor the striving after self-realization that fails to consider others. Rather, the obedience rendered to the Lord and the love owed to the neighbor set the tone for and determine the character of that capacity to make discriminating judgments. Such Christian discrimination can look over, sort out, and reformulate traditional rules and teaching in terms of their validity as Christian ethics.

In this probing and "proving" (RSV) (cf. Rom. 12:1–2) of the many forms of traditional ethical teachings, Christians must take care to maintain a good reputation in the eyes of outsiders. Those who do not belong to the Christian community are described as "those outside" (οἱ ἔξω) without associating any sort of pejorative judgment with this phrase (1 Thess. 4:12; 1 Cor. 5:12–13; Col. 4:5; Mark 4:11). Many such "outsiders" note carefully whether the deeds of Christians correspond to their words and whether they conduct themselves in a trustworthy manner. In this process they will form their opinions by the criteria that are generally considered appropriate for ethical conduct in that time and place. Christians are therefore not permitted to allow the suspicion to arise that they are misusing the freedom that has been conferred on them, and are living arbitrary, irresponsible lives. Rather, they must live "honorably" (εὐσχημόνως Rom. 13:13) and lead an orderly life (κατὰ τάξιν 1 Cor. 14:40). They are not to cause offense, but are so to conduct their lives that "outsiders," whether Jews or Greeks, receive a good impression. The apostle admonishes: "Give no offence to Jews or Greeks or to the church of God" (1 Cor. 10:32), and points to his own example: "just as I try to please everyone in everything I do, not seeking my own advantage but that of many, so that they may be saved" (v. 33). "Give no offence" (ἀπρόσκοπος) is accordingly used in the same sense as "please" (ἀρέσκειν). Carelessness or lack of consideration could have the result that the credibility of the gospel is damaged among the "outsiders," so that they reject the preached message and they would be deprived of salvation. Christians should not make themselves guilty of such an offence. That means, then, that their conduct must correspond to the generally accepted norms and stand up to the critical judgment of non-Christians. They must conduct themselves "wisely toward outsiders" (Col. 4:5), so as to make insightful judgments and to act accordingly.

Suggestions for Further Reading

Barth, Karl. *Christ and Adam: Man and Humanity in Romans 5.* Translated by T. A. Smail. New York: Collier Books, 1962.
Beker, J. C. "The Responsibility of Life in Christ." In *Paul the Apostle,* pp. 272–302. Philadelphia: Fortress Press, 1980.
Cranfield, C. E. B. *The Epistle to the Romans,* vol. 2, pp. 833–35. International Critical Commentary. Edinburgh: T. & T. Clark, 1979.
Hooker, M. D. "Interchange in Christ and Ethics." *Journal for the Study of the New Testament* 25 (1985): 3–17.
———. "ΠΙΣΤΙΣ ΧΡΙΣΤΕΩΣ." *New Testament Studies* 35 (1989): 321–42.
Johnson, L. T. "Romans 3:21–26 and the Faith of Christ." *Catholic Biblical Quarterly* 44 (1982): 77–90.

Käsemann, E. "A Critical Analysis of Philippians 2:5-11." In *God and Christ*, pp. 45-88. R. W. Funk, ed. New York: Harper & Row, 1968.

Kurz, W. S. "Kenotic Imitation of Paul and of Christ." In *Discipleship in the New Testament*, pp. 103-26. F. Segovia, ed. Philadelphia: Fortress Press, 1985.

Sanders, E. P. "One Body, One Spirit." In *Paul and Palestinian Judaism*, pp. 453-63. Philadelphia: Fortress Press, 1977.

Wedderburn, A. J. M. "Some Observations on Paul's Use of the Phrases 'in Christ' and 'with Christ.'" *Journal for the Study of the New Testament* 25 (1985): 83-97.

Williams, S. K. "Again Pistis Christou." *Catholic Biblical Quarterly* 49 (1987): 431-47.

Chapter Three

THE KINGSHIP OF GOD

Eschatology and Ethics

Jesus announced the approaching advent of the kingdom of God. The evangelist Mark summarized the central content of his message in the declaration: "The kingdom of God has come near, repent" (Mark 1:15). This is an appropriate summary of Jesus' proclamation. This statement is distinguished from the later eschatological message of the church in that it does not speak of the parousia of the Lord. On the other hand, it stands out from Judaism's ideas about the end time in that it contains no reference to the restoration of Israel's past splendor. What is the meaning of this proclamation and the call to repentance with which it is bound?

The "kingdom of God" was understood in the eschatological expectation of Judaism as the sovereign rule of the Lord and Creator of the world, which, to be sure, is already present though hidden, and which will become visible to all only at the end of history. Jesus adopted this concept of eschatological hope, but redefined it by giving it a new content. There is not a single word about the overthrow of foreign powers or of triumphing over the Gentile nations; the emphasis is exclusively on the fact of the coming of God's reign. In contrast to the Jewish ideas, its advent is not tied to this or that condition. It is neither integrated into a series of predetermined apocalyptic events, nor made to depend on Israel's obedience to the law, which supposedly could hasten the day when God's kingdom would begin. The definitive renewal of the world, the transformation of all things at the end of history, will not come about by human action, but is simply removed from the sphere of human competence. It comes through God's act alone, is entirely the result of God's miraculous intervention.

The question as to how this eschatological transformation will come about is answered by Jesus only in parables: "The kingdom of God is as if someone would scatter seed on the ground, and would sleep and rise night and day, and the seed would sprout and grow, he does not know how. The earth produces of itself (αὐτομάτη; it means a divine miracle), first the stalk, then the head, then the full grain in the head. But when the grain is ripe, at once he goes in with his sickle, because the harvest has come" (Mark 4:26–29). The parable does not describe a long process of gradual growth, but juxtaposes beginning and end, in order to emphasize the contrast. The farmer does not participate at all in what happens. The harvest comes, quite apart from his action or inaction. The growth of the seed, which leads to the miraculous harvest, is thought of as the miraculous activity of God.

The parables of the kingdom of God (Mark 4:1–34; Matt. 13:1–50; Luke 8:4–15) do not deal with a process within history that should describe the growth or building of the kingdom of God. They rather present a contrast, juxtaposing sowing and harvest, intended to portray the greatness of the divine miracle.

The kingdom of God is "at hand" (ἤγγικεν), that is, its beginning is in the near future. How near? According to the endtime expectations of Jewish apocalyptic, certain signs must become visible that indicate just how near the end is. Jesus rejects such demands for signs from which one could read just how late it is on the eschatological timetable. The kingdom of God will suddenly and unexpectedly be there (Luke 17:20), without anyone's being able to count on its arrival or calculate the time of its beginning. Still, for those with eyes to see and ears to hear, the signs of the coming kingdom are already there to be perceived: "But if it is by the finger of God that I cast out the demons, then the kingdom of God has come to you" (Luke

11:20 / Matt. 12:28). In Jesus' mighty deeds and healings of the sick, it can be recognized that the prophetic promises of the coming time of salvation (e.g., Isa. 35:5) are already being fulfilled: "the blind receive their sight, the lame walk, the lepers are cleansed, the deaf hear, the dead are raised, and the poor have the good news brought to them" (Matt. 11:5).

The coming of the kingdom of God brings salvation to the lost. By associating with publicans and sinners, sharing a table with them, and speaking to them of the gracious compassion of God, he makes clear to all eyes that the coming of the kingdom of God means salvation for the suffering and freedom to those who are bound. Jesus defends the saving power of his message against the objections of his critics by declaring that the angels, and even God, rejoice more over one lost sinner who is found than over the countless good people who suppose that they need no repentance (Luke 15:1–10).

———

Closely bound up with the announcement of the coming kingdom of God is the call to repentance: because God is about to make the final intervention in human affairs, the only adequate response is to abandon the false way of life previously followed and return to God. This call to repentance relates Jesus' preaching to that of John the Baptist, who demanded visible fruits of repentance (Luke 3:10–14), and who in turn had taken up the message of the biblical prophets: "As I live, says the Lord God, I have no pleasure in the death of the wicked, but that the wicked turn from their ways and live; turn back, turn back from your evil ways" (Ezek. 33:11). But Jesus' call to repentance, in contrast to John's, is not based on the near approach of the wrath of God, but names the only possible result that people could expect from the coming near of God's kingdom. This message communicates joy, as the parables of the treasure in the field and the pearl of great price show (Matt. 13:44–46). Everything is surrendered for the sake of the one treasure – and done with pure joy. But whoever puts the hand to the plow and looks back is not fit for the kingdom of God (Luke 9:62).

The invitation to the joy of repentance does not mean merely a change of attitude. With the words μετάνοια / μετανοέω (repentance / repent) the prophetic call to "return" is sounded again, which means much more than a change of thinking. The path of life previously followed leads away from the source of life. What is called for is a total reorientation that includes every area of activity and work.

This message met not only with responsive acceptance, it also aroused determined rejection from the side of the religious. When the Pharisees asked Jesus whether it is right to pay tribute to Caesar or not, they obviously thought they would be able to embarrass him. If he answered affirmatively, he would be suspect by the masses of his own people, who suffered bitterly under the foreign domination. But if he answered in the negative, he would appear to the Romans as a rebellious trouble-maker. Jesus' response was a surprise to his questioners: "Render to Caesar the things that are Caesar's, and to God the things that are God's" (RSV) (Mark 12:13–17). This means that whoever really gives to God what belongs to God—one's self, one's whole life, thought, relationships, and doing—can calmly and in good conscience also give to Caesar what he demands. Jesus thus urges his disciples to reject that struggle for place and power that everywhere prevails in human life. "But whoever wishes to become great among you must be your servant, and whoever wishes to be first among you must be slave of all" (Mark 10:43–44 par.).

———

Just as in the preaching of Jesus the near approach of the kingdom of God determines one's actions in the present, so also in the message of the early church, eschatology and ethics were bound most closely to each other. The unity of these two ideas must not of course be so understood as though every single statement of ethical content must always be provided with an eschatological basis. The ethical instruction of the earliest churches also included maxims of wisdom or commonly accepted rules for living. But as in the message of Jesus, so also in the early Christian proclamation, the general context of ethical instruction was determined by eschatology: "The night is far gone, the day is near. Let us then lay aside the works of darkness and put on the armor of light" (Rom. 13:12). Christians are people who belong to the day—that is, they live their lives in the horizon of the dawning day of the Lord. They must therefore "keep awake" and "be sober" (1 Thess. 5:5–6). What can be done stealthily in the darkness does not even come into consideration for Christians: reveling and drunkenness, debauchery and licentiousness, quarreling and jealousy. The appropriate response to the time is "to put on the Lord Jesus Christ" (Rom. 13:13–14). These words once provided the decisive factor for Augustine, as he was perplexed and pondered the further course of his life, with the result that he became a Christian (*Confessions* VIII, 12:28). Such words in fact leave no doubt: by pointing to the ultimate day of the Lord and the kind of life in the present for which it calls, one can derive clear directions for the leading of one's life.

As in the message of Jesus, so also in early Christian ethical instruction, the "kingdom of God" was understood in an eschatological sense—except when the phrase was used in a purely formal sense (e.g., Col. 4:11). Entrance into the future kingdom of God could be obtained neither by flesh and blood (1 Cor. 15:50), the unrighteous (1 Cor. 6:9–10), or any kind of evildoers (RSV) (Gal. 5:19–21; cf. also Eph. 5:5). Pointing to the future kingdom of God gives force to ethical admonitions. In its light it becomes clear how Christians are to regard their present conduct. "For the kingdom of God is not food and drink but righteousness and peace and joy in the Holy Spirit" (Rom. 14:17). Obviously the apostle Paul here appeals to a commonly accepted conviction (cf. also 1 Cor. 4:20), which is based on a firm connection between eschatology and ethics.

It is clear in this connection that an ethic motivated by eschatology is not a so-called interim ethic, which could claim validity only during that period in which people lived in the expectation of the nearness of the end of the world (see below, pp. 65–66). Neither Jesus' preaching nor the proclamation of the early church speak of the coming kingdom of God in the sense of apocalyptic ideas that deal with an imminent cosmic catastrophe. Their eschatological hope is not dependent on the calculation of some date, either in the immediate or distant future. Rather, the present is understood to exist under the sign of that which is to come, which is announced in the saving word of the gospel. The delay of the parousia therefore did not change the essential rightness of the announcement of the coming kingdom of God. Salvation and disaster depend rather on the decisive question posed by the proclamation of the approaching kingdom of God. In the light of its coming, what is to be perceived and done as God's will becomes clear: to repent and to believe (Mark 1:15).

The will of God can be learned from the law and commandments. Their teaching remains valid even in the horizon of the coming kingdom of God, but it is now understood and interpreted in the light of the eschatological expectation. When Jesus was asked by a rich young man what he must do in order to inherit eternal life, he responded by pointing him to the commandments: "You shall not murder; you shall not commit adultery; you shall not steal; you shall not bear false witness; you shall not defraud; honor your father and mother" (Mark 10:19 par). God's will must be done, in order to fulfill the condition for entrance into eternal life or the kingdom of God. Jesus did not think of calling the validity of the law into question. But he attacked the hypocrisy of those who supposed they had done enough when they had responded to the law's demand by casuistic interpretation and application.

The purity laws played an important role in everyday Jewish life. Still, one could comply with their requirements — so Jesus taught — and achieve only an external purification, without ever understanding what purity and impurity essentially is. For "there is nothing outside a person that by going in can defile, but the things that come out are what defile" (Mark 7:15). Evil resides and plays havoc within a person, where no cultic rite can counteract it. Purity is therefore not to be attained through ritual practices, but can exist only as purity of the heart (Matt. 5:8). By this rule Jesus radicalizes the demand for purity and gives it a new content.

Alongside the purity laws, the Sabbath commandment was of particular significance for the practice of a life obedient to the Torah. To be sure, the stories that deal with Jesus' conflicts over the Sabbath are mostly formulations by the Christian community, and represent the fallout of debates between the church and the synagogue. The nucleus of the tradition, however, certainly goes back to the historical Jesus, as can be perceived in the sayings of Jesus about the Sabbath. The scribes had determined exactly which activities had to be avoided on the Sabbath because they constituted work. Jesus broke through this network of casuistry with the word: "The Sabbath was made for humankind, and not humankind for the Sabbath" (Mark 2:27). While in the view of the rabbis the Sabbath could be violated only in a case where a life was acutely endangered, Jesus reversed the direction of thought: no longer does the demand of the law stand at the highest priority, but human beings and needs are valued more highly than the Sabbath commandment itself. The human person originated from the creative hand of God even prior to the Sabbath. To be sure, the Sabbath too is a gift of God and retains its basic validity, but in every case the greatest commandment has to do with the love to be shown to the neighbor.

Jesus directed a further word against the casuistic application of the Sabbath commandment: "Is it lawful to do good or to do harm on the Sabbath, to save life or to kill?" (Mark 3:4 par). By asking what is permitted on the Sabbath, Jesus avails himself of the same terminology used in the scribal discussion—that is, what is permitted and what is forbidden by the law. Formally, his statement seems to ask for a decision, but in fact, no choice is permitted, since obviously the answer can only be that one should do good, save life, and not destroy it—even on the Sabbath. An afflicted human being is to be helped under any and all circumstances (cf. also Matt. 12:11-12; Luke 14:5). Jesus thereby makes the love commandment a hermeneutical principle for the interpretation of the whole corpus of commandments. Their requirements are not fulfilled by an external obedience bound to legalism, but only by the love that recognizes and does the will of the creator.

So too the ethical instructions that are formulated as wisdom sayings are also conditioned by the eschatological character of Jesus' preaching. Thus the challenge "do not be anxious" is at first supported with the appeal to rational insight: "Look at the birds of the air—consider the lilies of the field" (Matt. 6:26, 28). Just as they neither labor nor are filled with anxiety, so also the disciples of Jesus should not worry and say

"What will we eat? What will we drink? What will we wear?"
(v. 31). The ultimate foundation of this exhortation is not, however, the clever insight of wisdom, but the view toward the
coming of the kingdom of God: "Strive first for the kingdom of
God and his righteousness, and all these things will be given to
you as well" (Matt. 6:33). Jesus' sayings about anxiety contain
neither a program for the solution of social problems nor a prohibition of work, but rather place all the questions of everyday
existence under the perspective of the coming kingdom of God.
In the horizon of this hope their appropriate place on the priority scale becomes visible, so that one perceives that it lies in the
power of no human being to secure one's own future by
becoming its lord. If rational insight permits one to recognize
that human anxiety in the final analysis accomplishes nothing,
still Jesus' saying does not give the last word to skeptical resignation. Rather, freedom from anxiety is attained only by the
path where life is led by trusting confidence: "Your heavenly
Father knows that you need all these things" (v. 32).

Fulfillment of the commandments will receive its proper
reward. In the preaching of Jesus, reward is spoken of in a fundamentally different way than in the context of legal religion
and piety, in which every act is performed with a view to its
anticipated acknowledgment and reward. Jesus says: "When
you have done all that you were ordered to do say, 'We are
worthless slaves; we have done only what we ought to have
done!'" (Luke 17:10). God demands an accounting for the goods
entrusted to his servants, because God asks them what they
have done with them (Luke 19:12-27; Matt. 25:14-30). Therefore
"love your enemies, do good, and lend, expecting nothing in
return. Your reward will be great, and you will be children of the
Most High" (Luke 6:35). At the Last Judgment those who will
be accepted are those unassuming people who were themselves
unaware that their deeds were a fulfillment of the divine will,
as is indicated by their amazed question: "'Lord, when was it
that we saw you hungry and gave you food, or thirsty and gave
you something to drink? And when was it that we saw you a
stranger and welcomed you, or naked and gave you clothing?
And when was it that we saw you sick or in prison and visited
you?' And the King will answer them: 'Truly, I tell you, just as

you did not do it to one of the least of these, you did not do it to me'" (Matt. 25:37–40). The reward given them does not consist in calculating their deeds and repaying them, but of entering into the joy of their Lord (Luke 19:12–27; Matt. 25:14–30). Whoever lives out of God's gracious gift knows that God's mercy has the last word.

Suggestions for Further Reading

Beasley-Murray, G. R. *Jesus and the Kingdom of God*. Grand Rapids: Wm. B. Eerdmans, 1986.

Bornkamm, G. *Jesus of Nazareth*, pp. 64–95. New York: Harper & Row, 1950.

Chilton, B., ed. *The Kingdom of God in the Teaching of Jesus*. Philadelphia: Fortress Press, 1984.

Chilton, B., and J. I. H. McDonald. *Jesus and the Ethics of the Kingdom*. Grand Rapids: Wm. B. Eerdmans, 1988.

Hiers, R. H. *Jesus and Ethics*. Philadelphia: Westminster Press, 1968.

Leivestad, R. *Jesus in His Own Perspective*. Minneapolis: Augsburg, 1987.

Perrin, N. *Rediscovering the Teaching of Jesus*. New York: Harper & Row, 1967.

Sanders, E. P. *Jesus and Judaism*. Philadelphia: Fortress Press, 1985.

Williams, J. G. "Neither Here Nor There: Between Wisdom and Apocalyptic in Jesus' Kingdom Sayings." *Forum* 5, 2 (1989): 7–30.

Willis, W., ed. *The Kingdom of God in 20th-Century Interpretation*. Peabody, Mass.: Hendrickson, 1987.

Following Christ

It is reported several times in the Gospels that Jesus addressed people with the call "Follow me!," challenging them to become his disciples and walk with him in his way (e.g., Mark 1:16–20; 2:14; Luke 5:1–11). Those who were chosen by this call stood up, left everything, and followed Jesus. As the Gospels portray him, Jesus was not only surrounded by crowds (e.g., Mark 1:39; 3:7; 5:24; Matt. 8:1; 14:13; Luke 7:9; 9:11; John 6:2), but also gathered a circle of disciples about himself, who accompanied him in his journey. Externally regarded, this picture is hardly to be distinguished from the associations in which rabbis lived together with their students. To be a disciple of a teacher meant not only to listen carefully to his teachings and to stamp them on their minds; the disciple lived constantly with his teacher and learned from him through the associations of the daily life they shared, until one day the student had successfully ended his period of study and was released from the school so that he could now pursue his own career as an independent teacher.

The relationship in which the disciples stood to Jesus was, however, of a fundamentally different sort than that of the students of a rabbi. While these had to seek out a rabbi and be accepted into his school in order to begin their study, and then could become his disciples only if they were found worthy, Jesus called his disciples to follow him. He did not instruct them with a view to their someday becoming independent teachers themselves who could take the place of their master; it would always be the case that Jesus is the Lord and they are the servants (Matt. 10:24–25). One is the master, so all the disciples must be brothers and sisters, and never allow themselves to be called "rabbi" like the Jewish scholars (Matt. 23:8). Jesus did not call disciples to follow him in order to establish a school or found an institution. He created no directives or prescriptions that were to serve his disciples as bylaws of an institution or the rule of an order. Rather, his call to discipleship stood under the sign of the coming kingdom of God. Discipleship was grounded in his word alone – its unqualified character finding its closest analogy in the calls of the Old Testament prophets. It was supported with no rationale, but was expressed as a demand with authority, to which the only right response could be acceptance and discipleship.

Discipleship, to which Jesus called individual followers, takes place in binding one's life and destiny to that of Jesus. The call to go with him was not directed indiscriminately to all, and did not insist that the only way to attain the coming kingdom of God was to become a disciple. Nevertheless, those addressed by Jesus' call knew that it applied to them personally, stopped them in their tracks, and called for a decision. The demand inherent in this call could not be put aside by any other responsibility, neither family ties nor the wish to be properly excused, not even the moral responsibility of burial of the dead before one begins the wandering life of a disciple. "Let the dead bury their own dead"—with this gruffly formulated command the radical call to discipleship is sounded forth, a radicality given with the commanding nearness of the kingdom of God. To follow Jesus meant to participate in his proclamation of the dawning kingdom of God and to place one's life under the compulsion of this task. For the sake of the kingdom—not on the basis of ascetic discipline or pious practices—it was commanded to harken to the call and leave everything. To follow Jesus includes severing oneself from all other ties (Luke 14:33), including those of one's family (Luke 14:26–27; Matt. 10:37–38), and even of hating one's own life (Luke 14:26).

While some obediently accept the unqualified call to discipleship, to others the challenge appears too severe (Matt. 8:19–22; Luke 9:57–62). To be sure, the so-called rich young ruler can guarantee that he has kept the Ten Commandments since he was a child (Mark 10:20 par.). But he was not able to obey the demand to sell all that he had, give it to the poor, and to enter into the life of discipleship (v. 21 par.), because he had many possessions. The directive given to him may not be understood as a universally applicable demand to everyone, as it was for example in the community of Qumran, which required all applicants to renounce all their property and deposit it in the common store of the community (see below, p. 79). Such a legal requirement is found neither in the preaching of Jesus nor in the teaching of the early church. There is no fundamentally negative judgment against earthly possessions; they are rather to be mobilized in the service of love for the good of others. Still, wherever the call of Jesus sounds forth, no other intention may block its path. His word can be heard as so harsh and difficult that one might think it must be avoided. But wherever it is heard and obeyed, there God is honored as the only Lord, the one who is to be feared, loved, and trusted above all things.

Those who choose to follow Jesus are not burdened with any additional ethical demands exceeding those that apply to all. Yet they receive their commission and promise for their chosen way directly from Jesus. He wants to make them "fishers for people" (Mark 1:17 par.) who will proclaim the glad tidings of the coming kingdom of God. The saying about "fishers for people" was a common one in the ancient world, but was always used in the derogatory sense of someone who used shady tactics to entrap others. As used in Jesus' call to discipleship, the metaphor is used positively, and apparently is derived from its connection with the call of the first disciples of Jesus, who were going about their business of fishing when Jesus called them. They are called to share Jesus' life and destiny, in order to be witnesses to the coming of the kingdom of God and to win people to this message.

To walk with Jesus in his way includes a readiness to suffer. This association is hardly to be characterized as an instance of an already developed life-style, the so-called wandering radicalism, as it was practiced here and there in the ancient world. It does not fit into comparable social forms of its environment, but is entirely determined by Jesus' call and the disciples' obedient response. Jesus' word points the way: "If any want to become my followers, let them deny themselves and take up their cross and follow me" (Mark 8:34 par.). Of course, the form of this saying present in the Gospels has been shaped in reference to Jesus' own crucifixion, and thus bears the stamp of the post-Easter Christian community; yet it is clear that an older formulation lies behind the present version, which binds discipleship to the readiness to suffer—whatever kind of suffering may be involved in individual cases of discipleship. For "a disciple is not above the teacher, nor a slave above the master" (Matt. 10:24). But whoever has left family and possessions for Jesus' sake will "receive a hundredfold now in this age . . . and in the age to come eternal life" (Mark 10:28–31 par.).

After Good Friday and Easter, discipleship to Christ takes on a new meaning. It is now directed to the exalted Lord. To follow Jesus means to believe and confess that he is the light of the world (John 8:12). Discipleship to Christ is not constituted by the resolute and persuasive conduct of those who make their own decision for it. Impressive examples of moral conduct also exist outside Christianity, not only in the ancient pre-Christian world but also in non-Christian society alongside the church. Discipleship to Christ is determined solely by hearing, accepting, and responding to the call that confesses him as the light of the world and lives by the power of this faith.

The call to discipleship no longer means, as it did in the time of the earthly Jesus, the demand to leave everything and literally follow Jesus wherever he goes. The message that Christ is the light of the world is directed to all people, and invites them to respond in faith and trust to this good news. Whoever steps into the light of Christ, who brings life to the lost world, and confesses that he is the source of light and life, is a disciple of Christ and walks behind the good shepherd, whose sheep know and respond to his voice (John 10:4–5). The 144,000 who, as portrayed in Revelation, represent the people of God at the end time, follow the Lamb even to the point of death—through suffering to glory (14:4). According to the Epistle to the Hebrews, Christ is the pioneer for his own, who has gone before them to prepare the way (2:9–10; 5:9, 20). He is the great high priest who has passed through the heavens (4:14–16), and is the "pioneer and perfecter of our faith," its beginning and end (12:2). He has gone ahead of us to prepare the way that his own are to follow to heavenly glory (see below, p. 185).

Discipleship to Christ becomes a description of Christian existence as such. It is of course true that the Pauline letters speak not of discipleship to Christ, but of being imitators of Christ: "Be imitators (μίμησις / μιμεῖσθαι) of me, as I am of Christ" (1 Cor. 11:1). This challenge could be misunderstood, as though the concept of mimesis were applied to Christ or the apostle in the sense of an ethical model—and therefore an unattainable goal. In fact, however, the apostle is urging his readers neither to copy his own conduct in its particular details, nor to take Christ as an example in the sense of mimicking the individual features of Jesus' life. Rather, it is a matter of living in a manner appropriate to the sovereignty of Christ, which means in word and deed to confess Christ, the King of kings, as Lord in one's own life (Phil. 2:5–11). The appeal to Paul as a model (1 Thess. 1:6; 1 Cor. 4:16; Phil. 3:17, as well as 2 Thess. 3:7, 9) is intended to serve as encouraging admonition to acknowledge the authority of the apostolic word and to bring one's life into line with it. To be an "imitator" of the apostle or of Christ means to follow the directive of his word. There is nothing said here about an example to be emulated in the sense of doing the same things as the model, but of following, in the sense that the confession of Christ as Lord is the directing and forming power for one's life. The Pauline concept of the imitation of Christ means nothing else than discipleship to Christ, which comes to realization in obedience to the exalted Lord. When Ephesians 5:1 calls for Christians to be "imitators of God," then that means "forgiving one another, as God in Christ has forgiven you, . . . and live in love, as Christ loved us" (Eph. 4:32; 5:2). Discipleship to Christ is accordingly oriented to the practice of the love commandment, the binding force of which comprehends every area of life.

Suggestions for Further Reading

Best, E. *Following Jesus: Discipleship in the Gospel of Mark*. Sheffield: JSOT Press, 1981.

Hengel, M. *The Charismatic Leader and His Followers*. New York: Crossroad, 1981.

Kingsbury, J. D. *Conflict in Mark*. Philadelphia: Fortress Press, 1984.

———. "On Following Jesus: The 'Eager' Scribe and the 'Reluctant' Disciple (Matthew 8.18–22)." *New Testament Studies* 34 (1988): 45–59.

Lohfink, G. *Jesus and Community*. Philadelphia: Fortress Press, 1984.

Räisänen, H. "Jesus and the Food Laws: Reflections on Mark 7.15." *Journal for the Study of the New Testament* 16 (1982): 79–100.

Schottroff, Luise, and Stegemann, W. *Jesus and the Hope of the Poor*. Maryknoll, N.Y.: Orbis Books, 1986.

Segovia, F., ed. *Discipleship in the New Testament*. Philadelphia: Fortress Press, 1985.

Theissen, G. *Sociology of Early Palestinian Christianity*. Philadelphia: Fortress Press, 1978.

Wengst, K. *Humility – Solidarity of the Humiliated*. Philadelphia: Fortress Press, 1989.

The Love Commandment

Which is the greatest commandment of all? This question, which was raised from time to time in pre-Christian Judaism (see above, pp. 14–15), finds a clear answer in the preaching of Jesus as it is reported in the tradition of the synoptic Gospels. As represented in the Gospel of Mark, essentially reproduced by Matthew, Jesus formulates the double commandment of love in which he unites Israel's confession of the one God (Deut. 6:5) with the commandment to love one's neighbor (Lev. 19:18), followed by the declaration that "there is no other commandment greater than these" (Mark 12:28-31). The scribe who had turned to Jesus with this question responds in agreement, by repeating the "Hear O Israel" and the commandment to love one's neighbor, commending them as much greater than all ritual worship and animal sacrifice.

The Markan form shows clear traces of having been composed in a way that reflects an explicit appeal to "heart, soul, mind, and strength," as well as an emphatic critique of the externals of ritual worship. This formulation reflects the interests of the tradition of the Hellenistic churches, which had in turn already been influenced by the ideas circulating in the Hellenistic synagogues. This was the original setting for the line of argument directed to reasonable judgment rather than authority, as well as for the point of view critical of the temple cult, both of which considered moral responsibility as more important than correct observance of the temple rituals. Although in its Markan form the saying is overlaid with some of the reflections of Christian tradition, its kernel can be traced back to Jesus himself. This is clear from the fact that the Lukan parallel, which has been formulated differently, belongs to an independent strand of tradition, which notwithstanding its independence still manifests the same central content in its formulation of the double commandment of love.

According to Luke 10:25-28 Jesus was asked by a scribal lawyer what he must do in order to inherit eternal life. This is the same question posed by the "rich young ruler" (see above, p. 44). The point is to determine the true will of God, which must be fulfilled in order to obtain salvation. Jesus responds with a counter question, which gives the dialogue the form of a scholastic dialogue: "What is written in the law? What do you read there?" It is then not Jesus, but the scribe himself, who comes up with the clarifying solution, in that he formulates a short (in comparison with Mark) version of the double commandment of love. The presuppositions present in the Jewish community's discussions of what constituted the essential elements of the teaching of the law as a whole (see above, pp. 14–15) allow us readily to imagine that a Jewish scribe could have made such a declaration. The affirmation of the oneness of God as well as the importance of the command to love the neighbor had already played a significant role in scribal discussions. Nevertheless, Jesus' standpoint clearly transcends such discussions when he makes the love commandment the one decisive requirement of the law: "The greatest commandment is this" (Mark 12:28); "There is no other commandment greater than this" (Matt. 22:38); "On these two commandments hang all the law and the prophets" (Matt. 22:40); "Do this, and you will live" (Luke 10:28).

In the double command of love each of the two commands is heard with its full weight, while at the same time the indissoluble unity of both commands is held fast. The command to love God is not absorbed into that of the love to neighbor, nor does the care expended on others simultaneously fulfill the obligation to grant God due love, as if it were the case that the unknowable God could only be loved as met in the human family. To be sure, the view is also affirmed that Christ himself is met in the suffering and oppressed (Matt. 25:31–46). But this insight can only be attained where the commanding majesty of God is humbly acknowledged and God is given praise by loving deeds. But where the first commandment is understood in its comprehensiveness that embraces the whole Decalogue, there it is clear at the same time that love directed to God cannot ignore the neighbor. For it is God who is honored when the neighbor is served in love (Gal. 5:13).

But who is my neighbor? In the answer that Jesus gives to this question, the love commandment receives no concrete application. All sorts of considerations were reflected upon in the rabbinic discussion of the question as to how far the love commandment should extend. Usually it was assumed that "neighbor" meant one's compatriots, members of the people of Israel. There were, however, both narrower and wider understandings of the term. The circle was drawn more narrowly in the religious associations, which considered "neighbor" in the strict sense to apply only to the members of one's own group, those who with serious commitment attempted to fulfill the whole law. A broader understanding of "neighbor" tended to prevail in settings of humanitarian considerations, especially as these were conceived in Hellenistic popular philosophy and synagogal discussions. One might even dare to advocate helping one's enemy who was in distress. Still, nowhere were such ideas considered to be included in the command to love one's neighbor in a way that knows no boundaries.

In view of the different definitions that the term "neighbor" had found, it is not surprising that a scribe directed to Jesus a question concerning the identity of the neighbor. Jesus responded by telling a story (Luke 10:30–37). On the deserted road from Jerusalem to Jericho a man was attacked and robbed. The robbers had beaten him half to death and left him lying by the road, wounded and bleeding. A priest came along the road, but he passed by on the other side; later a Levite did the same. Finally a Samaritan came down the road. Although the Samaritans, like the Jews, observed the Pentateuch as the binding law of God, hostility had existed between them for generations, for the Samaritans worshiped God at a different holy place than the Jews (John 4:20–24). Thus Jews and Samaritans did not associate with each other (John 4:9). One who was not only a foreigner but an enemy was the last person in the world from whom the severely wounded man could expect any help. But the unexpected happened. The Samaritan took care of the wounded man, washed and bound up his wounds, placed him on his donkey, and brought him to the nearest inn, so that further care could be provided for him there. The narrative concludes with the question, "Which of these three, do you think, was a neighbor to the man who fell into the hands of the robbers?" (v. 36). The answer is indisputable: "The one who showed him mercy" (v. 37).

The story is told from the perspective of the person who is being advised in his distress and pointed to others for support and help. The issue of "who is my neighbor" is then turned around, and becomes the question "to whom am I neighbor?" Priest and Levite refused to give the needed help, whatever reasons they may have given themselves for not interrupting their trip. There is probably no particular emphasis to be placed on the critical tone with regard to the temple ritual that could be seen here, although it should not go unnoticed that those who neglected to practice the loving deed were members of the temple staff. But if the failure of the temple personnel were to be noticed, one would then expect the contrast to be drawn by having the third person in the story to come by an Israelite layman. The parable portrays a contrast that works much more sharply: a foreigner, a Samaritan despised by Jews, comes by. He does not hesitate, he does what is needed. He thereby proved to be a neighbor to the one who had fallen among robbers. The final word calls for responsible action: "Go and do likewise" (10:37).

The universal validity of the command to love one's neighbor finds its clearest expression in the command to love one's enemies: "But I say to you that listen, love your enemies, do good to those who hate you, bless those who curse you, pray for those who abuse you" (Luke 6:27–28). The fourfold admonition confers upon the imperatives an urgency that cannot be missed. Without any qualification, we are urged to love, do good, bless, and pray. The series of verbs interpret each other. The deed of love is executed when the word of blessing replaces that of cursing, when doing good to another replaces hostility, and when insult is replaced with prayer for the other before God. The idea that one might turn helpfully toward people who were regarded as unworthy or even hostile was not altogether alien to the ancient world. But neither in Hellenistic nor Jewish scribal discussions was the word "love" used for this attitude.

The commandment of love as formulated by Jesus thus received its ultimate and most critical development in the directive to love one's enemies. It permits no distinctions between personal enemies and national enemies, everyday experiences, religious conflicts, or military operations. It speaks of enemies in the comprehensive sense, in whatever realms of life hostility may appear. The conquering power of love is limited by no boundary; it is made dependent neither on the consideration of whether the act is in behalf of people who are worthy of love nor on specifying the circle of potential recipients of helpful deeds. By naming even enemies as those to whom one should act in loving care, every hesitating deliberation is excluded as to whether the "neighbor" must first meet some qualification, as is usually supposed. The command of love knows no condition and no presupposition; it is valid for every place and every time.

The evangelist Matthew placed special emphasis on the command to love one's enemies by clothing it in the form of an antithesis and by placing it as the conclusion of the series of juxtapositions of what was said by the ancients and what Jesus says: "You have heard that it was said, 'You shall love your neighbor and hate your enemy.' But I say to you, love your enemies and pray for those who persecute you, so that you may be children of your Father in heaven" (5:43–45). This includes the command to love one's neighbor as it is given in the Old Testament (Lev. 19:18), but the opposite command is also included: "You should love your neighbor and hate your enemy." Although such a contrast is found nowhere in the pages of the Old Testament, this form is found in the texts from the Qumran community. In the Rule of the Community a fundamental norm is formulated: "to love all the sons of light, each according to his lot in the counsel of God, and to hate all the sons of darkness, each according to his guilt in the vengeance of God" (1QS 1:9–11). One's enemies are considered enemies of God, and are thus fundamentally to be rejected. In contrast, Jesus knows neither enemies nor those hated by God, and speaks of unbounded love. God's mercy knows no boundaries, for after all God lets the sun rise on all people, and God's blessing rests on all. The love of the Father applies to every person. Thus to be perfect, which is the final requirement, means "be merciful, just as your Father is merciful" (Luke 6:36).

Early Christian teaching held fast to this understanding of the love of enemies. As an expression of the love commandment it taught "bless those who persecute you; bless and do not curse them" (Rom. 12:14) and "do not repay evil for evil or abuse for abuse; but on the contrary repay with a blessing. It is for this that you were called, that you might inherit a blessing" (1 Pet. 3:9).

The love command has concrete action as its goal. What is required by love is not spelled out in advance in casuistic rules. As the example of the good Samaritan shows, when love encounters a need, it is capable of determining the appropriate action that will offer genuine help. This understanding is attained by virtue of the fact that love as the determining motive of every deed orients itself by the possibilities and experiences that are given in the situation. If love is the fulfilling of the law, then the commands of the laws are appropriated in the way that love directs, either affirming or rejecting them as love shows what is required.

Whoever acts on the basis of love deliberates on the proper course of action as issues are posed, for example, in the traditions about marriage and divorce (Mark 10:1–12 par.), about one's relation to governmental authority (Mark 12:13–17 par.), about the right use of money and property (Mark 10:17–27; Matt. 6:19–34). Because love is simply the commandment of God as such, the command that is always relevant and applicable, it can express its force by making probing evaluations and decisions with regard to traditional ethical doctrines, since it grasps the will of God in an absolute, unconditioned sense, and is capable of putting it into effect in concrete actions.

Such concretion is the intent of Jesus' saying, "So when you are offering your gift at the altar, if you remember that your brother or sister has something against you, leave your gift there before the altar and go; first be reconciled to your brother or sister, and then come and offer your gift" (Matt. 5:23–24). The unconditional priority of the love commandment over against the rules for the sacrificial ritual is here affirmed. Reconciliation with the brother or sister must under all circumstances be accomplished immediately, even if one is in the act of bringing a sacrificial offering when it occurs to one what it is that has troubled the relationship. No other commandment may stand in the way of reconciliation. Once this is accomplished, then the other commandment may receive its due. For afterwards, in accordance with the old Jewish Christian usage presupposed in this pericope, the offering was to be brought. All the commandments are interpreted with reference to the love commandment. It imposes the obligation on Jesus' disciples to be peacemakers and ministers of reconciliation, to overcome the differences that separate people, to promote mutual understanding, and to commit themselves in word and deed to peaceful cooperation among the people in their realm of influence.

The way in which the love command determines all realms of life is also illustrated by the parable of the unforgiving servant (Matt. 18:23–35). In response to his imploring the king, the servant was forgiven an unimaginably high debt. Soon thereafter he met one of his fellow servants who owed him the relatively small amount of one hundred denarii. A manual laborer could normally earn one denarius per day (Matt. 20:2). The servant to whom the money was due bruskly rejected the debtor's request for patience and threw him into prison until he should pay what was owed. But the other servants, who had observed the proceedings, reported to the king what had happened. The king called in the unmerciful servant, demanded that he explain why he had not had compassion on his fellow servant, and turned him over to the torturers until he should pay what he owed. "So"—thus the parable concludes—"my heavenly Father will also do to every one of you, if you do not forgive your brother or sister from your heart" (Matt. 18:35). To grant or to deny love to the neighbor thus affects one's relationship to God. After all, Jesus had taught his disciples to pray "and forgive us our debts, as we also have forgiven our debtors" (Matt. 6:12).

Suggestions for Further Reading

Borgen, P. "The Golden Rule, With Emphasis on Its Usage in the Gospels." In *Paul Preaches Circumcision and Pleases Men*, pp. 99–114. Trondheim: Tapir, 1983.

Crossan, J. D. "Parable and Example in the Teaching of Jesus." *New Testament Studies* 18 (1971–72): 285–307.

Furnish, V. *The Love Command in the New Testament*. Nashville: Abingdon, 1972.

Klassen, W. *Love of Enemies: The Way of Peace*. Philadelphia: Fortress Press, 1984.

Patrick, M. W. *The Love Commandment: How to Find Its Meaning for Today*. St. Louis: CBP Press, 1984.

Perkins, P. *Love Commands in the New Testament*. New York/Ramsey: Paulist Press, 1982.

Piper, J. *Love Your Enemies: Jesus' Love Command in the Synoptic Gospels and the Early Christian Parenesis.* Cambridge: Cambridge University Press, 1978.

Schottroff, L., et al. *Essays on the Love Commandment.* Philadelphia: Fortress Press, 1978.

Stendahl, K. "Hate, Non-Retaliation and Love." *Harvard Theological Review* 55 (1962): 343–55.

Chapter Four

THE NEW
RIGHTEOUSNESS

The Ethics of the
Sermon on the Mount

The Sermon on the Mount (Matt. 5-7) presents us
with a well thought out and carefully constructed
composition, in which the evangelist Matthew has brought
together different traditions under the heading of the "better
righteousness" or the "new righteousness." The theme and content of the individual sections frequently change and are often
only loosely connected with each other, as can be seen especially
clearly in chapter 7. One saying is joined to another, without
being connected by any apparent train of thought. The section
begins with the admonition not to judge, in order not to be
judged oneself (v. 1). Verse 6 directs that holy things not be
given to dogs. Without any transition, the next sentence adds:
"Ask, and it will be given to you; seek, and you will find; knock,
and the door will be opened for you." Then a general rule
follows in v. 12: "In everything do to others as you would have
them do to you." A single speech with a connected train of
thought can hardly have been constructed by stringing together
such a series of unrelated sayings. The Sermon on the Mount
does not contain the stenographic report of a self-contained
discourse given on one occasion, but traditions that have been
developed, formed, and set forth under the authority of Jesus

in order to develop legitimate teaching in his name for the Christian community.

The special character of this composition becomes clearly apparent when it is compared with the shorter composition called the Sermon on the Plain in Luke 6:20-49. Like the Sermon on the Mount, it begins with a series of beatitudes, though here there are only four, and they are juxtaposed to a corresponding series of four woes. These are followed by brief topical collections of sayings dealing with, among other things, love of enemies, compassion, and the relation to one's brother or sister in the fellowship of Jesus' followers. As in the Sermon on the Mount, the conclusion is formed by a challenge to obedient response to the message of Jesus. We therefore have here a compactly composed speech that circulated in the oral tradition. We should then think of Matthew's having had such a traditional composition available to him in the tradition of Jesus' sayings that came to him. He filled out this concise frame-work with other material, in part taken from the collection of Jesus' sayings shared by Luke (Q) and found in other contexts in Luke's Gospel, and partly from the oral tradition that did not belong to Q. Thus the Lord's Prayer in Luke is located at the beginning of chapter 11; the sayings about anxiety have parallels in Luke 12:22-31, and the twin saying about the narrow and wide gates is placed by Luke at 13:23-24.

The keynote of the whole composition of the Sermon on the Mount is sounded by the text "unless your righteousness exceeds that of the scribes and Pharisees, you will never enter the kingdom of heaven" (5:20). It is therefore a matter of recognizing and living out the righteousness that must be fulfilled as the entrance requirement for the kingdom of God. It is this righteousness for which one must strive (6:33). These words take up ideas that were expressed in the Psalms of the Hebrew Scriptures. The question "Who can approach God's holy mountain and dwell in God's holy place?" receives the response: "Those who walk blamelessly, and do what is right" (Ps. 15:2; see p. 11, above). The Sermon on the Mount makes contact with this stream of tradition and wants to set forth a somewhat catechetical presentation of what it means to live and do the "new righteousness."

This theme of the "new righteousness" is the structuring principle of the Sermon on the Mount. The introduction portrays Jesus as climbing up a mountain in order to speak to his disciples (5:1-2). Just as the law was once proclaimed from Mount Sinai, so now the authoritative interpretation of the law will again be presented from a mountain. The new righteousness surpasses the old, and takes its place. At the same time, the introduction to the Sermon on the Mount also points forward to the conclusion of the Gospel: the resurrected Lord commissions his disciples to go into all the world and teach the nations to observe all that he has commanded them (28:16-20). This teaching of Jesus by which the community is to order its life is set forth in the Sermon on the Mount.

The introduction is followed by the Beatitudes (5:3-12). In union with Jesus, God's new world has broken in—this is also the tenor of the following verses about the salt of the earth and the light of the world (5:13-16). Only after the indicative affirmation of the mercy of God has been proclaimed is the imperative meaning of the new righteousness set forth, in six antitheses (5:17-48). The Sermon on the Mount presents ethical instructions only as they are embedded within the framework of the good news of the dawning kingdom of God.

Chapter 6 illustrates the right kind of worship, as it should be practiced by Jesus' disciples, under the headings of alms, prayer, and fasting (6:1-18). This then leads into instruction on the path of discipleship that concerns how those who follow Jesus deal with wealth and anxiety (6:19-34). Chapter 7 then adds a series of aphorisms and admonitions, and then four urgent warnings: the narrow and wide gates (7:13-14), false prophets (7:15-20), those who only say "Lord, Lord," (7:21-23), and finally the double parable of the builder (7:24-27). At the end, it is reported that the people "were astounded at his teaching, for he taught them as one having authority, and not as their scribes" (7:28-29). The ethical instruction set forth in the Sermon on the Mount evoked different responses. Some hearers reacted with shock, lack of understanding, and opposition, while others accepted Jesus' words with obedience, and became his followers.

The significance of the Sermon on the Mount for Christian life may be seen more clearly in dialogue with its history of interpretation. By assessing and debating with the various interpretations, the meaning of the ethic developed in the Sermon on the Mount can be determined more precisely.

(1) An interpretation advocated in the Middle Ages sought to comprehend the Sermon on the Mount as an ethic of the perfect. Whoever wants to belong to the group of "perfect" should learn from the Sermon on the Mount the standard by which they must live. While the laity were required to follow the Decalogue and the love commandment, the monks sought to fulfill the stricter ethic of the Sermon on the Mount. The Reformation raised a protest against such a two-level ethic. It emphasized that the message of the Sermon on the Mount was not addressed to a narrow circle of "perfect" who distinguish themselves from others by a higher ethic, but calls all to repentance.

(2) As interpreted in the Reformation, the Sermon on the Mount was primarily an ethic of repentance. The law brings the awareness of sin; thus the new righteousness is also to be understood from the point of view that it holds before the eyes of Christians the reality that they cannot be saved by their own deeds but only by the grace of God. Accordingly, the demands of the Sermon on the Mount are ultimately unfulfillable. They only provide the mirror image of the fact that the sinner can receive salvation only by the merciful acceptance of God.

It is in fact the case that the intention of the Sermon on the Mount is not to give Jesus' disciples any occasion to boast about their works, as though they had done everything necessary to realize the new righteousness, and thus to make a claim on salvation. The Sermon on the Mount is doubtless to be heard also as a call to repentance. Still—as especially the concluding section makes plain—it brings before the eyes of Jesus' disciples the command of God as something that is to be heard and done, and thus not only intends to call to repentance, but to give clear ethical instruction.

(3) Yet another interpretation would like to understand the Sermon on the Mount in the sense of an ethic of law. In this view, Jesus' command surpasses the law of Moses by requiring

a higher standard of righteousness. In the Reformation period the so-called fanatics wanted to put into practice the ethic of the Sermon on the Mount, rigorously understood, even if it required violence. At the turn of the century, Tolstoy, the Russian philosopher of religion, advocated a consistently legalistic understanding of the Sermon on the Mount. He wanted to understand the prohibition of retaliation as the key to its interpretation, and to derive from this a rule that denied to the Christian any sort of resistance. Instead of resistance, the Christian could only respond with unqualified love for the enemy. Christians were prohibited from taking any oaths or committing themselves to any institutions in this world; they are rather called to exercise a critique against all institutions. But in such an understanding, which ultimately opens the door to anarchy, it is overlooked that the Sermon on the Mount does not develop a program of legal demands, but places its ethical directives under the sign of the promise of salvation. The claim [*Aufruf*] made by its ethical demands can therefore only be rightly understood when seen or heard inseparably with the acclamation [*Zuruf*] of the good news of salvation.

(4) The idealistic interpretation attempts to avoid the mistake of the legalistic interpretation. It explains the Sermon on the Mount as being misunderstood when it is interpreted literally, since it only intends to call forth a new attitude that can be applied in the modern situation as well. One's attention should therefore not remain fixed on the particulars of the individual commands, but one should look for the basic ethos and attempt to operate by the corresponding attitude in one's own life. This interpretation directs us away from any sort of legalism as the means of coming to terms with the Sermon on the Mount. Still, its message is not completely grasped by this approach, for the Sermon on the Mount intends not only to evoke a new attitude, but calls for doing the concrete will of God in every area of life.

(5) At the beginning of our century, Albert Schweitzer and other exegetes recognized that the center of gravity of Jesus' message was provided by eschatology. Since Schweitzer thought Jesus expected the end of the world in the near future, he inferred that the ethic of the Sermon on the Mount must be

described as an "interim ethic" (see above, pp. 43–44). The ethic of the Sermon on the Mount was supposed to be exceptional, valid only for the brief period prior to the consummation of history. It could not be generalized once it became clear that the parousia was delayed. Liberal-minded Christianity as advocated by Schweitzer must therefore renounce the effort to equate its own faith directly with the teaching of Jesus. Rather, it should be acknowledged that the ethical is simply the essence of religion as such. To this interpretation it must be objected that neither the evangelists' view of the Sermon on the Mount nor that of their churches can by any means be considered an "interim ethic." The Gospel of Matthew is already aware of the delay of the parousia and wants to make clear in the face of this situation how the Sermon on the Mount should still come to expression in the lives of Christians.

(6) The Sermon on the Mount has received particular attention within the contemporary efforts toward an ethic of peace. In the context of this discussion, people attempt to take seriously the compulsory character of its commands. Still, its message is only appropriated in a one-sided manner when only a few key statements are taken from their context and set forth as directives for concrete political action. The Sermon on the Mount impresses on its hearers the necessity for radical obedience, but it develops no political program. The call to discipleship implicit in the Sermon on the Mount provides a combination of devotion to this world and distance from it, and it is only when this call to discipleship determines the responsibility of Christians in their secular conduct will they be able to perceive their political responsibilities and make adequate decisions.

Each of the different types of interpretation emphasizes different aspects, and each is important. Yet one-sided interpretations must be corrected. The Sermon on the Mount can be understood neither as an elitist ethic for a few "perfect," nor as some sort of excessive legalistic demand. It calls for neither an idealistic attitude nor is it an interim ethic of a past day that can now only evoke a general religious disposition. It does not want merely to strengthen the call to repentance by offering us a list of impossible demands that make us feel guilty, like the traditional guides for the examination of conscience used prior to confession. Nor may individual sayings be taken from their context and used as rules of practical reason that may be incorporated into a political program. The critical counter-questions raised by each of the types of interpretation therefore lead back to the text: What is the meaning of the ethical instruction of these sayings of Jesus? And how do they relate faith and deed to each other?

Careful study of the Sermon on the Mount reveals that there are comparable Jewish teachings to many of its ethical statements, teachings that have a long history of oral tradition behind them before they were later written down in the Mishnah and the Talmud. Matthew 5:28 declares that whoever looks with lust on a woman has already committed adultery with her in his heart. The same kind of argument was made by the rabbis: "Whenever any one [lustfully] looks at a woman, it is the same as if he had slept with her" (Kalla Rabbath 1). Matthew 6:26 says, "Look at the birds of the air: they neither sow nor reap nor gather into barns, and yet your heavenly Father feeds them." In a comparable manner, rabbinic teaching says "Have you ever . . . seen a wild animal or bird working at a trade? Yet they receive their food without anxiety" (m. Qidd. IV.14). To the rule found in Matthew 7:2, "the measure you give will be the measure you get," one may compare as a Jewish parallel "by the measure one uses, one will be measured (that is, by God)" (b. Meg. 12b and elsewhere).

An especially clear example is offered by the Golden Rule of Matthew 7:12: "In everything do to others as you would have them do to you; for this is the law and the prophets." There are parallels to this not only in the Jewish world, but in the Hellenistic-Roman world as well. Already Isocrates of Athens, in the fourth century B.C.E., taught "Do not do to others that which angers you when they do it to you" (Nicocles 61). Jewish teachers contemporary with Jesus taught: "What is hateful to you, do not to your neighbor" (b. Sabb. 31a) (see above, p. 14). And in Hellenistic Judaism the positive form of the rule is found in the *Letter of Aristeas* 207 (about 100 B.C.E.) "As you wish that no evil should befall you, but to be a partaker of all good things, so you should act on the same principle toward your subjects" (see above, p. 14). This advice has been probed by centuries of experience and thus can be handed on as tried and true teaching.

The ethic of the Sermon on the Mount is based to a considerable extent on traditions that were already present in Palestinian and Hellenistic-Jewish traditions. Ethical instruction makes use of a rich treasure of experiences, in order with their help to describe the conduct that should be regarded as the right response to the divine command. Against this background of traditional statements and wisdom the special character inherent in the ethic of the Sermon on the Mount is seen all the more clearly. Not only were insights and points of view that were already current in the environment taken up and affirmed, but also in many cases—as especially the antitheses of 5:21-48 show—widely accepted views that resulted in a relaxation of the divine command were decisively rejected and contrasted with the authoritative declaration of the word of Jesus.

———

In order rightly to understand the ethical instructions of the Sermon on the Mount, they must be considered in the context of the whole composition: Jesus addresses his disciples and juxtaposes to the old righteousness the new righteousness of the coming kingdom of God. It is therefore not a matter of quantitatively exceeding the deeds of the scribes and Pharisees. The new righteousness is of a fundamentally different kind than the old, because it is free of the effort to establish one's own piety by striving to fulfill conditions understood in a legalistic manner. On the contrary, the new righteousness is borne along by undivided trust in the heartening pledge of God's acceptance.

The Sermon on the Mount begins with the beatitudes that promise salvation, and only then develops ethical instructions on this basis (cf. the relation of indicative and imperative in Paul, below, pp. 108-10). The more terse introductory announcement of salvation, as found in the Lukan Sermon on the Plain, is expanded by the evangelist Matthew. While in the Lukan formulation the disciples are addressed directly—"Blessed are you . . ." — , in Matthew the form has been changed to the third person, a form that is inherently of general applicability: "Blessed are the poor in spirit. . . ."

The poor, who are the subjects of the first declaration, are the poor in spirit—an expression found in comparable statements in the writings from Qumran (1QH 14:7)—referring to people who hold nothing in their hands, but reach out with empty hands to be filled by the grace of God. The expression thus does not necessarily refer either to economic poverty or deprivation. The poor, like the hungry, crying, and persecuted, are not blessed on the basis of the nature of their everyday lives, but because of their trusting acceptance of God's gracious turning to them, because they anticipate the coming kingdom of God as the gift of their heavenly Father.

As the first section of the beatitudes speaks of people who in a particular situation of distress place their hope in the saving help of God, the second section focuses on people who have accepted the message of the dawning kingdom of God and who have oriented their conduct to this hope. Blessing is pronounced on the merciful, the pure in heart, the peacemakers, and the persecuted. They are not put off by being given promises of some uncertain future, but the blessing of salvation is pronounced upon them in the here and now.

The immediately following verses also speak of this gracious turning of God toward his people: "You are the salt of the earth. . . . You are the light of the world" (5:13–16). This is not an appeal for people to try to be the salt of the earth or the light of the world, but the declaration is simply made: you are this. Everything depends on not losing the salting power already there, otherwise the salt is good for nothing. Everything depends on letting the light shine, otherwise darkness prevails. The message of salvation, as expressed in the beatitudes and the pronouncements about salt and light, provides the keynote for all the following ethical instruction of the Sermon on the Mount.

What the new righteousness means is elaborated in the six antitheses of the second part of chapter 5. Of these, the third, fifth, and sixth have parallels in the Gospel of Luke, though they are not found there in antithetical form, but as direct declarative statements. These were then obviously taken over by Matthew and reformulated by him to correspond to the antitheses already present in his tradition. Jesus sets his authoritative "But I say to you . . ." over against both Scripture and tradition, in order thereby to lay bare the radical will of God. But this means, as the evangelist formulates it, not that the word of Scripture is destroyed, but fulfilled (5:20) – that is, interpreted in accord with its real intention. Thereby a sharp distinction is made between the new righteousness and the old by means of the contrast "not guilty until y is done" vs. "guilty already when x is done." The fifth commandment, "you shall not kill," is violated not first by the act of murder, but already by the angry word directed against the brother or sister. And not first the act of adultery, but already the lustful look is a transgression against the sixth commandment, "you shall not commit adultery."

The series of antitheses is constructed on an ascending scale that leads finally to the commandment of perfection – that is, to a life that is ruled entirely by the grace of God (5:48; see above, p. 57). The parallel to the fifth antithesis reads in Luke: "If anyone strikes you on the cheek, offer the other also; and from anyone who takes away your coat do not withhold even your shirt" (6:29). The evangelist Matthew emphasizes the contrast to the Old Testament law of strict retaliation, "An eye for an eye, a tooth for a tooth" (*ius talionis*, see above, p. 9). In place of retaliation he places unqualified love, which is expressed in the prohibition of retaliation. For if evil is met with no opposition but is patiently accepted and suffered, it loses the possibility of finding any point of contact to generate more evil.

That it is ultimately wiser to suffer violence than to perpetrate it on others is one of those insights derived from the experience of life that was expressed in different ways in the ancient world – in the philosophical tradition of the Greeks as well as in the scribal discussions of the Jews. But Jesus did not formulate clever rules for the pragmatic experience of living, but declares the binding will of God that directs one to a way of life entirely alien from the world's. For how can one get along in this world if one consistently lives by this model? Jesus' word is not separable from the one who speaks it: the meaning of what he says is understood only through faith in him.

In the same manner, in the final antithesis the love commandment is concretized in the command to love one's enemy (see above, p. 56). This is not merely a matter of agreeing that enemies exist and one can have opponents. But where their curse is met with words of blessing and prayers to God in their behalf, there hostility loses the space in which it can effectively operate. This is the only way in which evil is overcome by good. The compelling force of the ethical instruction of the antitheses is neither a matter of the illumination commended by the insights of practical wisdom, nor is it something that can be forced by legal measures. Only as discipleship to Jesus do such actions prepare the way for the coming kingdom of God, in that Jesus' disciples by their own actions performed in weakness praise the Father in heaven and give him the glory.

The call "do not be anxious," as elaborated in the second half of chapter 6, does not intend to encourage a casual or passive attitude, as though one could dispense with all plans and forethought for the future (see above, p. 46), but it makes clear: on whatever you set your heart, that is your God. For "where your treasure is, there your heart will be also" (6:21). This is the way the real priority in our life is recognized. For persons of "little faith," God is not a factor to be reckoned with. But to believe means to set oneself before the claim of God's will and to trust in God's word with an undivided heart.

Chapter 7 describes the meaning of discipleship: to take the path that goes through the narrow door, and to avoid the broad road that supposedly leads on to the goal by a simple and pleasant route (7:13–14). The demand to harken to the word of Jesus comes to expression once again in the twin parable of the wise and foolish builders (see above, p. 31). Those who build their house on the sand do in fact seem to have an easier and less expensive job of it. But when the storm and rain come, the house built on sand will be shattered. In the hour of crisis, only the one who has built on the solid rock will dwell secure and stable. Only the one who follows Jesus' teaching will be like the wise man who has found firm ground on which to base his life.

The Sermon on the Mount closes with a contrast between the teaching of Jesus and that of the scribes. Their statements were always open to further discussion, contradiction, more refined support, new perspectives on the question, and alternative responses. His words were spoken with authority and set forth the unconditioned will of God with absolute validity.

The ethic of the Sermon on the Mount, then, is not set forth as a collection of rules for living based on commonly accepted wisdom, but the proclamation of the dawning kingdom of God and the invitation to discipleship to Jesus. To be sure, many traditional insights that had proven their validity in general experience were taken over and built into the overarching framework of the Sermon on the Mount. But all these statements are now securely inserted within the context provided by the proclamation of the new righteousness, which is to determine the whole lives of disciples. Its teaching may be summarized in five brief concluding theses:

(1) The Sermon on the Mount begins not with the demand of the law, but with the gracious promise of the beatitudes. This glad tone struck at the beginning echoes throughout all the following sections.

(2) The Sermon on the Mount elaborates the promise [*Zuspruch*] as well as the demand [*Anspruch*] of the grace of God. Just as the love of God is unqualified, so also the life to which the disciples are called in following their lord is a life of unqualified love. This is the way the new righteousness becomes operational, the Golden Rule is brought to reality, and love of the enemy is expressed in suffering, blessing, and prayer.

(3) The Sermon on the Mount demands from the disciples of Jesus undivided obedience to the will of God. That means: I am not yet obedient when I have done this or that heroic act. I can turn the other cheek, give my shirt as well as my coat to my opponent—but without love it means nothing (1 Cor. 13). The examples introduced in the antitheses are intended to show that the will of God, as interpreted by Jesus, is not a matter of performing this or that individual deed, but is a matter of offering one's whole self in the service of God.

(4) The much discussed question of whether one can translate the Sermon on the Mount into political action, or whether it is inappropriate to make such an attempt, is an issue that is falsely posed. The instructions of the Sermon on the Mount offer no rules that clarify the situation without further

ado. By their radicality, they expose the ways of this world for what they are and juxtapose them to the will of God. Their call, however, is not to some sphere of private inwardness, but challenges to a trusting attempt to carry them out in the sphere of everyday life. Mindful of the words of their Lord, the disciples of Jesus are called to establish peace and reconciliation among people, politics, business, economics, and every realm of life.

(5) Thus the Sermon on the Mount is at once both good news and a call to repentance. It is a constant reminder to Christians of how far they have fallen short, and throws them back on God's grace, which alone can be the foundation of the new righteousness and the resource by which it can be lived.

Suggestions for Further Reading

Betz, H.-D. *Essays on the Sermon on the Mount*. Philadelphia: Fortress Press, 1985.

Bornkamm, G. "The History of the Exposition of the Sermon on the Mount." In *Jesus of Nazareth*, pp. 221-25. New York: Harper & Row, 1960.

Davies, W. D. *The Sermon on the Mount*. Cambridge: Cambridge University Press, 1966.

Davies, W. D., and D. C. Allison. *The Gospel According to Saint Matthew*, vol I. International Critical Commentary. Edinburgh: T. & T. Clark, 1988.

Fuller, R. H. "The Decalogue in the New Testament." *Interpretation* 43 (1989): 243-55.

Guelich, R. A. *The Sermon on the Mount*. Waco: Word Press, 1982.

Kingsbury, J. D. "The Place, Structure, and Meaning of the Sermon on the Mount within Matthew." *Interpretation* 41 (1987): 131-43.

Lapide, Pinchas. *The Sermon on the Mount: Utopia or Program for Action?* Maryknoll, N.Y.: Orbis Books, 1986.

Luz, U. *Matthew 1-7*. Philadelphia: Fortress Press, 1989.

McArthur, H. K. *Understanding the Sermon on the Mount*. New York: Harper, 1960.

Moo, D. J. "Jesus and the Authority of the Mosaic Law." *Journal for the Study of the New Testament* 20 (1984): 3-49.

Strecker, G. *The Sermon on the Mount*. Nashville: Abingdon Press, 1988.

Windisch H. *The Meaning of the Sermon on the Mount*. Philadelphia: Westminster Press, 1951.

Ethical Implications
of the
Story of Jesus

The ethical applications that had already been made to the stories about Jesus in the oral tradition (see above, p. 29) were adopted by the evangelists and strengthened by their own redactional work. The evangelist Mark, the first to compose a written account of Jesus' work, suffering, death, and resurrection, gave special emphasis to the discipleship motif. Thus the story of the healing of the blind man was provided with a concluding comment that the healed man, whose faith had been acknowledged by Jesus, followed him on his way (10:52). By this means Mark shifts the accent from the miraculous deed itself to its significance for discipleship.

Just as the two pairs of brothers whom Jesus called from their fishing business at the very beginning of his public ministry left everything and went after him (1:16–20), so the good news of the gospel invites the reader to follow Jesus in his way. Since the time of fulfillment has dawned, the call goes forth to respond to the gospel in faith and repentance (1:15). Those in this world who have property at their disposal are more hesitant than others to take this call seriously. How hard it is for those who have riches to enter into the kingdom of God (10:24 par.)! The evangelist takes up the sharp word of Jesus, that it is easier for a camel to go through the eye of a needle than for one who has riches to enter into the kingdom of God (10:25). Still, just as Jesus had not made it an absolute and universal rule that they must abandon all their property, so also the evangelist makes no legalistic demand for a general renunciation of possessions. The refusal of the rich to become Jesus' followers because of what they must give up raises the anxious question from the disciples, "Then who can be saved?" The evangelist responds: "For mortals it is impossible, but not for God; for God all things are possible" (10:27 par.).

Whoever follows Jesus cannot want to lord it over others, but is called to serve them, for "whoever wants to be first must be last of all and servant of all" (9:35). Thus even children, who have been pushed aside so brusquely by their elders, have their place in the fellowship around Jesus (10:13–16 par.). Whoever receives a little child in Jesus' name, receives Jesus himself and the one who sent him (9:37). Jesus himself gave his disciples a model of what servanthood means: "For the Son of Man also came not to be served but to serve, and to give his life as a ransom for many" (10:45). Following Jesus includes readiness to suffer and to bear one's own cross (8:34 par.). The destiny of the community, which they must experience in the last times, is characterized by threat and persecution, which will inevitably come (chap. 13). But precisely under the pressure of faintheartedness and suffering, the community is called to remain true, alert, and to endure, for the beginning of the eschatological woes announces that the end is near (13:8 par.). Then the Son of man will appear and gather his elect from the four winds, from the end of the earth to the end of heaven (13:27 par.). Thus the warning: "Therefore, keep awake—for you do not know when the master of the house will come" (13:33 par.).

In the Gospel of Matthew the meaning of Jesus' teaching is emphasized much more strongly than in the Gospel of Mark, which Matthew used as one of his sources. The teaching of Jesus is elaborated in the extensive discourses composed by the evangelist from his traditional materials: the Sermon on the Mount (5–7), the missionary discourse (10), the parables discourse (13), the instructions on church life (18), the speech against the scribes and Pharisees (23), and the eschatological discourse (24–25). The risen one sends forth his disciples into the world with the commission to spread his word into every place and to teach all peoples to observe all that he has commanded them (28:20). In Jesus' teaching all that the law and the prophets had said finds its fulfillment. This means that the new righteousness does not nullify the word of the old covenant, but reveals its true intention and brings to fulfillment what had been announced in the writings of the Old Testament. Just as the evangelist repeatedly binds the narrative of Jesus' deeds explicitly to the realization of the prophetic promises, so he sees Jesus' teaching in the light of the fulfilled words of Scripture.

The call to discipleship, as expressed in the Gospel of Mark, is taken up by the evangelist Matthew and related to the repeated admonition to bring forth good fruit. In the last judgment people will be judged according to what they have done or neglected to do, according to whether their conduct has been determined by obedience or disobedience. It is not enough to say "Lord, Lord" — what counts is doing the will of the Father who is in heaven (7:21–23). That is why the warning against false prophets urges: "You will know them by their fruits" (7:16). A good tree can be distinguished from a bad one precisely by the fact that it brings forth good fruit (7:17–20).

The requirement to produce good fruit had found no response from the people to whom the vineyard had been entrusted. That is why it will be taken away from the bad vineyard keepers and the kingdom of God will be given to a people who will bring forth fruit (21:43). But they also must pass the test. The future judgment, in which sheep will be separated from goats, is yet to come, and its verdict has not yet been announced. No one may slumber in false security, supposing that he or she cannot miss out on salvation, as though one's present conduct made no difference. Just as the scribes and Pharisees were charged with not taking seriously for themselves the words of legal piety of which they were the advocates and thus show themselves to be hypocrites (6:2, 5; 15:7; 23:13, 15, etc.), so also the disciples are reminded that deed must be consistent with word. Piety that is done for show, with human applause as its motive, is rejected just as is the talkative enthusiasm that is satisfied with a lot of high-sounding religious words.

The whole of the law and the prophets find their crowning summary in the double commandment of love (22:40). It is precisely in loving conduct that the will of God is fulfilled. The love commandment thus serves as a critical principle in the proper understanding of the law. Just as reconciliation with the brother or sister has a higher priority than carrying out the law of sacrifice (5:23–24), so all formal public religious practice is measured by the love commandment. It had in fact already been clearly said by the prophets that God wants mercy and not sacrifice (9:13; 12:7; Hos. 6:6). This does not mean that either public worship, Sabbath, or the other commandments are nullified, but only makes clear that without love they are nothing, and that their meaning can only be grasped and put into practice from the point of view of the double commandment of love.

The express emphasis on the commandment of love preserves the ethic developed in the Gospel of Matthew from a legalistic misunderstanding. The definitive interpretation of the will of God is so understood in terms of love, that mercy always has the last word. Because the love commandment should determine human relations in every aspect of life, the ordering of church life is also to be adjudicated by it. If anyone has a problem with a brother or sister in the Christian community, he or she should first try to work it out in direct communication. Only if this fails is the matter to be brought before the whole congregation (18:15–17). Just as the good shepherd seeks the lost sheep in order to bring it safely back home, so it is also the will of the heavenly Father that not one of these little ones be lost (18:14).

In Luke's two-volume work the life and relationships of Christians are considered from the perspective of history understood as the story of God's saving action in the world. The time of Jesus represents the time of the fulfillment of God's promises. "Today this Scripture has been fulfilled in your hearing" —with these heartening words Jesus addressed the hearers in the synagogue at Nazareth (Luke 4:21). The "acceptable year of the Lord" has dawned, the time of fulfillment has arrived. The Christian community goes its way under this confident banner. In Luke's theology the original eschatological expectation has receded in the light of the fact that the end did not come as originally expected. Therefore what is called for is loyal perseverance, in order not to be led astray and to lose oneself amid the dangers of this world.

Among the dangers that the community must overcome are the external threats that can shatter the firmness of its faith. But power to persevere is conferred by the presence of the Spirit, which leads the community. The Lord will not abandon his own, but will give them a mouth and wisdom so that their opponents cannot withstand or contradict (21:15). But the dangers that derive from internal temptations can be even more threatening than those posed by external persecution. That is why the admonition is repeatedly given against surrendering oneself to earthly possessions and riches: "Be on your guard against all kinds of greed, for life does not consist in the abundance of possessions" (12:15). Warning examples are offered by the rich farmer, who wanted to build larger barns to preserve his wealth, without ever thinking of his last hour (12:16–21), and by the rich man who never noticed poor Lazarus at his door (16:19–31). Whoever attends to these warnings will be concerned to handle earthly possessions responsibly.

Although the poor are pronounced blessed (6:20), Luke too by no means calls for a universal and absolute renunciation of property. But still, earthly goods may not be used merely for one's own self-realization, but are there for the purpose of helping others. Thus the rich publican Zacchaeus, who became a follower of Jesus, did the right thing when he gave half of his property to the poor (19:8). After all, one should use unrighteous mammon in order to make friends (16:9). But woe to the rich (6:24), for they stand in the great danger of losing themselves amid the cares of this world.

The proper fruits of repentance, which are also called for in Luke's theology (3:8), should be manifest above all in public and political life. Luke is thus concerned to emphasize that Christians may not be suspected of anything like fomenting revolution. The Roman authorities were not guilty of the condemnation of Jesus nor of the persecutions suffered by the earliest church, although local authorities sometimes gave in to the pressure of their accusers. By reporting Paul's appeal to Caesar in order to secure justice, Luke intends to affirm the effectiveness of the Roman judicial system (Acts 25:10–12). But however much Luke may emphasize the loyal conduct of Christians, he is also aware of the boundary beyond which they may not pass: "We must obey God rather than any human authority" (Acts 5:29).

In obedience to God's will, Christians seek to form their lives in such fashion that each one is there for the other. This dominant idea shapes the narrative given in Acts of the life of earliest Christianity. The first church in Jerusalem is so portrayed as to give an ideal picture of Christian fellowship, especially in the summaries of Acts 2:42–47 and 4:32–35. There it is told how the first Christians lived together in harmony and peace, gathered for worship and prayer, and shared all their earthly goods with each other. This sharing of goods is sometimes described as an early Christian communism, but this designation is not an appropriate label. To be sure, individual claims to private property were renounced, but there was no systematic organization founded nor provision made for regulating a common means of production. Rather, what happened was—as the individual examples show (Acts 4:36–37; 5:1–11)—that various members of the community sold their property and placed the proceeds in the community treasury. This kind of renunciation of private property has a history-of-religions parallel in the Qumran community, which required of those who wanted to join that they place their personal assets at the disposal of the whole community (1QS 1:11–12; 6:2–3). One can easily imagine that in earliest Christianity, conditioned by their view of the nearness of the end, the critical attitude toward wealth and property led some members of the church to give their goods to the poor or to the church. But there is no evidence of an organized program by which the lives of the first Christians were directed.

Luke intends to describe the unique fellowship in which the first church lived together. It is clear that traditional regulations such as those found in the community at Qumran, and traditional critiques of wealth, may have provided points of contact from which he could develop his description. But, above all, Acts is dependent on ideas that had long since been advocated in Greek philosophy and had been developed as the outline of an ideal society. This view portrays a group of people bound together with ties of equality, wisdom, and mutual friendship, in which none say that anything belongs exclusively to them, but everything belongs to everyone in common (Aristotle, *Nic. Eth.* 1168b). The picture of earliest Christianity is intended to show that those hopes were realized in their life together. Of course their manner of life is not presented as a model that would become a binding regulation for all churches, but nevertheless is intended to show in exemplary style how a fellowship in which everyone shares with everyone else could actually be realized in the life of the church.

Suggestions for Further Reading

Achtemeier, P. *Mark.* 2 ed., revised and enlarged. Philadelphia: Fortress Press, 1986.

Barth, G. "Matthew's Understanding of the Law." In *Tradition and Interpretation in Matthew,* pp. 58–164. Günther Bornkamm, Gerhard Barth, and Heinz Joachim Held, eds. Philadelphia: Westminster Press, 1963.

Danker, F. W. *Luke,* revised and enlarged. Philadelphia: Fortress Press, 1987.

Kee, H. C. *Jesus in History: An Approach to the Study of the Gospels.* 2 ed. New York: Harcourt, Brace, Jovanovich, 1977.

Kingsbury, J. D. *Matthew.* 2 ed., revised and enlarged. Philadelphia: Fortress Press, 1986.

Krodel, G. *Acts.* Philadelphia: Fortress Press, 1981.

Martin, R. "Salvation and Discipleship in the Gospel of Luke." *Interpretation* 30 (1976): 366–80.

Meier, J. P. *The Vision of Matthew: Christ, Church and Morality in the First Gospel.* New York: Paulist Press, 1979.

Moxnes, H. *The Economy of the Kingdom: Social Conflict and Economic Relations in Luke's Gospel.* Philadelphia: Fortress Press, 1988.

Schweizer, E. "The Portrayal of the Life of Faith in the Gospel of Mark." *Interpretation* 32 (1978): 387–99.

Via, D. O. *The Ethics of Mark's Gospel—In the Middle of Time.* Philadelphia: Fortress Press, 1985.

Chapter Five

DIRECTIONS FOR THE EVERYDAY LIFE OF CHRISTIANS

The Right Way

In accordance with the Old Testament and Jewish understanding, also in early Christianity the life and conduct of people was described simply as "the way." God is director of the human sojourn. Wherever God's will is observed, there the path goes in the right direction. The standard teaching was, "commit your way to the Lord; trust in him, and he will act" (Ps. 37:5). Blessing is bestowed upon those who obediently follow God's commandments. But a curse will fall on those who do not harken to the voice of the Lord and who despise his ordinances (Deut. 28). Human life can therefore succeed only when it proceeds on its course oriented by God's direction and strives toward the goal that God has established.

Early Christian ethical instruction attempted to describe more accurately the way that Christians must go in their everyday lives. They thus adopted the moral instruction that was generally taught in the synagogues of the Hellenistic world (see above, pp. 21–23). Since it all depends on pointing out the right way to live one's life, ethical preaching and teaching as they were communicated in the early Christian communities, could also simply be called "the way" (Acts 9:2, 23; 19:9; 22:4; 24:14, 22). By bringing the false way before one's eyes as a warning example and by designating the right way as the only road that is to be followed, memorable guidance is provided that leads to the shaping of everyday life and can be a help in the tasks that must constantly be faced.

"My ways in Christ" is what the apostle Paul calls the ethical instruction that he has taught "everywhere in every church" (1 Cor. 4:17). His fellow workers whom he sent to various churches also taught these "ways." Thus when it is said that Timothy will remind the Corinthians of Paul's "ways," this is by no means merely a reference to the personal life-style of the apostle, although he can also incidentally use himself as a model for the churches (e.g., 1 Cor. 11:1). The comment "as I teach them everywhere in every church" makes it absolutely clear that he is here referring to his instruction of his fellow Christians in ethical matters. After all, their conduct is finally to be oriented toward the commands of the Lord Jesus (1 Thess. 4:2). God's will for Christians is simply that they live holy lives (1 Thess. 4:3). Because they through baptism have become the property of God and the Lord, so that they now belong to him and are therefore "holy," their lives should correspond to this "sanctification" that they have already experienced. What this concretely means is seen in the delineation of the "ways in Christ Jesus": to abstain from immorality and not be misled into impure ways, to follow the call to holiness and to live as they are led by the Spirit (vv. 4–8).

When Paul refers to the "ways in Christ" without further explanation, he presupposes an idea already familiar to the churches, an idea filled with a definite content. As minority groups within the world of late antiquity, they had to be instructed concerning what the will of God requires and warned against conduct that violates that will. In this regard the determining factor is the command of the Lord, whose sovereignty points the way in the right direction. Thus the moral instruction of the earliest churches is to be understood under the rubric of the "ways of the Lord," which were again and again impressed upon the memory of the early Christians, and which must have had a firm place in their teaching. We can in large measure infer the content of this teaching from allusions found in the letters of the New Testament. Just as Paul from time to time can incidentally refer to "my gospel" (Rom. 2:16), by which he means the good news that he preaches in all his mission work by means of creedlike formulae, so "my ways in Christ" refers to the central affirmations of early Christian instruction as he had communicated it in his churches.

The contents of this instruction are for the most part determined by traditions that were already in circulation, taken over from the environment and reformulated so that they now correspond to the Christian way of life and become a vehicle for its communication. To these contents belong the "virtue catalogues" and "vice catalogues" found in several places in early Christian literature. In Romans 1:29–31 a long list of practices and attitudes are enumerated that are to be rejected: wickedness, evil, covetousness, malice, envy, murder, strife, deceit, malignity, gossiping, slandering, hostility to God, insolence, haughtiness, boasting, inventiveness in evil, disobedience to parents, foolishness, faithlessness, heartlessness, ruthlessness. Comparable tabulations are found in Matthew 15:19; Mark 7:21–22; Romans 13:13; 1 Corinthians 5:10–11; 6:9–10; 2 Corinthians 12:20–21; Galatians 5:19–21; Ephesians 4:31; 5:3–5; Colossians 3:5, 8; 1 Timothy 1:9–10; 2 Timothy 3:2–5; Titus 3:3; 1 Peter 2:1; 4:3, 15; Revelation 21:8; 22:15. By branding evil conduct with a series of such negative labels, it is not the case that a description is being offered of concrete circumstances in this or that church to which a particular letter is addressed. Although there is much to be criticized concerning the conduct of Christians in the various churches, still there never was a single church in which such a mass of unhappy circumstances was present. The lists were rather taken over from catechetical tradition that had been used in instructing Christians to an appropriate style of life.

The same is true of the lists of positive qualities, the "catalogues of virtues," such as Galatians 5:22–23: "But the fruit of the Spirit is love, joy, peace, patience, kindness, generosity, faithfulness, gentleness, self-control." Comparable tabulations of virtues are found in 2 Corinthians 6:6; Ephesians 4:2–3, 32; 5:9; Philippians 4:8; Colossians 3:12; 1 Timothy 4:12; 6:11; 2 Timothy 2:22; 3:10; 1 Peter 3:8, 2 Peter 1:5–7. In these series too, traditional teaching is taken up that describes how the Christian life should be characterized by a list of statements. From time to time the accent is placed on a particular virtue by the way the list is arranged. The foremost "fruit of the Spirit" is love, which heads the list in Galatians 5:22. Occasionally the first or last item in the list is emphasized because it is of particular importance for the wider context, as in Romans 1 the emphasis on the contrast of righteousness and unrighteousness influences the way Romans 1:29 is presented (see above). By the citation of such catalogues the congregation is reminded of the "ways of Christ" in which they had been instructed. The allusion to the familiar catechetical teaching strengthens the concrete admonition, in order to impress upon the readers the obligation of right Christian conduct by the repetition of traditional material.

The tradition of the catalogues of virtues and vices came to the early Christian congregations from their environment, from the Hellenistic synagogues in particular. The Cynic-Stoic popular philosophy had developed certain lists of vices and virtues—especially the so-called cardinal virtues. These "cardinal virtues"—wisdom (φρόνησις), modesty (σωφροσύνη), courage (ἀνδρεία), and justice (δικαιοσύνη)—were then more precisely explained by means of related concepts. To them were contrasted the cardinal vices: foolishness (ἀφροσύνη), licentiousness (ἀκολασία), injustice (ἀδικία), and cowardice (δειλία). They were then likewise characterized more precisely by the addition of related statements. In the discussions of popular philosophy no systematic analysis of these concepts was undertaken; praiseworthy and blameworthy conduct was described simply by assembling loosely connected lists. The language was accommodated to everyday speech, and even coarse expressions were not avoided, in order to translate philosophical reflections into directives for concrete action. Such listings of ethical ideas could be of service in the ethical instruction that was taught to Jews and proselytes in the synagogue, in order to explain the commandments of God contained in the Scriptures with the help of expressions current in the everyday Hellenistic world.

Catalogues of ethical terms are also found in the writings of the Qumran community. In their teaching that was much influenced by dualistic ideas, light is contrasted with darkness, and the ways that please God are juxtaposed with the ways that belong to the spirit of falsehood. On the positive side, that means—as expressed in the Manual of Discipline—

> a spirit of humility, patience, abundant charity, unending goodness, understanding, and intelligence, [a spirit of] mighty wisdom which trusts in all the deeds of God and leans on his great loving kindness; a spirit of discernment in every purpose, of zeal for just laws, of holy intent with steadfastness of heart, of great charity towards all the sons of truth, of admirable purity which detests all unclean idols, of humble conduct sprung from an understanding of all things, and of faithful concealment of the mysteries of truth (1QS 4:3–6).

But on the other side, it is said:

> But the ways of the spirit of falsehood are these: greed, and slackness in the search for righteousness, wickedness and lies, haughtiness and pride, falseness and deceit, cruelty and abundant evil-ill-temper and much folly and brazen insolence, abominable deeds [committed] in a spirit of lust, and ways of lewdness in the service of uncleanness, a blaspheming tongue, blindness of eye and dullness of ear, stiffness of neck and heaviness of heart, so that man walks in all the ways of darkness and guile (1QS 4:9–11).

The intention of these two lists is to urge and facilitate the recognition of what God's command is and what it means. In anticipation of the imminent divine judgment, a warning is raised against disdaining the commandments. People are admonished to walk in the right way, so that they can stand in the judgment. The listing of pious conduct on the one side and evil deeds on the other is intended to instruct one in what obedience to the law looks like concretely. Such contrasts correspond to the picture of the Two Ways, as it was portrayed in the Jewish legal teaching at the time of Jesus and the first Christians. In this picture, the way of righteousness was described in contrast to the way of violence (1 Enoch 91:18–19). The good way of light is to be distinguished from the evil way of darkness (2 Enoch 30:15). Just as the Hellenistic popular philosophy referred to the fable that told of Hercules standing at the crossroads, so the pious can say in the words of Rabbi Johanan ben

Zakkai: "Go forth and see which is the good way to which a man should cleave. . . . Go forth and see which is the evil way which a man should shun" (Aboth 2:9).

———

The New Testament documents do not yet presuppose a catechism of the Two Ways, which was first formulated at the beginning of the second century C.E. in the early Christian catechetical tradition. It is documented in both the *Didache*, the "Teaching of the Twelve Apostles," and in the *Letter of Barnabas*. The *Didache* begins with the sentence: "There are two ways, the one of life and the other of death, and there is a great difference between the two ways" (1:1). Then the way of life is described:

> First, "thou shalt love the God who made thee; secondly, thy neighbor as thyself; and whatsoever thou wouldst not have done to thyself, do not thou to another." Now, the teaching of these words is this: . . . "Thou shalt commit no murder; thou shalt not commit adultery"; thou shalt not commit sodomy; thou shalt not commit fornication; thou shalt not steal; thou shalt not use magic; thou shalt not mix any deadly poison; thou shalt not procure abortion, nor commit infanticide, "thou shalt not covet thy neighbor's goods"; thou shalt not commit perjury, "thou shalt not bear false witness"; thou shalt not speak evil; thou shalt not bear malice. Thou shalt not be double-minded nor double-tongued, for to be double-tongued is the snare of death. Thy speech shall not be false nor vain, but completed in action. Thou shalt not be covetousness nor extortionate, nor a hypocrite, nor malignant, nor proud, thou shalt make no evil plan against thy neighbor. Thou shalt hate no man; but some thou shalt reprove, and for some shalt thou pray, and some thou shalt love more than thine own life. (*Didache* 1:2–2:7; translation from Loeb Classical Library).

This composition blends into one unit the double commandment of love, declarations from the Ten Commandments, instruction that is also found in the Sermon on the Mount, as well as echoes of material also found in the catalogues of virtues and vices that circulated in oral tradition. The later summary arranged according to a catechetical point of view reflects one result of early Christian ethical instruction in which the way of life is held up against its forbidding counterpart, the way of death.

> First of all, it is wicked and full of cursing, murders, adulteries, lusts, fornications, thefts, idolatries, witchcrafts, charms, robberies, false witness, hypocrisies, a double heart, fraud, pride, malice, stubbornness, covetousness, foul speech, jealousy, impudence, haughtiness, boastfulness. Persecutors of the good, haters of truth, lovers of lies, knowing not the reward of righteousness, not cleaving to the good nor to righteous judgment, spending wakeful nights not for good but for wickedness, from whom meekness and patience is far, lovers of vanity, following after reward, unmerciful to the poor, not working for him who is oppressed with toil, without knowledge of him who made them, murderers of children, corrupters of God's creatures, turning away the needy, oppressing the distressed, advocates of the rich, unjust judges of the poor, altogether sinful; may ye be delivered, my children, from all these. (*Didache* 5:1–2)

The rather oppressive fullness of this list partly overlaps with the preceding portrayal of the way of life. In both places the warnings and threats are intended to direct one to the way of life. In the long series of prohibitions and demands various elements from the oral tradition have been inserted into the schema of the two ways. We thus can recognize clear echoes of the double commandment of love, references to the early Christian vice catalogues, as well as warnings taken from the ethical instruction of the popular philosophy. As the similar section in the *Letter of Barnabas* shows, a two ways catechism was constructed by early Christianity in this pattern, which placed an impressive commentary alongside the teaching of Jesus: the way through the narrow gate, which alone leads to life, must not be missed, and one must not be misled into adopting as one's course the supposedly easier way through the wide gate and broad street. For "the gate is narrow and the road is hard that leads to life; there are few who find it" (Matt. 7:13–14).

Thus the early Christian instruction on the right way has its historical setting in the midst of a broad stream of late antique and early Christian tradition. Already present were lists of virtues and vices, documented on the one hand in the popular philosophical discussions, and advocated on the other hand in the Jewish interpretations of the law. Fixed forms of catechetical tradition thus developed early in Christian history, which at the beginning of the second century led to the formulation of a two ways catechism. The moral teaching reflected in the New Testament documents thus rests in great part on traditions already present in its environment, but these had not yet been structured into a catechism of ethical instruction on how one should live one's life (see below, p. 215).

The long, unsystematic, loosely connected lists that cover the range from abstractions to concrete actions, show in pragmatic illustrations that the important thing is to recognize the ways of Christ and to walk in them. They thereby provide extensive descriptions of what it means to live one's life "in the Lord" and where his ways are abandoned. Even though it is the case that the individual ideas aim at concrete conduct and decisive action, the presentation of catalogues and lists still avoids attempting a casuistic decoding and classification of the divine will, as though it were directed to a certain number of conceivable individual cases, even if this number is thought of as very large. Early Christian exhortation does not intend to advocate a righteousness based on works, but to give direction for the conduct of Christians, which they are to pursue with persistence, patience, and perseverance. The task of determining this way in the context of their given situation remained their own responsibility. But it is the responsibility of those whose lives are oriented by the guidebook of catechetical instruction, which will enable them in their particular situation to decide what is commanded by their Lord.

Suggestions for Further Reading

Aune, D. E. "Paraenetic Forms." In *The New Testament in its Literary Environment*, pp. 19–96. Philadelphia: Westminster, 1987.

Betz, H. D. "Excursus: A Catalogue of Vices and Virtues." In *Galatians*, pp. 281–83. Philadelphia: Fortress Press, 1979.

Borgen, P. "Catalogues of Vices, The Apostolic Decree, and the Jerusalem Meeting." In *The Social World of Formative Christianity and Judaism*, pp. 126–41. J. Neusner, P. Borgen, E. Fredrichs, and R. Horsley, eds. Philadelphia: Fortress Press, 1988.

———. *Paul Preaches Circumcision and Pleases Men, and Other Essays on Christian Origins*. Trondheim: Tapir, 1983.

Collins, J. J. *Between Athens and Jerusalem*, pp. 158–62. New York: Crossroad, 1983.

Doty, W. "Catalogues and Lists." In *Letters in Primitive Christianity*, pp. 57–59. Philadelphia: Fortress Press, 1973.

Schweizer, E. "Traditional Ethical Patterns in the Pauline and Post-Pauline Letters and Their Development (lists of vices and house-tables)." In *Text and Interpretation*, pp. 195–209. Ernst Best and R. McL. Wilson, eds. Cambridge: Cambridge University Press, 1979.

Stowers, S. K. *The Diatribe and Paul's Letter to the Romans*. Chico: Scholars Press, 1981.

Suggs, M. J. "The Christian Two Ways Tradition: Its Antiquity, Form and Function." In *Studies in New Testament and Early Christian Literature*, David Aune, ed., pp. 60–74. Leiden: E. J. Brill, 1972.

Zaas, P. "Catalogues and Context: 1 Corinthians 5 and 6." *New Testament Studies* 34 (1988): 622–29.

The Responsibility of Conscience

The first Christians had to account for their decisions regarding the extent to which they could adopt traditional materials already present for their ethical orientation, and when they must formulate new moral directives. When they adopted different stances to particular ethical questions than their surroundings, they had to give a reason for doing so. They not only had to attain sufficient clarity about the requisite decisions, they also had to be able to explain to outsiders the determining power that shaped their convictions about how their lives were to be shaped. They thus sought to express not only the freedom of faith but also its binding obligations, by following the counsel of the apostle Paul to "test everything" and "hold fast to what is good" (1 Thess. 5:21). The confidence of their faith disclosed to them a broad horizon within which they could form their judgments, and opened to them the prospect of bringing within view the multiplicity of possibilities, so that they could carefully reflect on what would prove itself as good, or even the best.

Everything in the environment was weighed and tested, and wherever truth, justice, and goodness were to be found, it was considered important for the orientation of Christians' lives (Phil. 4:8; see below, p. 215). Arguments from reason also carried weight. Then, after careful probing of the traditional ideas that came to them and decisions were made as to what was an appropriate expression of Christian faith, care had to be taken to make the results understandable to the general membership of the church. Because this task could not be done once for all but was constantly renewed by the changing demands of everyday life, the question of how God's will could be recognized and done was always posed afresh. Early Christian ethics was therefore no closed system, but was constantly exposed to correction as warranted by the "measure of faith" (Rom. 12:3).

In order to recognize the demand of the will of God, one must harken to the voice of conscience. The apostle Paul, who repeatedly makes use of the concept of "conscience," probably adopted it from the Hellenistic synagogue, which in turn had already been influenced by its usage in Stoic philosophy. The Old Testament Scriptures do not use the word "conscience," though the idea to which the Greek term points is found there. This is seen, for example, in distinctions between good and evil as well as the awareness that humanity has fallen into guilt, which is perceived by "conscience" (Gen. 3). The word "conscience" declares: "I am aware of myself." Conscience critically examines whether I have made the right decision and acted responsibly. It judges according to moral norms and lets me know when I have violated them—partly as the judge who condemns past transgressions, partly as the watchman who forewarns of and attempts to hinder potentially wrong decisions and causes one to reflect on its objections. Its voice does not simply repeat what transpires in my own thinking and striving, but stands independently over against it, in order from this distance to sound a warning note. People who think responsibly will not suppress this voice, but will allow it to be heard and will listen to it.

Paul uses the concept of conscience in different contexts, in some of which it is a matter of recognizing God's will and translating it into action. Since a conscience has been given to every human being, all know that they are called to a responsible manner of life. For the Jew, the command of God is made known in the law; but the gentiles also know God's will and are thus responsible in the same way. For them—so the apostle argues—the requirement of the law is written on their hearts, "while their conscience also bears witness and their conflicting thoughts will accuse or perhaps excuse them" (Rom. 2:15). In the conscience, it is the demand of God that comes to expression, and can be heard clearly enough that no one can make the excuse that there was no way to know what should be done. The warning voice of conscience is thus a critical, but by no means infallible, court. It can have limited insight, or even be mistaken. The final court of appeal is God alone (1 Cor. 4:4). In the apostle's understanding, conscience does not represent an awareness of duty and norms that can be absolutized, but rather a critical self-awareness that provides a check on the sincerity of our own thinking and activity, and thus sharpens the responsibility that all persons have as they stand before God.

An illustrative example of how the Christian should attend to conscience is offered by the extensive discussion of the question of whether or not Christians may eat meat sacrificed to idols (1 Cor. 8–10). Paul thereby clearly distinguishes himself from the understanding of the issue advocated in the Jewish communities of that time. To them the eating of meat that had not been slaughtered according to the regulations of the Torah, or even to participate in events that took place within the precincts of a pagan temple, appeared out of the question. In contrast, Paul makes his decisions on the basis of the freedom of the Christian who is persuaded that the whole earth belongs to the Lord and who thus considers it unnecessary to inquire into the origin and preparation of the food placed before him or her. "Everything is permitted" —the apostle can affirm his basic agreement to this motto current among the Corinthian Christians (NRSV: "all things are lawful," 1 Cor. 10:23).

Still, with this response only one side of the problematic of the issue was brought into view. The other side is determined by the consideration of how the proposed action affects the people concerned. Not every Christian was persuaded by the insight that "no idol in the world really exists" (1 Cor. 8:4). Many shared the anxious fear that behind the idols the demonic powers were at work, powers with which it is dangerous to come in contact. They were afraid that they might be venturing into their danger zone. They are therefore considered to have a weak conscience (1 Cor. 8:7, 10, 12). They were simply unable to share the valid knowledge that however many "gods" and "lords" there may be in this world, for the believer there is "one God, the Father, from whom are all things and for whom we exist, and one Lord, Jesus Christ, through whom are all things and through whom we exist" (1 Cor. 8:6). Those who on the basis of this knowledge consider themselves to be "strong" may not sin against their brother or sister by their conduct intended to challenge others, but which in fact becomes an obstacle to them. Whoever does not take the weak conscience of a brother or sister into consideration, but in proud superiority eats "idol meat" that has been sacrificed in a pagan temple, sins against that person. By such conduct the weak conscience of the other person is brought into danger, which could even result in a loss of faith.

By the position that he takes on this issue, Paul has given an answer that is of fundamental significance for the understanding of Christian ethics. To be sure, the Christian lives in the freedom that comes through faith. This freedom would simply degenerate into lack of consideration, even recklessness, if love is not the guiding norm of one's conduct. "Knowledge puffs up," because it arouses the feeling of proud superiority; love alone, which takes the other into consideration, "builds up" (1 Cor. 8:1). For Christians, moral decisions are not made on the basis of a scrupulous discrimination among the objects in this world with which they have to do. They are not obligated to subject the things in this world to arbitrary objective tests, as prescribed by the purity regulations of the Old Testament. Love alone, which attends to the possible endangering of the conscience of the other person, provides the orientation by which one can make responsible decisions. The thesis, "everything is permitted," remains valid. It is limited, however, by the insight guided by love, that not everything serves what is good. "Everything is permitted," but not everything leads to building up the community of faith. Therefore no one should simply seek what is good for oneself, but what is good for the other (1 Cor. 10:23–24).

What concrete conclusions should be drawn from this fundamental consideration? The apostle offers no legalistic directions that claim to be valid for all time. He rather gives illustrative examples of how the responsible conscience directed by love points the way to right Christian conduct. Basically – this principle is affirmed once again – Christians need not conduct an investigation to determine the origin of the meat served at public functions, nor be concerned with the qualities that are inherent in the things with which they have to do in this world. It is not necessary to burden one's conscience by raising such questions (1 Cor. 10:27). The situation will look different, however, if someone at the meal points out: "This has been offered in sacrifice" (v. 28). To be sure, Christian freedom allows the believer even in this case to go ahead and enjoy the meat, and to do so without scruples. But now the decision is no longer a matter of Christian freedom, but of love, which takes into consideration the weak conscience of the other (v. 29). Love has a higher priority than knowledge. It seeks not its own good, but the edification of the other. Christians are therefore called to do everything to God's glory and to provoke no offense to Jews, to Greeks, or to the church of God (vv. 31–32).

How this *responsibility of Christians* is to be exercised is explained by the apostle in fundamental affirmations that he prefaces to the comprehensive ethical section of the Letter to the Romans (12:1–2). This hortatory section, which as paraclesis includes within itself the notes of encouragement and comfort, is based on the declaration and promise of God's mercy. In apostolic instruction, the compassion of the God who has already turned in love toward the life of the believer comes to expression as the guide for the believer's own life. They are to offer their bodies – that is, themselves, with all that they are and do – as a living sacrifice to God, holy and well-pleasing to God.

The whole life of the Christian is thus described as an act of worship. What has been declared "holy" is withdrawn from ordinary human use and is dedicated to God's use as God's own property. The temple precinct, which is marked off from the profane sphere, is the site where offerings "well-pleasing to God" are presented. But Paul uses these cultic concepts, which were familiar to everyone in the ancient world, in a sense that leaves every cultic meaning far behind. The distinction always presupposed between "sacred" and "profane" is here broken. There is no talk here of a particular temple and its partitioned-off, consecrated space, but of the whole length and breadth of human life, in which all one's doing and being is involved. There is no longer any sacred area given special honor as the site of worship and sacrifice. The whole world is the place in which Christians carry out their worship in the midst of everyday life.

Paul characterizes this worship as "reasonable service" (λογικὴ λατρεία), and thereby uses a Stoic concept that calls for living in accord with the universal reason that permeates the universe. Presumably this expression, like much else in his thought, came to him by way of the Hellenistic synagogue, which in turn sought to use the idea to communicate the proper knowledge and worship of God. Reasonable reflection, which strives to determine and do the will of God, is thus explicitly commanded. But the question remains in ethical decisions as to how Christians can arrive at well-founded judgments and corresponding actions. Paul first responds to this question with a negative restriction, which is then followed by a positive rule. Christians, who in the freedom of faith can survey everything in their environment with a probing look and can learn from this dialogue, must not however subject themselves to the formative influence of this world, but must give heed to the warning not to let the world press them into its own mold. They should rather be guided by the renewing of their judgment which they experience by the power of faith. This "renewing" includes human reason, and its capacity to make well-grounded decisions. While in another passage Paul says of the non-Christian gentiles that their powers of perception and judgment have become vain and futile (Rom. 1:21, 28), here he speaks of the transforming power of God that applies specifically to the human capacity for reflective thought.

The level-headed perspective on the world, as it opens itself to the gaze of Christian faith, awakens and sharpens the aptitude for critical thought. This does not lead to the production of a specifically Christian doctrine of social ethics, according to which the order of human life could be regulated. The sample of traditional ethical views presented for inspection is oriented to one question alone, what is the "good and acceptable and perfect" will of God (Rom. 12:2).

Suggestions for Further Reading

Bornkamm, G. "Faith and Reason in Paul." In *Early Christian Experience*, pp. 29–46. New York: Harper & Row, 1969.

——. "On the Understanding of Worship." In *Early Christian Experience*, pp. 161–79. New York: Harper & Row, 1969.

Conzelmann, H. *An Outline of the Theology of the New Testament*, pp. 173–84. New York: Harper & Row, 1969.

Engberg-Pedersen, T. "The Gospel and Social Practice According to 1 Corinthians." *New Testament Studies* 33 (1987): 557–84.

Horsley, R. A. "Consciousness and Freedom Among the Corinthians: 1 Corinthians 8–10." *Catholic Biblical Quarterly* 40 (1978): 574–89.

Käsemann, E. "Ministry and Community in the New Testament." In *Essays on New Testament Themes*, pp. 63–94. Naperville: Alec R. Allenson, 1964.

Keck, L. E. *Paul and His Letters*, pp. 84–98. Philadelphia: Fortress Press, 1979.

Stendahl, K. "The Apostle Paul and the Introspective Conscience of the West." In *Paul Among Jews and Gentiles and Other Essays*, pp. 78–96. Philadelphia: Fortress Press, 1976.

Theissen, G. *Psychological Aspects of Pauline Theology*. Philadelphia: Fortress Press, 1986.

——. *The Social Setting of Pauline Christianity*, pp. 121–43. Philadelphia: Fortress Press, 1982.

Willis, W. *Idol Meat in Corinth: The Pauline Argument in 1 Corinthians 8 and 10*. Chico: Scholars Press, 1985.

Male and Female

In early Christianity the relationship of man and woman experienced a fundamental transformation, which stands out clearly from the views that prevailed in its surroundings. The general view was that men were more highly regarded than women. To be sure, a spectrum of different relationships existed in various settings, that were not evaluated everywhere the same in either Judaism or the Hellenistic-Roman world. Still, the dominant view was that a woman's place was lower than a man's, and that she should therefore be subservient to him (Josephus, *Contra Apion* 2:201). A prayer is handed on in the rabbinic tradition in which the man praises God three times each day that he was not born a gentile, a woman, or a common man untrained in the rabbinic lore (t. Ber. 6:18). This particular statement certainly may not be generalized. But it still expresses in extreme form the general view that men are superior to women.

In order to hold a legitimate synagogue worship service, at least ten men must be present—the number of women is irrelevant. The testimony of a woman was not recognized in court. And when a marriage suffered hard times, the power to decide concerning a divorce rested solely with the husband. One of the topics of the scribal discussions was the grounds that must be present if a man wants to release his wife. The condition mentioned in Deuteronomy 24:1, that he "finds something objectionable about her," was seen as fulfilled by the school of Shammai if the woman had committed adultery. By contrast, the school of Hillel considered the woman to have already given sufficient occasion for divorce if she did something contrary to good manners, such as going about with her hair down or allowing dinner to burn (m. Git. 9:10).

In the Hellenistic world too, it was considered an incontestable rule that the woman was subordinate to the man and must resign herself to following his instructions. However, a decision concerning divorce could be made by the woman as well as the man. But the ancient world knew many examples of marital faithfulness and sincere love between husband and wife, as is documented by an enormous number of gravestones and inscriptions. Although in terms of legal rights the woman was at a disadvantage in comparison to the man, in many houses and families it was the woman who played the decisive role.

In the preaching of Jesus men and women were addressed in the same way. Human beings are not essentially neuter, but "from the beginning of creation God made them male and female" (Mark 10:6). To be sure, the narrow circle of disciples that followed Jesus about was composed of men. But women were also closely associated with him (Luke 8:1-3). His helping and healing deeds were conferred on men and women alike, without anywhere making any distinction. His sayings and parables deal with both men and women, with nowhere a suggestion that men have the higher rank. The joy in seeking and finding the lost is described in the same way for the shepherd who brings his sheep safely home as for the woman who again holds her lost coin in her hand (Luke 15:1-10).

In the light of the dawning kingdom of God the distinctions and separations that have been erected by human beings fall away. To all, both women and men, the announcement of the good news goes forth as a call to repentance and renewal. Jesus was not hesitant to go against the custom of his times and to speak with women in public (Luke 7:36-50; Mark 14:3-9). Wherever he turns to people who have lost their way and have been excluded from association with others, he addresses them both with forgiveness for their guilt and direction for their future life. To the woman taken in adultery, whom Jesus does not condemn, the challenge is directed: "Go your way, and from now on, do not sin again" (John 8:11).

According to the reports of all the Gospels, women, whose testimony was not accepted in the courtroom, were the first witnesses of the Easter message (Mark 16:1-8 par.). Along with the disciples, who were called by the appearances of the risen one to form the community of the new covenant, they confessed that the Lord had indeed risen (Luke 24:34). Thus the evangelists show by many examples that women and men belong together as members of the church of Jesus Christ. Just as the call to repentance and faith goes forth to all, so baptism was administered to both men and women. They participated together in the celebration of worship, without the number of men or women present playing any role. The prophetic word can be spoken by women as well as men (1 Cor. 11:1–16). In the same way, the service of love was sometimes performed by men, sometimes by women. The operative conviction was: "There is no longer Jew nor Greek. There no longer slave nor free, there is no longer male nor female, for all of you are one in Christ Jesus" (Gal. 3:28).

In the declaration that male and female are one in Christ Jesus, the joyful experience came to expression that is based on the new creation in Christ effected by the Spirit. Possibly the apostle Paul is here adopting a quotation that had its origin in the self-confidence of spirit-inspired enthusiasm. It could sound as if all the distinctions that exist in human society had been trivialized and become null and void. In some Gnostic circles such an understanding was developed and put into practice forthwith, so that one either ascetically turned away from all worldly involvement, or drew the opposite inference and with the elation of freedom's belief that all is permitted, surrendered to libertine conduct. The apostle Paul can agree neither with the one conception nor the other, as especially is shown in his extensive debate with the views advocated by the spirit-inspired enthusiasts in the Corinthian church. He has no doubt that all-embracing unity in Christ actually exists, but he is also constantly aware that Christians must adjust to the rules that define decency and order, as they are acknowledged throughout the world.

Over against the Corinthians, Paul seeks to explain why it is necessary for a woman who speaks prophetically in the congregational worship to do so with her head covered, while a man need not conform to this rule (1 Cor. 11:2–6). Obviously the apostle directs his comments to the views of spirit-filled enthusiastic groups in the congregation who see the matter differently, and introduces a variety of material from different perspectives to support his argument. Among these is the view current in his setting, according to which the man does not need to cover his head because he is the image and reflection of God's own glory, but the "glory" of the woman is derivative from that of the man (v. 7). "For," he continues, "man was not made from woman, but woman from man. Neither was man created for the sake of woman, but woman for the sake of man" (v. 8). But then it appears that in the very act of copying down this explanation Paul himself perceives that, while to be sure it corresponds to the current opinion, it does not give appropriate expression to the unity of man and woman grounded in Christ. He thus corrects himself as he continues, "Nevertheless, in the Lord woman is not independent of man or man of woman. For just as woman came from man, so man comes through woman; but all things come from God" (vv. 11–12). In view of this knowledge of how things are "in the Lord," decisions can no longer be made on the basis of higher or lower rank, but only by acknowledging that the generally accepted custom does carry some weight in the way Christians order their own lives. Paul argues that individual congregations should not deviate from the practice that prevails in all the churches (v. 16).

The apostle does not here follow a united line of argument, but swings back and forth between the views presupposed in the culture and the conviction that "in the Lord" man and woman are one. His judgment also alternates between views based on his ethical principles and views based on practical conduct as experienced in the church. These distinctions are conditioned principally by the variety of presuppositions given by, on the one hand, contacts with Jewish-Christian Palestinian traditions, and on the other hand by the views prevailing in the Hellenistic gentile churches. The abrupt order directing women to be silent in the churches (1 Cor. 14:34–35) is in tension with the statement that obviously assumes that women also can be given the charisma of prophetic speech (1 Cor. 11:5), and thus should be considered a post-Pauline statement later inserted into this context of the Corinthiar letter (see below, p. 142). Irrespective of these differing opinions and practices, the conviction was everywhere held fast that by baptism men and women had been made one in Christ. This is the explanation of the fact that the almost universally acknowledged rule that women were to be subject to men was preserved in the ethical doctrine of early Christian instruction, but newly understood on the basis of partnership in the spirit of love grounded in Christ (see below pp. 142–43). This is an illustration of the phenomenon that the social relationships that formed the structure of the contemporary way of life were seen in a fresh light and changed as they were subordinated to the unity founded "in the Lord."

The eschatological message of the dawning kingdom of God, as proclaimed both in the preaching of Jesus and in the witness of the earliest church, reveals the will of God as set forth in creation for the good of humanity. Thus, in distinction from the views prevailing in the culture, an understanding of the unity of man and woman in marriage was advocated, an understanding based on the gospel. While in both Jewish and Hellenistic-Roman law a marriage could be dissolved at any time, usually to the detriment of the woman, Jesus taught that God had created humanity as a unity of male and female in order that they might live together in partnership their whole life long (Mark 10:6–7). In the creation story of the Old Testament, it is said that a man shall leave his father and his mother and be joined to his wife, and that the two shall become one flesh (vv. 7–8; Gen. 2:24). The conclusion drawn from this text is "therefore what God has joined together, let no one separate" (v. 9). According to the account of the synoptic Gospels, this is Jesus' response to the question of a Pharisee who asked whether it was permitted for a man to divorce his wife (Mark 10:2 par.). This formulation lets it be recognized, however, that the wording has been shaped by the church as it handed on the traditional story, since neither by Jews nor Greeks was it contested that a man could divorce his wife. A question directed to Jesus could not have dealt with "whether," but only with the question of "how." But in place of naming the expected conditions under which a marriage could be dissolved, Jesus responds with a strict prohibition of divorce as such.

By conceiving marriage as a unity of husband and wife that, in the intention of the creator is indissoluble, Jesus attributes a dignity to marriage that it received neither among the Jews nor the Greeks. The Christian community remained aware of the binding significance of this understanding, and brought this insight to expression as they adapted it to the situation with explanatory comments unique in both the Jewish and Hellenistic world. If in the Greco-Roman world a woman could in some circumstances divorce her husband, in Christ it is permitted neither to the man nor to the woman to dissolve a marriage. For "whoever divorces his wife and marries another commits adultery against her; and if she divorces her husband and marries another, she commits adultery" (Mark 10:11-12).

When Jesus and the first Christians advocated the indissolubility of marriage, they knew very well the weakness and failures of humanity. For the provision for divorce in the law reveals something about the hardness of human hearts (Mark 10:5 par.). But also for Christians situations can emerge in which despite good will the unity of a marriage can no longer be maintained — whether because the non-Christian partner is no longer willing to continue the marriage (1 Cor. 7:15), or whether through repeated adultery, described as "unchastity," the unity of the marriage is destroyed (Matt. 5:32; 19:9). The early Christian community thus inserted a so-called adultery clause, and sought thereby in view of persistent hardheartedness to open up a viable way in certain conditions, in order to be able to bring an unbearable situation to an end. The intention was that with the help of these additions, Jesus' teaching could be brought into passable agreement with the reality of the imperfections of human life, as they also emerge among Christians. In this process it is made clear that in the exalted dignity attributed to the institution of marriage, which so clearly distinguishes the Christian view from that of their contemporaries, no new law is being erected, no new burden that people will not be able to bear. The ethical orientation is not provided by legal prescriptions, but is attained from the freeing power of the new creation, in order to form the unity of man and woman so that it corresponds to the original intent of the creator.

———

Quite apart from the fact that marriage was held in very high esteem in both the preaching of Jesus and in the apostolic teaching, each of them also affirmed that the intentionally chosen celibate state is also deserving of respect. In this regard, too, a clear distinction from the views prevalent in the contemporary culture is discernable. In the Judaism of that time, it was the practically unanimous understanding that marriage was a binding obligation of the law of God in order to propagate life on the earth in obedience to the creator's command. Only the community of Qumran, which advocated a constant state of priestly ritual purity for itself, deviated from this general understanding and required celibacy of its members. Over against the ascetic tendencies promoted and practiced in some groups of the Hellenistic world, the statements of the New Testament stand in contrast, in that they neither prescribe legalistic rules nor express any dualistic rejection of this world, but base their teaching on eschatological motivation. For the sake of the kingdom of heaven — so says a saying of Jesus in the Gospels — marriage can be renounced (Matt. 19:12), just as in the period of final eschatological distress the ties of family can be broken (Luke 12:53; Matt. 10:35–36; and elsewhere). And the apostle Paul considers it to be commendable to remain unmarried in order to devote oneself wholly to the Lord. He thereby expresses neither a devaluation of marriage nor an ascetic attitude, for he advises married couples not to deny each other, but to respond to the partner's conjugal expectations (1 Cor. 7:3–5). But whoever has received the charisma of remaining unmarried may do so, in view of the coming eschatological distress. For all Christians, however — whether single or married — the instruction applies equally that they live their lives aware that the time is short, so that those who have marriage partners should live as if they had none. "For the present form of this world is passing away" (1 Cor. 7:29–31). Marriage, which is to be seen as the good gift of the creator, belongs to the transient reality of this world. When the dead are raised, they will neither marry nor give in marriage, but will be as the angels in heaven (Mark 12:25 par.).

Suggestions for Further Reading

Balch, D. L. "1 Cor 7:32–35 and Stoic Debates About Marriage, Anxiety, and Distraction." *Journal of Biblical Literature* 102 (1983): 429–39.

Bartchy, S. *Mallon Chresai: First Century Slavery and the Interpretation of 1 Corinthians 7:21.* Missoula: Scholars Press, 1973.

Brooten, B. "Early Christian Women and Their Cultural Context." In *Feminist Perspectives on Biblical Scholarship,* pp. 65–91. A. Y. Collins, ed. Chico: Scholars Press, 1985.

Collins, R. F. "The Unity of Paul's Paraenesis in 1 Thess. 4.3–8. 1 Cor. 7.1–7, A Significant Parallel." *New Testament Studies* 29 (1983): 420–29.

Elliott, J. K. "Paul's Teaching on Marriage in 1 Corinthians: Some Problems Reconsidered." *New Testament Studies* 19 (1973): 219–25.

Fiorenza, E. S. *In Memory of Her.* New York: Crossroad, 1983.

MacDonald, D. R. *There is No Male and Female.* Philadelphia: Fortress Press, 1987.

Waetjen, H. *A Reordering of Power: A Socio-Political Reading of Mark's Gospel.* Minneapolis: Fortress Press, 1989.

Walker, W. O. "The 'Theology of Woman's Place' and the 'Paulinist' Tradition." *Semeia* 28 (1983): 101–12.

Yarbrough, O. L. *Not Like the Gentiles: Marriage Rules in the Letters of Paul.* Atlanta: Scholars Press, 1985.

Chapter Six

THE NEW CREATION
IN THE LIFE
OF THE BELIEVER

Justification and the New Life

"So if any one is in Christ, there he is a new creation; everything old has passed away, see, everything has become new" (2 Cor. 5:17). With these words the apostle Paul describes the new life in which believers participate when they are baptized into Christ. In the cross of Christ, the amazing exchange has taken place: God "made him to be sin who knew no sin, so that in him we might become the righteousness of God" (2 Cor. 5:21). The preaching of the gospel makes known this event that creates salvation (Rom. 1:16–17). Where this message is accepted in faith, there it is grasped that the righteousness acceptable before God is received as the gift of divine mercy only in faithful trust in the redemption given through Christ, not by vain works that attempt to establish one's own righteousness.

"Christ alone," "grace alone," "faith alone" correspond to one another, as the Scripture teaches in the example of Abraham. Paul appeals to the report in Genesis, in which it is said that Abraham believed God, and this was reckoned to him as righteousness (Gen. 15:6=Rom. 4:3; Gal. 3:6). The faith of

Abraham means that, despite all appearances, he relied on the promise of God and thereby allowed room for God's act. He held the word of God to be more real than all that his eyes could see, and thus placed himself in the only right relationship to God, a relationship that is reckoned to him as righteousness, accepting the communion with God that is graciously bestowed on those who put their trust in God.

With this understanding of the righteousness of God the apostle refers not only to the Old Testament, but also at the same time takes up affirmations of the faith as it was commonly confessed in the early Christian creeds. In a creedal statement adduced at the end of Romans 4, it is said that Christ "was handed over to death for our trespasses and raised for our justification" (Rom. 4:25). The passive voice points to God as the actor in the event of the death and resurrection of Christ. Forgiveness of sins may not be related only to Jesus' death, nor justification only with his resurrection. Both belong together as one statement. Forgiveness of sins as the liberating, justifying act of God is assured on the basis of the cross and resurrection of Christ.

Paul also takes up traditional formulations when he reminds the Corinthian church that the name of the Lord Jesus Christ is named over those who are baptized and the Spirit of God is given to them. The old state of affairs is no longer valid, but "you were washed, you were sanctified, you were justified" (1 Cor. 6:11). The washing that occurred in baptism means that sins have been taken away; sanctification means that God has accepted the baptized person as God's own; and justification means that God has allowed the new creation to become a reality.

Also in Romans 6:3 the apostle introduces an affirmation from common Christian doctrine, "that all of us who have been baptized into Christ Jesus were baptized into his death." By using the expression "do you not know" to remind the church of instruction they had already received, he seeks to make clear that baptism has effected a break with the past that means an irreversible renunciation of sin. If sin was once able to establish its worldwide power through the disobedience of Adam, now its lordship has been broken by the obedience of Christ (Rom.

5:12–21). If Christians are united by baptism with the death and resurrection of their Lord, then the change of lordships that has been accomplished must have consequences for the whole life of the believers. This is what Paul means by the words, "therefore we have been buried with him by baptism into death, so that just as Christ was raised from the dead by the glory of the Father, so we too might walk in newness of life" (Rom. 6:4).

Spirit enthusiasts understood baptism to be a guarantee of the resurrection that had already been experienced, through which the divine saving powers had already become effective. In contrast to such an understanding Paul emphasized that our resurrection still lies before us, and will become reality only at the future eschatological resurrection (Rom. 6:5). Those who have been baptized, who have died with Christ to old humanity and the lordship of sin, stand between the resurrection of Christ and the coming resurrection of the dead. Their lives are determined by victory over the powers of this age won by the death and resurrection of Christ and are lived out under the sign of the resurrection of the dead still to come. If in the past they were slaves of impurity and unrighteousness, this time is now gone forever. Now it is a matter of proving the meaning of the new life in experience and in the exclusive service of righteousness (Rom. 6:19–23).

In Pauline theology, the Christian ethic is developed as the formation of the new creation in Christ appropriated in baptism. Both the promise of the gospel and the demand of the moral exhortation were always concerned to make clear that the reconciliation grounded in Christ and received on the basis of his act can never be supplemented or improved upon by our own actions done through faith in the gospel. Just as salvation for the world is already accomplished in the event of the cross and resurrection of Christ, so at the beginning of the Christian life stands the event of baptism, in which the old self is crucified with Christ and the new person is subjected to the resurrected Lord. Just as Christ died and was raised once for all, so the Christian is baptized only once. The proclamation of justification, however, which must be preached again and again, is a constant reminder to the baptized Christian of the new creation that God has called into being, and challenges them to be always determined by the foundation laid in baptism, so that in trusting faith and obedient life this foundation may be constantly reappropriated.

In the Pauline theology we find pairs of formulations with almost the same vocabulary, the one being a statement, the other being a command. Indicative and imperative, promise announcing salvation and challenge to responsible life, are in this way related most closely to each other: "If we live by the Spirit, let us also be guided by the Spirit" (Gal. 5:25). On the one side we are told, "we have died to sin" (Rom. 6:2). On the other side, we are challenged, "therefore do not let sin exercise dominion in your mortal bodies, to make you obey their passions" (Rom. 6:12–13); "for sin will have no dominion over you" (Rom. 6:14). The imperative "clean out the old yeast so that you may be a new batch" is bound to the indicative "as you really are unleavened" (1 Cor. 5:7). The apostle is alluding to the custom of every Jewish household, where all leaven was removed before the feast of the Passover, so that in memory of the exodus of Israel and its liberation from Egyptian bondage only unleavened bread would be eaten during the festival. Thus Christians, who confess that Christ is the Passover lamb sacrificed for them, as a sign of the new festival of life that has already begun in Christ, must take leave of the old selves and live their lives only under the sign of the new life. The declaration "you have clothed yourself with Christ" (Gal. 3:27) refers to the new creation that has occurred in baptism. To it there is the corresponding challenge, "put on the lord Jesus Christ" (Rom. 13:14).

How is this juxtaposition of indicative and imperative to be understood? Is the emphasis placed on the indicative, which declares the gift of new life? That could easily lead to the assumption that, in view of the overwhelmingly glorious fact of belonging to Christ there is no need for further exhortations. An imperative would then seem entirely redundant, since the Christian has already decisively broken with sin. This would then mean that commands calling for ethical living had been added because the apostle was compelled to bring his high-flying ideals into some kind of correspondence with sober reality. But if one wants to place the emphasis primarily on the imperative, the preceding indicative is then greatly weakened, for the words that announce salvation as already accomplished are then taken back and limited. Or is it the case that the apostle intends to describe a movement that begins with the indicative and that is made effective by being continued in the imperative? Thereby a development would be suggested that begins with God's act and gradually leads toward greater and greater perfection by ethical living through a process of continual admonition. None of these attempts to explain the Pauline relationship of indicative and imperative do justice to the matter, however. This relationship must be so described that both sides of the equation receive their full value.

In order to determine the interrelationship between indicative and imperative in Paul, it must be noted that the same concepts and vocabulary are used on both sides of the dialogue. Therefore, neither side may be emphasized at the expense of the other, but each must be explained on the basis of the close relationship in which it stands to the other. On the one side it is said: "You have received salvation in Christ, you are really dead to sin, so that you are no longer its prisoner." As Paul's own words express it, "and those who belong to Christ Jesus have crucified the flesh with its passions and desires" (Gal. 5:24). On the other side, it is not denied that the powers, sin, law, and death, which Christ has already conquered, are still present and active. Therefore Christians must in their own lives carry on the struggle between flesh and Spirit, between the independent self-will of the human ego and the determination of the new life by God's act. The compelling might of the powers, to which the Christian once had no choice but to serve as a slave, has now been broken. They can therefore now be successfully resisted, so that the imperative is now directed to Christians who no longer live "according to the flesh," though they still live "in the flesh" – that is, in the network of earthly, human existence (Gal. 2:20).

Thus when the imperative demand is expressed in precisely the same words used for the formulation of the indicative declaration, no qualification is placed against the statement that believers have truly died to sin and do in fact live in the Spirit. But this only leads to the conclusion that they should direct their lives by the Spirit. "So," says Paul, "you also must consider yourselves dead to sin and alive to God in Christ Jesus" (Rom. 6:11). Because the new life the Christian has received is still hidden, it is necessary to hear both the announcement of salvation received in Christ and its challenge to renewed life. This gift received in faith has as its goal the formulation of the new life in the believer—the life that has already become reality in Christ.

The new life of the believer exists in a tension determined by the "already" of the new creation and the "not yet" of the final consummation. The freedom in which Christians presently stand in the world is described by Paul in the words, "the appointed time has grown short; from now on, let even those who have wives be as though they had none, and those who mourn as though they were not mourning, and those who rejoice as though they were not rejoicing, and those who buy as though they had no possessions, and those who deal with the world as though they had no dealings with it. For the present form of this world is passing away" (1 Cor. 7:29–31). These statements appear to resemble those philosophical statements in which people with a philosophical education could describe the freedom of action gained by their perspective on life. In Stoic teaching, everything depended on not allowing oneself to be determined by external events, but by internal sovereignty of one's own reflection resolving how one could make right decisions in harmony with the universal reason (see above, pp. 18–20). The required freedom is only to be realized by distancing oneself from the world, by which one may not be too impressed either by joy or sorrow. Only those who let their hearts be touched neither by external events nor by the goods and enticements of this world will be able to bear patiently their inevitable destiny and preserve their inner distance from the world, so that they can lead lives directed by the reasonable insight and serene confidence.

But despite the fact that comparable expressions are present in Paul's statements and the ideas of Stoicism, the apostle's line of argument differs from the Stoics in that it is not grounded on rejection of the world but on the eschatological perspective: the time is short, the end is near, the parousia of the Lord is expected soon. It is for this reason that Christians must be aware that the world has no lasting substance. The darkness and uncertainty of the present is illumined by the light of the coming Lord.

This expectation, directed to the breaking in of God's new world, may be compared with the pictures of the end found in Jewish apocalypticism. In view of the end that is soon breaking in, the present is thought of as a transitory state, while the future is thought of as representing the eternal world. "For," as the Syrian Apocalypse of Baruch says,

> everything will pass away which is corruptible, and everything that dies will go away, and all present time will be forgotten, and there will be no remembrance of the present time which is polluted by evils. For he who now runs runs in vain, and he who is happy will fall quickly and be humiliated. For that which will be in the future, that is what one will look for, and that which comes later, that is what we shall hope for. For there is a time that does not pass away (44:9-11).

While the apocalyptic expectation longs for an unchanging future that will be different from the transient present, the eschatological basis of hope presented by the apostle Paul is filled with the confidence of faith. The hope of Christians is directed toward the coming of their Lord, in whom they confess their faith as the crucified and resurrected Christ. Under the sign of his lordship there thus stands both the insight that the time is short as well as the ethical admonition to keep a critical distance between oneself and the world that is passing away, but at the same time challenges to be active in the world with deeds of love.

Christians are permitted to back away from this commission neither by a dualistic rejection of the world as evil nor by a flight in which they turn away from involvement in it. The expectation of the coming consummation that grew out of their confession of faith in Christ adds tremendous weight to their ethical direction. Without this confidence, the Christians would be like the others, who have no hope (1 Thess. 4:13), and would be victimized by the prevalent attitude of "let us eat and drink, for tomorrow we die" (1 Cor. 15:32). The conviction that one belongs to the Lord drives out skepticism and frees one to daily works of love. Paul thus speaks at one and the same time of a critical distancing from the world and of a life that exists in the midst of the world's everydayness in confident security. He brings this tension to expression even in the context of 1 Corinthians 7:29–31, where he quite consistently uses the same verb in both the first and second part of each clause: have, as though you did not have; cry, as though you did not cry; rejoice, as though you were not rejoicing; deal with the world as though you were not dealing with it. With Christ's death and resurrection the future has already begun, so that the insight that this world is passing away no longer calls forth fear and anxiety, but enables one to separate penultimate from ultimate, important from ultimately important. Thereby neither marriage nor joy nor sorrow nor the buying of things is fundamentally denied, but the door is opened to the perception of Christian freedom, which makes possible responsible dealing in and with the world.

The eschatological basis of ethical instruction in the context of Pauline theology affirms that the future salvation has already come near (Rom. 13:11). All the same, the confidence of this expectation is not dependent on calculating how far advanced the hands of the world clock may be. Whether the Lord will return during the lifetime of the apostle, or only after his death, is a matter of no importance. The decisive thing alone is the conviction that one belongs to the Lord, who has delivered his own from darkness and placed them in the clear light of day. They cannot therefore continue in the works of darkness, but must put on the armor of light (Rom. 13:12; see above, p. 42). For the Christian, the right perspective on the world is not oriented to apocalyptic speculation, but to christological motivation. For "if we live, we live to the Lord, and if we die, we die to the Lord; so then, whether we live or whether we die, we are the Lord's" (Rom. 14:8).

Suggestions for Further Reading

Bornkamm, G. "Baptism and New Life in Paul." In *Early Christian Experience*, pp. 71–86. New York: Harper & Row, 1969.

Bultmann, R. "The Sacraments." In *Theology of the New Testament*, vol. I, pp. 133–44. New York: Scribner's, 1951.

——. "The Theology of Paul," In *Theology of the New Testament*, vol. I, pp. 190–345. New York: Scribner's, 1951.

Byrne, B. "Living Out the Righteousness of God: The Contribution of Rom 6:1–8:13 to an Understanding of Paul's Ethical Presuppositions." *Catholic Biblical Quarterly* 43 (1981): 557–81.

Dahl, N. "The Doctrine of Justification." In *Studies in Paul*, pp. 95–120. Minneapolis: Augsburg, 1977.

Kümmel, W. G. *The Theology of the New Testament*, pp. 224–28. Nashville: Abingdon, 1973.

Tannehill, R. *Dying and Rising With Christ*. Berlin: Töpelmann, 1966.

Wagner, G. *Pauline Baptism and the Pagan Mysteries*. Edinburgh: Oliver & Boyd, 1967.

Watson, N. "Justified by Faith; Judged by Works—An Antinomy?" *New Testament Studies* 29 (1983): 209–21.

Wedderburn, A. J. M. *Baptism and Resurrection*. Tübingen: J. C. B. Mohr, 1987.

Westerholm, S. "Letter and Spirit. The Foundation of Pauline Ethics." *New Testament Studies* 30 (1984): 229–48.

Christian Existence "in the Body"

In accord with its Old Testament heritage, early Christian anthropology understands human existence in its bodily nature as the good creation of God. In contrast, the view dominant in the Greek world distinguished two parts in the human being, the soul as the higher element and the body as the lower. While the body is transient and perishes, the soul is immortal and is freed by death from its earthly prison. The biblical view considers each person's existence as one undivided whole, experienced as mortality and responsibility before God. The anthropological concepts "spirit," "soul," "body," and "flesh" do not therefore describe different organs or parts of human beings, but regard persons as a whole from different perspectives, one living creature who can be the subject, and also the object, of one's own decision and action.

This holistic perspective, which is taken over from the language of the Old Testament and developed further, comes to clearest expression in Pauline theology, especially in Paul's use of the concept "body" (σῶμα). Paul can still sometimes use "body" to refer only to the physical body of a person, as for example in 1 Corinthians 13:3 when he says that one can give one's body to be burned, or Galatians 6:17 where Paul mentions the marks (wounds) that he bears on his body. He can write, as he does to the Corinthians, that he is absent in body but present in spirit (1 Cor. 5:3). Nevertheless, even in these statements the body is not seen merely as a part of the person, that could be distinguished from one's real self, for it is precisely in the body that people encounter their fellow human beings and develop relationships with them. On the one hand Paul can say, "do you not know that *your bodies* are members of Christ" (1 Cor. 6:15), and on the other hand, "now you are the body of Christ and individually members of it" (1 Cor. 12:27). The human "I" is not distinguished from its body; just as "I" have a body, so "I" also am a body.

What one does with, or lets happen to, his or her body, is a matter of personal self-experience. Paul concludes from this insight: "Therefore do not let sin exercise dominion in your mortal *bodies* to make you obey their passions. No longer present *your* members to sin as instruments of wickedness, but present *yourselves* to God as those who have been brought from death to life, and present your members to God as instruments of righteousness" (Rom. 6:12–13). The body is therefore not an external attachment to the real self, as it was frequently understood in the Greek world according to the common distinction of external form and internal content, so that the "kernel" of the immortal soul could distance itself from the "husk" that enclosed it. Moral responsibility for Paul was a matter of the deeds of the body, by no means merely concerned with mental reflection and spiritual attitude. Moral responsibility had to be realized in bodily existence and confirmed with deeds.

With this understanding of the concept "body," Paul emphasizes that human beings are not free to dispose of themselves as they choose, but are subject to a Lord. As "body," the human being stands under the claim of the creator, with the demand "present yourselves to God" (Rom. 6:13). If one rejects this claim, one does not find oneself in a realm of independent, freely chosen action. Rather, one comes under the lordship of powers and dominions, is forced under the yoke of sin, so that one's body becomes a "body of sin" (cf. Rom. 6:6, where the NRSV equates "old *self*" with "sinful *body*," [σῶμα] τῆς ἁμαρτίας) to which one is in bondage and subject to death (Rom. 7:24). Nevertheless, even as sinners human beings remain God's creatures, who are called back to obedience to God their creator. Christ suffered death in the body (διὰ τοῦ σώματος, Rom. 7:4), in order that our bodies might no longer be slaves to sin, but might belong to the Lord (1 Cor. 6:13). When human beings become aware that they are to live their lives as creatures of God, they perceive that a point of orientation has been given for their lives and are enabled to perceive and do the will of their creator.

Since there is no such thing as human existence apart from the body, the apostle Paul conceives of the resurrection of the dead as the raising of the body. Unlike the Greeks, Paul does not long for the release of the soul from the body, but is fearful before the prospect of the destruction of the earthly dwelling, and expects a reclothing in the heavenly dwelling, so that he will not be found naked (2 Cor. 5:1–4). If in our earthly existence we have a "natural body" (σῶμα ψυχικόν), which as such is exposed to the dangers of the evil powers that dominate this life, we will then have a "spiritual body" (σῶμα πνευματικόν) that is determined by the life-giving Spirit of God and can therefore be called a "glorious body" (σῶμα τῆς δόξης, Phil. 3:21). In this line of thought Paul departs from his customary manner of speaking shaped by the conceptuality of the Old Testament, and makes use of the Hellenistic expressions that distinguish between an earthly "soul" (ψυχή) and a heavenly "spirit" (πνεῦμα). Still, even in these statements the body is not thought of merely as an external "husk." Rather, the "spiritual body" describes human existence in God's new creation that begins with the resurrection of the dead. Here too, in his thinking about the resurrection of the dead, Paul holds fast to his understanding of the wholeness of human beings.

The hope of bodily resurrection has consequences for how the Pauline ethic is understood. The Christian has a living Lord, whose resurrection was not an isolated event, but the beginning of the eschatological resurrection of the dead. By baptism, Christians are incorporated into the body of Christ, so that they are now members of it. The present bodily existence of the Christian therefore stands between the incorporation into the body of the resurrected Lord and the future resurrection of all the dead, which will be a resurrection of the body (1 Cor. 6:14). So how could one fall prey to the erroneous idea that one can do whatever one pleases with one's own body? In the hope of the resurrection of the dead, Christians are aware that their body belongs to the resurrected Lord, so that life is now lived by looking to him. Paul can call the body a "temple of the Holy Spirit" (1 Cor. 6:19), which may not be profaned. Those who close themselves off from this insight dismember the body of Christ—that is, they separate Christ's members from his body and deliver them over to the dominating authority of the powers that rule in this world. Against this the apostle can only cry out "Never!" (1 Cor. 6:15). For wherever people think they can live without God and independently take charge of their own lives, there, even in their sharpest ideas and most exalted plans, they are nothing more than "flesh" (σάρξ) that in its frail transitoriness is subject to death. For Christians, however, the operative principle is no longer the independent will of the "flesh" to self-rule, but the rule and power of the Spirit of God.

———

The bodily existence of Christians is thus seen by Paul in its positive aspect of requiring moral responsibility of them. Christians cannot concur with the view that everything regarding their Christian life is already taken care of by the fact that they have received the Spirit and have experienced its powerful effects. Rather, they are called to praise God in all areas of their life with their bodies (1 Cor. 6:20).

The apostle had to defend this evaluation of bodily existence against an arbitrary libertinism. In the Corinthian church, the enthusiastic motto was circulated, "Everything is permitted" ([NRSV: "All things are lawful"] 1 Cor. 6:12). In this case the slogan was used to support the practice of sexual relations with a near relative. The argument was as follows (1 Cor. 6:13): just as food is for the stomach and the stomach was made for food, but in God's will both are destined to pass away, so also the body can be given over to intercourse with prostitutes. Sexual acts involve only people's bodies, which are doomed for destruction anyway, in contrast to the true self, the immortal spirit (πνεῦμα).

To begin with, the apostle finds something with which he can agree: everything is in fact permitted, "all things are lawful." The freedom of Christ is universally valid. But this freedom may not be misused. Even if everything is permitted, not everything serves a good purpose. And although everything is lawful, I still may not become the slave of anything (1 Cor. 6:12). Paul takes up an idea he had already developed in a previous context. "All things are yours"—he had declared these encouraging words to the Corinthians, and had in mind their awareness of being disciples of a particular teacher, as well as "things present and things to come." But then he adds the further consideration: "You belong to Christ, and Christ belongs to God" (1 Cor. 3:21–23.) He thus makes clear that Christian freedom may not be hemmed in by legalistic rules. But Christians are still bound to the Lord who conferred this freedom on them. Only by belonging to him can freedom be sustained and preserved. What does this fundamental insight mean for the Christian's attitude toward sexuality?

By rejecting the libertine misunderstanding of the affirmation that "everything is permitted" with the response that not everything serves a good purpose, the apostle had already rejected the rationale on which it was based. When one says that food and stomach both belong to this temporal world destined for destruction, one by no means may conclude that in the same way sexual activity only involves the transient bodily organs and is unrelated to the true self of the person. Union with a prostitute by no means affects only the external "husk" of one's true spiritual self; it involves the body of the person— one's real self in the wholeness of personhood. Therefore no one can say that one can casually give the body over to prostitution; one must rather say, "the body is meant not for fornication but for the Lord" (1 Cor. 6:13). Paul relates this to the hope for the bodily resurrection of the dead. "God raised up the Lord and will also raise us up by his power" (1 Cor. 6:14). Instead of "us," Paul could just as well have said "our bodies," since in his view human life exists only as bodily existence, the resurrection of the dead can only be thought of as bodily existence, accomplished by the life-giving power of God the creator. When this connection is made, however, Christians may never conduct their life as though the body were irrelevant or only a physical object that could be disdained. They must rather consider the reality that the body is no longer at their disposal, because Christ is Lord over it.

Paul provides no casuistic reflections that give details as patterns of sexual conduct that are permitted and those that are denied to the Christian on this basis. He holds fast to the freedom given him by the Lord. But whoever is united in bodily existence with the Lord, cannot also give the body over to unity with a prostitute. Sexual relations mean that two people are really united — "one flesh" in the biblical idiom, but the Pauline theology would make the expression even more pointed: "one body." Other sins are outside the body. But traffic with prostitutes is sin against one's own body. Thus in no case can relations with prostitutes be considered acceptable conduct. The Christian is not only spiritually united with the Lord, but in the Pauline way of thinking is also incorporated into one body with him.

Just as the apostle, in his debate with libertine ideas is by no means guided by a dualistic attitude that is hostile to the body, but on the contrary by a positive perspective on bodily existence that derives from his view of the resurrection of the dead and of belonging to Christ, so his rejection of ascetic tendencies is derived from the same presuppositions. Like the libertines, advocates of ascetic tendencies disdain the body, but draw different conclusions from their view. They have a low opinion of marriage, and counsel "do not touch a woman" as an item of their advice (1 Cor. 7:1). Here too the apostle can at first agree that it is commendable not to be bound to a wife. But his advice is not based on any contemptuous attitude toward bodily existence. Neither legalistic nor ascetic motives prompt Paul to this judgment, but exclusively the expectation of the imminent parousia of the Lord.

Marriage is not defamed, but is described as the bodily unity of man and woman who give themselves to each other according to the will of the creator, in order to become one flesh

(1 Cor. 6:16). That means, however, that married couples should not refuse one another—except by agreement for a brief period, in order that they might devote themselves to prayer without distraction (1 Cor. 7:5). "For the wife does not have authority over her own body, but the husband does; likewise the husband does not have authority over his own body, but the wife does" (1 Cor. 7:4). If they close the door to this insight and force themselves to turn away from each other, they open the door to the temptations devised by Satan (1 Cor. 7:5). In that Paul speaks of the mutual obligation that each of the partners owes to the other, he bestows no higher rank on the husband than on the wife, but acknowledges that man and wife have the same responsibility and duty, which they fulfill in accordance with the will of their creator.

The few comments that Paul devotes to homosexuality also proceed from this conviction that Christians in their bodily existence know that they belong to the Lord and must fashion their conduct accordingly. Early Christian vice catalogues also sometimes warn against indecent acts and pederasty (1 Cor. 6:9; 1 Tim. 1:10) as offences that prohibit entrance into the kingdom of God. With this evaluation early Christian teaching follows the judgment current in Judaism. While in the Hellenistic environment pederasty and homosexual relations were not considered scandalous, for Jewish ethics the command of the creator was considered binding, so that sexual conduct had to conform to this command. In Jewish teaching, a close relationship was seen between idolatry and sexual perversion: "Shun unlawful worship. Worship the Living One. Avoid adultery and indiscriminate intercourse with males" (Sib. Or. 3:764–66). Paul shares this understanding, but he neither engages in argumentative deliberations nor threatens homosexuals with future punishment. He considers homosexual activity already widespread in ancient society as a sign of the judgment of God already breaking in. "Therefore God gave them up in the lusts of their hearts to impurity, to the degrading of their bodies among themselves" (Rom. 1:24). "For this reason God gave them up to degrading passions. Their women exchanged natural intercourse for unnatural, and the same way also the men giving up natural intercourse with women, were consumed with passion for one another. Men committed shameless acts with men and received in their own persons the due penalty for their error" (Rom. 1:26–27).

———

As members of the body of Christ Christians must demonstrate the gift of freedom and the moral responsibility that comes with it in their bodily existence. They may not allow themselves to be misled by the false conclusion that the sacrament of baptism confers salvation in such wise that it can never be lost, so that one's personal conduct makes no difference (1 Cor. 10:1–13). Rather, the warning example of the disobedient people of Israel should make them conscious of the fact that in their belonging to Christ they are freed and called to belong to the Lord and to keep his commands.

Just as baptism concerns the whole person and makes the power of the new creation effective, so also does the celebration of the Lord's Supper. In 1 Corinthians Paul also had to oppose a fanatically spiritualistic sacramentalism based on the view that salvation was already tangibly present, available in the power of the Spirit that could be possessed as an object and not be lost. This "puffed up" attitude (1 Cor. 4:6, 18–19; 8:1) comes to expression in the celebration of the Lord's Supper especially in the fact that members of the congregation who had to come late and could not bring any food with them went away hungry, because in the elation of their own spiritual enthusiasm some feasted and celebrated, but did not notice the others. The apostle directed that people should satisfy their hunger at home before the worship service, and that the Lord's Supper be celebrated in an appropriate manner (1 Cor. 11:33).

The Lord's Supper could only be celebrated in an appropriate manner—so Paul argues—when all members of the congregation are conscious that they participate in the body of Christ that was given up for them, and that they belong together as members of the body of the Lord and therefore also bear responsibility for their bodily welfare. In the apostle's formulation of the words of institution pronounced at the celebration of the Lord's Supper, he gives special emphasis to the concept of "the body" by relating the expression "for you" not with the saying about the cup (Mark 12:24 par.), but with the statement pronounced about the bread (see above, p. 28). "This is my body that is for you"(1 Cor. 11:24). In 1 Corinthians 10:16–17 we see the reason for this emphasis. There the apostle first cites an early Christian formula that declares that the cup over which the blessing is spoken confers participation in the blood of Christ, and that the bread that is broken gives participation in the body of Christ. The two parallel statements are so presented that the one that deals with the bread and body is in the final position, allowing an explanation to be appended that gives it special emphasis: "Because there is one bread, we who are many are one body; for we all partake of the one bread" (10:17). The significance of the "body" concept shifts from christology to ecclesiology. All who receive the bread at the celebration of the Lord's Supper and thereby participate in Christ's body are, as members of the church, members of the one body of Christ and therefore bound to one another, so that each must look after the other and no one can be a Christian by one's individual self. From this insight, however, the ethical obligation flows: the bodily existence of Christians places them in union with their brothers and sisters and makes them responsible for each other. To eat and drink only for one's own edification, enjoying food and drink without thinking of the others who remain hungry, is absolutely excluded. Whoever participates in the body of Christ has the obligation to share their bread with those who are hungry.

Suggestions for Further Reading

Bornkamm, G. "Lord's Supper and Church in Paul." In *Early Christian Experience*, pp. 123–60. New York: Harper & Row, 1969.
Bryne, B. "Sinning Against One's Own Body: Paul's Understanding of the Sexual Relationship in 1 Corinthians 6:18." *Catholic Biblical Quarterly* 45 (1983): 608–16.
Countryman, L. William. *Dirt, Greed and Sex. Sexual Ethics in the New Testament and Their Implications for Today.* Philadelphia: Fortress Press, 1988.
Gundry, R. H. *Soma in Biblical Theology with Emphasis on Pauline Anthropology.* Cambridge: Cambridge University Press, 1976.

Jewett, R. *Pauline Anthropological Terms.* Leiden: E. J. Brill, 1971.

Käsemann, E. "On Paul's Anthropology." In *Pauline Perspectives,* pp. 1–31. Philadelphia: Fortress Press, 1971.

Pearson, B. A. *The Pneumatikos-Psychikos Terminology in 1 Corinthians.* Missoula: Scholars Press, 1973.

Scroggs, R. *The Last Adam: A Study in Pauline Anthropology.* Philadelphia: Fortress Press, 1966.

———. *The New Testament and Homosexuality.* Philadelphia: Fortress Press, 1983.

Trompf, G. W. "On Attitudes toward Women in Paul and Paulinist Literature: 1 Cor 11:3–6 and its Context." *Catholic Biblical Quarterly* 42 (1980): 196–215.

Justification and the Final Judgment

In Jewish apocalyptic the expectation of a universal judgment at the end of time had developed. On that day all the peoples of the earth must appear before the judgment seat of God, or of his authorized representative sent from heaven, so that they can be properly repaid for their evil deeds. The old world will pass away, and in its place the new world of God will appear, a world in which the righteous will live in eternal joy and blessedness. At the last judgment, each one must give an account of how they have lived. Each person will be charged with both evil deeds and sins of omission, but good deeds will also be remembered on that day. "Many" – so the book of Daniel teaches –"of those who sleep in the dust of the earth shall awake, some to everlasting life, and some to shame and everlasting contempt" (Dan. 12:2). How both nations and individuals have conducted their lives will be read forth from books kept by the recording angels, after which sentence will be pronounced. The godless are contrasted with the righteous: the saved are led away to eternal blessedness, the others are condemned to eternal destruction.

God's judgment is pronounced without respect of persons; it is just and without appeal. It is thus important that one's earthly life be lived in view of this pronouncement to be made at the end of time. Israel was given the law, so that all persons could orient themselves to God's command and live their life on the basis of that knowledge in such a manner that it would be able to stand in the day of God's probing judgment (see above, p. 13). The pious may take comfort in the knowledge that with the gift of the Torah they have been given the possibility not only of perceiving what is just and right, but also of living in accord with these commands, so that at the end they will have good works to exhibit and can enter into eternal life.

In the teaching in the synagogue, the reminder of future judgment was bound up with the exhortation to a pious life corresponding to the conditions of the law. A parenetic application was thus made of the judgment theme, in order to impress upon all that they had to take care to have accumulated a sufficient number of meritorious works to exhibit before God's judgment seat. There, deeds of merit will be weighed against transgressions. The judgment to be pronounced will be determined according to which side the scale tilts. If meritorious deeds outweigh the bad, the person will be pronounced righteous. But if the number of transgressions is greater, the person is judged as a blasphemous doer of evil. Only in a case when the scale is exactly evenly balanced can it happen that the merciful God adds a small supplement to the credit side of the scale, so that the balance tips in the person's favor.

This parenetic application of the judgment theme comprised an important part of the Hellenistic-Jewish missionary preaching. It attempted to win gentiles by challenging them to turn away from the vanity of idolatry to the worship of the one true God. Emphasis was given to this invitation to conversion by speaking of the future judgment before which every person must appear. Everyone must take care to conduct their life so that they can one day give account before God's probing judgment. Traditions that were widespread in the world of the orient could be united with this preaching of repentance and conversion. It had been taught in ancient Egypt that after death the soul of the individual must stand before the court where the dead are judged and give information on things done and left undone during its lifetime (see above, p. 12). A specific catalogue of questions that will comprise this final investigation was already provided to the living, so that they could live their lives accordingly. Responsible hearers of this kind of preaching must conclude from it that they had better live according to the divine law, the necessary presupposition for receiving an affirmative decision in the last judgment.

Pious Jews were concerned to fulfill the commandments and perform deeds of charity to their fellow human beings, in order to provide a treasury of merit that would be at their disposal on that day when the good and bad deeds of their lives are placed on the balance. The seriousness with which life is lived, the sincerity of acts of worship, the study of the law, and the careful following of all its commands is for the purpose of gaining advocates that will be able to speak in their behalf when the end of all days arrives and the last judgment begins. The awareness of having someday to stand before God's final judgment confers binding force on the moral responsibility of religious people. And the confidence of being able to live a righteous life on the basis of precise knowledge of the Torah and conscientious observance of its prescriptions strengthened the hope in which they walked their life's course and looked forward to that last day.

In early Christian preaching the announcement of future judgment was mostly undertaken by means of concepts taken over from Jewish instruction and missionary preaching. All peoples and every individual will have to stand before God's judgment. Surrounded by throngs of angels, God or his Anointed will take his place on the throne. Books will be brought out, and what all individuals have done during their lifetime will be read forth. Then judgment will be pronounced — either as acquittal, which opens the way to eternal life for the righteous, or condemnation, which delivers the evil over to eternal damnation. These two possibilities constitute the only options. The decision will either be that the blessed will inherit the kingdom of the heavenly Father prepared for them from the foundation of the world (Matt. 25:34), or the damned will hear the pronouncement: "You that are accursed, depart from me into the eternal fire prepared for the devil and his angels" (Matt. 25:41). In view of this last judgment, all must be careful to shape their life so that later entrance to eternal life will be granted.

Early Christian missionary preaching made extensive use of ideas and statements that came to it from the synagogue. It too bound together the preaching of judgment and repentance, and demanded that vain idolatry be renounced and only the one true God be served. In 1 Thessalonians the apostle Paul mentions the content of missionary preaching, and specifically describes it with concepts that obviously go back to formulations that were originally Jewish: "how you turned to God from idols, to serve a living and true God" (1 Thess. 1:9). However, early Christian preaching supplemented this usual demand for repentance, in that it bound it to the confession of Christ. Thus to the traditional expression there was added the expectation of the return of Christ, whom God had raised from the dead. He will save his own from the coming wrath (1 Thess. 1:10). Thereby not only is christological support given to the eschatological expectation, but also a new content is provided for the statement made about the last judgment. To be sure, the seriousness of the last judgment and every person's responsibility before it are explicitly named: God's wrath is imminent. But those are saved from it who hold fast to Jesus as their savior. He will be their advocate before God's judgment throne. He has been raised from death to life and will appear from heaven on the last day to redeem his own.

The certainty of the coming redemption thus confers on Christian preaching the character of a recruiting invitation and the announcement of a heartening promise. To be sure, it is not left in doubt that God will inquire how people have conducted themselves during their earthly lives. But the final word is no longer dependent on whether or not they are able to produce a sufficient list of good works and accomplishments to their credit, for believers can trust that Jesus as their savior will deliver them from the annihilating wrath of the judgment. Thereby the moral requirement incumbent upon Christians is not reduced in the slightest; on the contrary, the knowledge of God's holy will obligates one to be obedient to God. But this obedience is no longer weighed and examined as meritorious deeds that earn credit; it is the consequence of the certain hope that the Lord who has already liberated his own people will also be present on the last day to redeem them.

Among those doctrinal elements that according to Hebrews 6:1–2 constitute the content of early Christian instruction, priority belongs to "repentance from dead works and faith toward God, instruction about baptisms, laying on of hands, resurrection of the dead, and eternal judgment." From this listing one can again clearly perceive how early Christian missionary preaching was linked to Jewish traditions. Those who turn away from the dead works that characterize pagan existence and are converted to faith in the one true God, and are received into the Christian community through baptism and the laying on of hands, will lead their lives henceforth in the hope of the resurrection of the dead and in the expectation of eternal judgment. As in the Jewish tradition, the themes of the resurrection and the last judgment obviously belong to those elementary items of instruction that were to be communicated to every member of the community. The awareness that one would have to stand before God's judgment on the last day sharpened the sense of responsibility of leading one's life in such a manner that God's will is fulfilled. But faith in the God who forgives sins for Christ's sake gives confidence for the day of the final examination. Since the exalted Christ will sit on God's throne as the eschatological judge, the hope of the believers may rest secure in the fact that Christ is not only the judge, but also the savior, who saves from the wrath to come (1 Thess. 1:9–10; Phil. 3:20).

———

The question of how the idea of judgment and the hope of eschatological salvation are related to each other is in need of a fundamental clarification. The early Christian ideas concerning judgment are not consistent in themselves, but take over previously existing Jewish materials of different kinds and unite them with affirmations of Christian confession, without always creating sufficient clarity about their mutual relationship. Sometimes God, sometimes Christ, is presented as the judge (Rom. 14:10; 2 Cor. 5:10). Some passages speak of the final separation achieved at the last judgment (Matt. 13:24–30, 36–43,

47–50); other passages speak of the necessity of being able to present fruits by which the righteous are recognized (Matt. 7:16–20). Just as in Judaism, the demand for good works plays a role (Rev. 14:13), for they will be asked for in the last judgment in order to grant an appropriate reward (Matt. 7:2; Jas. 2:13). But if redemption happens entirely through Christ's saving act, then the idea of a future judgment must be rethought from the ground up.

The relation between justification, which is granted the believer for Christ's sake, and the final judgment, which calls everyone before God's throne, found its needed clarification in the context of Pauline theology. At first it even seems that in Paul, too, both ideas simply stand beside each other without being related. If the doctrine of justification is considered the specific Pauline development of the preaching of the gospel (see above, pp. 105–7), one could easily jump to the conclusion that the statements about the coming judgment according to works is an idea taken over from Judaism preserved by the apostle but not really integrated into his theology. But references to the coming judgment are found much too frequently in the apostle's letters for them to be merely traditional material he has unintentionally adopted without their having any real significance for his own theology. Just how are justification and future judgment to be related to each other?

Paul shares with the first Christians the expectation of the coming judgment and the hope that Christ will appear as the savior of his own (1 Thess. 1:9–10). The apostle emphasizes that God's wrath on Jews and gentiles reveals the universal guilt of humanity (Rom. 1:18–3:20). He radicalizes the traditional concept of judgment into the conviction that no human being will be justified before God by the works of the law (Rom. 3:20), and combines this affirmation with the doctrine of justification by faith (Rom. 3:21). God accomplishes the justification of human beings by grace alone, since they are always in need of God's justifying pronouncement of acquittal. What justification means is grasped only when the lost condition of humanity is recognized, which becomes obvious when they stand before God's judgment. Then it is clear that justification occurs exclusively through God's gracious turning to humanity, and can be received only by faith.

In combination with the catalogues of vices he takes over from tradition (see above, pp. 83–84), Paul repeatedly warns of the pronouncement of condemnation in the last judgment: the unrighteousness will not inherit the kingdom of God (1 Cor. 6:9–10), "those who do such things will not inherit the kingdom of God" (Gal. 5:21). The expression "inherit the kingdom of God" is used by Paul only in formulations he has taken from the tradition (see above, p. 43); they thus existed prior to the apostle's own teaching. He retains them in order to underscore the warning that is expressed in the lists of vices. Whoever is disobedient to God's commands can waste the chance of supreme happiness. The old rule that one finally reaps what one has sown holds true. Thus all who sow to their own flesh and place their trust in their own capabilities and possibilities will finally reap corruption. But whoever sows to the Spirit and thereby trusts in God's gracious act will receive eternal life (Gal. 6:8).

On all these places the reference to judgment serves as a cautionary warning not to gamble away salvation by disdaining God's word and will in a reckless, arbitrary carelessness. It is always the case that morally irresponsible actions can lead to hearing God's sentence of condemnation at the final judgment. But in Paul's understanding it could never be the case that a human being—even the most pious one—could earn salvation by his or her own works. Only through the gracious compassion of God can there be deliverance from condemnation (Rom. 8:1). Since in this central affirmation the apostle makes a fundamental distinction between his views and all Jewish ideas about judgment, justification, and justice, there is never any room in his ethical discussions for casuistic considerations, as though one could determine how one could be pronounced righteous in the judgment by clever calculation and corresponding conduct. Even if one has a good conscience, this never means that the pronouncement of acquittal has already been made; judgment remains exclusively God's business (1 Cor. 4:4–5). Salvation happens entirely for Christ's sake; it is secure. At the end of days nothing new will be revealed that has not already been pronounced as already valid. "Who will bring any charge against God's elect?" So the apostle pictures the challenge going forth in the courtroom of the last judgment. But every accusation must lapse into silence, for "It is God who justifies. Who is to condemn? It is Christ Jesus, who died, yes, who was raised, who is at the right hand of God, who indeed intercedes for us" (Rom. 8:33–34).

Thus the expectation that by the exhibition of meritorious works and fulfilling of commandments one might someday be able to stand before God's judgment can no longer be the motive of Christian ethics. Rather, there grows out of the announcement of justification already experienced the claim that determines the whole life of believers and holds them to the task of doing right and not becoming weary in well-doing (Gal. 6:9).

Suggestions for Further Reading

Beker, J. C. *Paul the Apostle. The Triumph of God in Life and Thought.* Philadelphia: Fortress Press, 1980.

Boring, M. E. "The Language of Universal Salvation in Paul." *Journal of Biblical Literature* 105 (1986): 269–92.

Donfried, K. P. "Justification and Last Judgment in Paul." *Interpretation* 30 (1976): 140–52.

Gibbs, J. *Creation and Redemption.* Leiden: E. J. Brill, 1971.

Jewett, R. *The Thessalonian Correspondence. Pauline Rhetoric and Millenarian Piety.* Philadelphia: Fortress Press, 1986.

Käsemann, E. *Commentary on Romans.* Grand Rapids: Wm. B. Eerdmans, 1980.

———. "Justification and Salvation History in the Epistle to the Romans." In *Perspectives on Paul,* pp. 60–78. Philadelphia: Fortress Press, 1971.

Kreitzer, L. J. *Jesus and God in Paul's Eschatology.* Sheffield: JSOT Press, 1987.

Lincoln, A. T. *Paradise Now and Not Yet.* Cambridge: Cambridge University Press, 1981.

Roetzel, C. *Judgment in the Community.* Leiden: E. J. Brill, 1972.

Wimbush, V. L. *Paul, the Worldly Ascetic: Response to the World and Self-Understanding According to 1 Corinthians 7.* Macon, Ga.: Mercer, 1988.

Chapter Seven

THE WORLDLINESS
OF FAITH

Christians and the Political Order

The first Christians lived in the expectation that this world would soon end and that God's kingdom would be established in the near future. Nevertheless, this world remains God's creation, in which Christians are to live out the meaning of their faith in deeds as well as prayer, through their conduct as well as through their confession. The bearers of political power exercise the functions of their office not on the basis of its having been founded and agreed upon by human beings, but by God's will—whether they are aware of it or not. God has made arrangements for the protection of human life and for the regulation of the functioning of society according to law and justice. Thus Christians, like everyone else, must give heed to the political authorities and conform to their rules.

The ethical instruction of the early Christian congregations could take up and develop the rules that had already been developed in the Hellenistic synagogue with regard to how people of faith should be related to the political order. This teaching, in turn, had already combined traditional biblical teaching with current Stoic views, and had developed the interpretation that a just political structure is represented by the good order corresponding to the Logos. Among the mass of possibilities of political structures, wherever citizens receive their appropriate share and place within the great body of human society, and is concerned there to fulfill their responsibilities for the welfare of all, there the insight of reason is followed. From their side, the authorities of the state will recognize the upright conduct of its citizens, will reward specially meritorious acts with public praise, and with the help of the taxes and tribute it receives will see to it that the arrangements and institutions for the general welfare are created and maintained. But whoever violates these laws or independently resists their directives must fear the punishing hand of the state. It is God's will that those who hold political office and have its power at their disposal, by praise and encouraging support, but also by blame and even punishment, insist on compliance with the law binding on all citizens, and thus maintain the legal order by which alone human society can in the long run endure.

In the context of the parenetic discussion in his letter to the Romans, the apostle Paul also deals with the conduct of Christians with regard to government authorities (Rom. 13:1-7). No more, but also no less, is required of them than of any other responsible citizen. Everyone must be subject to government authorities, because these have been established by God. This demand for subordination is placed at the beginning of the discussion (Rom. 13:1), and is later repeated (v. 5), in order to underscore its general validity. This introductory thesis is followed by the inferences that may be drawn from it: whoever withstands this governmental authority withstands the will of God, and will receive the consequences of this resistance (v. 2). On the other hand, those who fulfill their duty with regard to the government have nothing to fear. It is presupposed that those who practice justice and do good, receive praise, not punishment (v. 3). The state bears the sword as God's servant, and for the execution of justice; it will be used only to give evil-doers their just deserts. But the orders of the state authorities should be followed not merely from fear of the sword, but for the sake of conscience, which knows how to perceive and attend to the cause of justice (v. 5).

After the repetition of the opening declaration that everyone should be subject to the governing authorities, the statement is appended that whatever is owed to anyone should in fact be paid, since every citizen, the Christian included, pays the required taxes and delivers the required tribute. Thereby the prescription of the law is fulfilled and due respect is rendered as in the proverb: "Taxes to whom taxes are due, revenue to whom revenue is due, respect to whom respect is due, honor to whom honor is due" (v. 7).

These instructions are not to be seen as a tractate that provides philosophical reflections on the nature and responsibility of the state, of the sort repeatedly found in ancient discussions. Paul is developing an aspect of early Christian exhortation, speaking to the church about how Christians should conduct their lives in the world. These statements do not have in view particular people who exercise governmental authority, but develop general principles that Christians might use in any time and place to find their way.

In Romans 13:1-7 Paul is making use of a traditional unit of exhortation in which—as can be seen by a careful examination of each verse—there is not a single word that can be described as specifically Christian. To be sure, there are references to God, to the service owed to God, and to conscience, but neither Christ nor Christian love is mentioned. Rather, the instruction is expressed in traditional terminology that originated in the synagogue. It is the one God and Lord of the world who has placed the rulers of the empires of this world on their thrones and who establishes the limits of their power and authority. The Jewish wisdom literature had said about the kings, rulers, and judges of this world: "It is the Lord who gave you your authority; your power comes from the Most High. He will put your actions to the test and scrutinize your intentions" (Wis. 6:3-4). And Rabbi Hanania (ca. 70 c.e.) taught: "Pray for the welfare of the government, for except for fear of it, we would already have eaten each other alive" (Aboth 3:2). God has established the political order—so it was taught in Jewish doctrine—in order that people might live together without the violence of the wicked giving them the upper hand. God's will is honored when the power of the state is acknowledged as having been instituted by God and prayer is made in its behalf that those in power may daily fulfill its task of maintaining justice.

In Romans 13:1–7 Paul obviously takes over ethical instruction that had already been given a definite form and inserts it as a distinct block of material into his exhortation directed to the church. The apostle is not interested in presenting theoretical reflections about the structures of authority in the world and the place of various officials within it, but wants to set forth how Christians should conduct themselves in the particular setting in which they live. In the Hellenistic-Roman world the local authorities were called ἐξουσίαι (authorities), whose task it was in their respective communities to exercise the authority of state power, to enforce the law and maintain justice. Their directions, intended to promote the general welfare, were to be followed also by Christians. Paul is not here thinking of a case in which there could be a conflict of conscience in which the Christian would be compelled to choose between obeying God or obeying human authorities—in which case the Christian must choose the former. Paul is thinking in terms of normal circumstances, as they were in the Roman empire as he wrote, when things had finally returned to normal after a series of wars and civil conflicts, a situation perceived by the inhabitants of the Mediterranean world as the blessing of peace.

But why does the apostle adopt the customary expressions and statements of this point of view, in order to use them to address the issue of how Christians should conduct themselves with regard to the state? The question of the substantive basis for this rather hardheaded and matter-of-fact treatment of an important issue—unique in the apostle's teaching—cannot be answered without considering the larger context to which this section belongs.

———

The instruction to which this section dealing with the Christian's political relationships belongs stands under the rubric "worldly worship," which the apostle has given to this last section of the Letter to the Romans. The multitude of individual exhortations, tried-and-true rules of experience, some of which are taken from Israel's wisdom tradition, are all placed under the guiding theme that Christians should offer their bodies—their whole selves, in all areas of doing and being—as living sacrifices that are holy and pleasing to God (Rom. 12:1; cf. above, pp. 93–94). The freedom of faith sharpens the sober capacity to judge and discriminate, so that it is able to sort through the abundance of current traditions, directives of conventional wisdom, and demands of the day, and decide what is the will of God for that situation, and do it. Wherever Christ is confessed as Lord and God's renewal of the whole person occurs, there the freedom and power to act in the world is given, action that is guided by true reason and the inventive power of love.

———

That the instructions brought together in Romans 13:1-7 have been shaped by their origin in tradition and conventional wisdom is clear not only from a comparison of them and analogous pieces from the contemporary Hellenistic-Jewish environment. It is confirmed by comparing them with similar didactic sections found in other early Christian literature. In the extensive directions provided by 1 Peter for the conduct of the Christian life, there is also a section that prescribes the attitude they should have toward the state. It is there commanded that Christians be subject to every human institution for the Lord's sake (1 Pet. 2:13). The key word, "be subject," is found here as in Romans 13:1, and recurs in Titus 3:1, which also speaks of being submissive to rulers and authorities. The household code in 1 Peter (2:13–3:7) supplements the traditional general rule with a specifically Christian motivation by appealing to the commanding authority of the Lord. The offices of kings and governors is entrusted to them for a limited time, for the maintenance of the general welfare in this world. They would have no power if it were not given them from God (John 19:11). The Lord alone holds all power in his hands, and through his word directs his own to obey the government authorities. Christians have to fulfill God's will, in that they, despite being called names and encountering hostile suspicions, show their Christian freedom by their readiness to serve and fulfill their civic responsibilities as servants of God. Thus the concluding sentence declares: "Honor everyone. Love the family of believers. Fear God. Honor the emperor" (1 Pet. 2:17). In the Hellenistic world, the Roman emperor was also simply called "king" [The NRSV here translates the usual Greek word for "king" as "emperor."] The structure of the Roman state, which stood under his control, was generally understood as established by God, and therefore to be honored by all. While enthusiasts and extremists, on the basis of excessive eschatological expectations or utopian hopes were inclined toward disparaging the present order, Christians respect the government authorities as the gift of God's patience, who does not want this world to revert to chaos.

Early Christianity also knows that normal conditions do not always prevail and that dangerous threats to the faith can arise in which the obedience owed to God requires that the totalitarian claim of human authorities must be resisted (see above, pp. 78 and 196). Thus the parenetic remarks on the conduct of Christians in regard to the state authorities may not be evaluated as though they were legalistic directives, valid without change for every time and place. The state is neither given a warrant that permits it to deal arbitrarily with its citizens, nor is limitless obedience demanded from its citizens. Christians have the responsibility to critically determine in their own experience where the honor due to God alone sets boundaries to any human claim to obedience.

———

In the course of history the structures of political order have undergone fundamental transformations with the result that in the modern democratic state neither the relationship of emperor and subject that was presupposed by early Christianity nor the sacrosanct authority of the ruler in the time of the Reformation any longer exists. All citizens participate in the responsibility for the fortunes of the commonwealth. Nevertheless, the directions provided by early Christian instruction on the conduct of Christians vis-à-vis the state are still valid under the conditions of modern government. God has given the secular order—regardless of its constantly changing form—the task of defending the world against anarchy and making it possible for humanity to live together in peace. The holders of political office are there in order to guard the law and to oppose evil. Christians, as citizens of whatever country, must respect this commission and conscientiously fulfill its obligations.

The fifth thesis of the Barmen Declaration of 1934 appeals expressly to 1 Peter 2:17. It emphasizes that the ethical teaching of the earliest Christians even today presents us with the right orientation for our own decisions. Its instruction is summarized in a matter-of-fact view of the state that presents both the authority of its commission and the responsibility of Christians:

> The Bible tells us that according to divine arrangement the state has the responsibility to provide for justice and peace in the as yet unredeemed world, in which the church also stands, according to the measure of human insight and human possibility, by the threat and use of force.
>
> The church recognizes with thanks and reverence toward God the benevolence of this, his provision. She reminds men of God's Kingdom, God's commandment and righteousness, and thereby the responsibility of rulers and ruled. She trusts and obeys the power of the word, through which God maintains all things.
>
> This positive affirmation is followed by the limitations by which the task of the state on the one side and the church on the other are subject and distinguished from each other: "We repudiate the false teaching that the state can and should expand beyond its special responsibility to become the single and total order of human life, and also thereby fulfill the commission of the church.
>
> We repudiate the false teaching that the church can and should expand beyond its special responsibility to take on the characteristics, functions, and dignities of the state, and thereby become itself an organ of the state. (Translation from *Creeds of the Churches*, rev. ed. edited by John H. Leith [Richmond: John Knox Press, 1973], 521)

Suggestions for Further Reading

Bammel, E. "Romans 13." In *Jesus and the Politics of His Day*, pp. 365–83. E. Bammel and C. F. D. Moule, eds. Cambridge: Cambridge University Press, 1984.

Borg, M. "A New Context for Romans XIII." *New Testament Studies* 19 (1972): 205–18.

Bruce, F. F. "Paul and 'the Powers that be.'" *Bulletin of the John Rylands Library* 66 (1983–84): 78–96.

Cullmann, O. *The State in the New Testament.* New York: Scribners', 1956.

Dunn, J. D. G. "Romans 13.1-7. A Charter for Political Quietism?" *Ex Auditu* 2 (1986): 55–68.

Furnish, V. *The Moral Teaching of Paul: Selected Issues* (2d ed., rev), pp. 115–39. Nashville: Abingdon, 1985.

Käsemann, E. "Principles of the Interpretation of Romans 13." In *New Testament Questions of Today,* pp. 196–216. Philadelphia: Fortress Press, 1969.

Morrison, C. *The Powers That Be: Earthly Powers and Demonic Rulers in Romans 13:1-7.* Naperville: Alec R. Allenson, 1960.

Stein, R. "The Argument of Romans 13:1-7." *Novum Testamentum* 31 (1989): 325–43.

Wengst, K. *Pax Romana and the Peace of Jesus Christ.* Philadelphia: Fortress Press, 1987.

Christians at Home and in the Family

"And whatever you do, in word or deed, do everything in the name of the Lord Jesus, giving thanks to God the Father through him" (Col. 3:17). It was according to this guideline that the members of the earliest Christian congregations sought to lead their lives and to fulfill the responsibilities that home and family set before them. The instructions directed toward the problems of everyday living were crystalized in the tables of household duties (*Haustafel,* so named since Luther). These are sections of New Testament ethical instruction formed according to a traditional outline, the details of which could be elaborated in various ways. Women and men, children and parents, slaves and masters, are all addressed with their respective responsibilities. The oldest such context is presented by Colossians 3:18–4:1; Ephesians 5:22–6:9 offers a version expanded by commentary. Although the comparable constructions in the Pastoral Letters and 1 Peter (1 Tim. 2:8–15; 6:1–2; Titus 2:1–10; 1 Pet. 2:13–3:7) are not literarily dependent on Colossians and Ephesians, with regard to their content they manifest many points of contact, which are to be explained by the fact that they are all dependent on a common store of oral catechetical tradition that had attained a fairly fixed form and content. Such traditions are also the basis of the corresponding sections found in the writings of the apostolic fathers (Did. 4:9–11; Barn. 19:5–7; 1 Clem. 21:6–9; Pol. *Phil.* 4:2–6:2).

In terms of their content, the prescriptions found in the *Haustafeln* are not original creations of the Christian movement, but are based on traditional tenets of common wisdom derived from experience that had already found a wide circulation in the environment of early Christianity. The understanding of their message requires a careful investigation of the models they have used as well as the changes that were made to these models when they were adopted by Christian teachers.

The contemporary philosophical instruction spoke often of the duties that were incumbent upon any person who wanted to live responsibly. Proper conduct in relation to women and children, friends and one's fellow human beings, one's nation and the state, as well as the respect due the gods was described in detail. Thus Epictetus, a Stoic philosopher whose career spanned the end of the first and the beginning of the second centuries C.E. (see above, p. 19), taught that a good disciple is one who comes to him with the desire to live as a religious person, as a philosopher, and as a concerned human being, and who wants to know his or her duties (τὸ καθῆκον) to the gods, to parents, brothers and sisters, one's own country, and friends (Diss. II, 17:31). Ethical instruction is supposed to make clear what is required as proper conduct to both gods and human beings. The advice of the teacher reads as follows: "maintaining with his associates both the natural and the acquired relationships, those namely of son, father, brother, citizen, wife, neighbor, fellow traveler, ruler, and subject" (Diss. II, 14:8). All persons must reflect on the task given by their state in life, and philosophy is the key to perceiving this. As Seneca had already said in the first century C.E., philosophy gives to each person the advice appropriate to one's situation. It teaches the husband how he should conduct himself in relation to his wife, teaches the father how he should rear his children, just as it teaches the master how he should direct his slaves (*Epistulae Morales* 94:1).

Such ethical directives for daily life were taken over by the Hellenistic synagogue from the contemporary popular philosophy, and, with appropriate changes, were used by the Jews in their moral instruction. Instead of respect for the gods, they now spoke of obedience to the one God, whose commands were to be followed. Duties to one's native country receded into the background. The didactic poem of Pseudo-Phocylides (see above, pp. 22–23) presents a series of duties that are to be fulfilled in marriage, in the rearing and education of children, in relation to friends and relatives, as well as in the treatment of slaves (175–227). In this process one can detect a distancing from some views that prevailed in the surrounding world, and an emphatic rejection of others, such as the exposure of newborn children, abortion, and homosexual relations.

From the command to honor one's father and mother, Philo of Alexandria (see above, p. 22) derives a host of regulations presumed to be implicit in it, namely, "necessary laws drawn up to deal with the relations of old to young, rulers to subjects, benefactors to benefited, slaves to masters" (*Decal.* 165). The parents represent the upper group—rulers, benefactors, and masters—while children represent the lower class of disciples, subjects, those who receive help, and slaves. The lower class is to respect the upper class, and the superior group is to care for their subordinates (ibid. 165–67).

Josephus, who at the end of the first century wrote a history of the Jewish people in which he attempted to make their faith understandable to the Hellenistic world, presents an enumeration of the Jewish laws and prohibitions that begins with the command to worship God. He then continues with proper conduct in marriage, the education of children, the burial of the dead, names love to parents, and then concludes with the duties that concern relationships to friends and foreigners (*Against Apion* 198–210).

Early Christian instruction had at its disposal a rich collection of traditional rules for conduct preserved in the Hellenistic popular philosophy, which was mediated primarily through the synagogue. However, the particulars of what Christians could consider decent and commanded by God had to be thought through and formulated afresh. As in Judaism, so also in Christianity, there could obviously no longer be any talk of cultic obligations to the gods. Nor were their commands related to patriotism; proper conduct in relationships with government authorities was mostly treated in other contexts, in a separate item of instruction (see above, pp. 131–32). Ethical instruction concentrated on appropriate conduct in one's immediate sphere of life, in which one found oneself together with members of the family, slaves, and masters. Such a focus meant that no social program was developed by which the existing social order might have been changed from the ground up. It was rather acknowledged that Christians too were obligated to do what was generally expected from people who were concerned to live responsible lives.

In Colossians 3:18–4:1 one can clearly see the manner in which early Christian ethical instruction both adopted traditional materials and reformulated them. Not only the content of individual admonitions, but the reference to what is fitting and what is generally acceptable corresponds to the current mode of moral instruction "as is fitting" (3:18, ὡς ἀνῆκεν); "this is your acceptable duty" (3:20, εὐάρεστον); "justly and fairly" (4:1, τὸ δίκαιον καὶ τὴν ἰσότητα). Still, the usual basis for right conduct has been formulated anew by the repeated reference to the commanding authority of the Lord, so that the instruction now reads: "as is fitting in the Lord" (3:18) and "this is your acceptable duty in the Lord" (3:20). "Fearing the Lord" is mentioned (3:22); one's work is to be done "as done for the Lord" (3:23), whose final judgment of rewards and punishments is called to mind (3:24–25; 4:1), and the charge is given "you serve the Lord Christ" (3:24). The phrase "in the Lord" that is repeatedly added as the grounding of ethical instruction is not a mere superficial phrase added in order to make the traditional instruction more acceptable to Christians. It is rather an indication that all living, thinking, and acting of believers is to be subordinated to the sovereignty of the Lord.

With the words "in the Lord," at the same time a critical principle is given that facilitates the determination of which ethical directives are to be regarded as binding on the community and how they are to be understood as an expression of the obedience due to the Lord. The authority of the Lord comes to expression in the fact that all members of the community are addressed; for all have been baptized in his name and therefore belong to him in the same way. While the traditional instruction of popular philosophy was directed primarily to the man, the Christian *Haustafel* is controlled by the idea of a partnership determined by love. Women and men, children and parents, slaves and masters are addressed in terms of their mutual responsibility that is to be expressed in their love for each other.

What instruction does the *Haustafel* give for the individual members of the community? In Colossians 3:18–4:1, the outline of which is followed in the parallel passage Ephesians 5:22–6:9, the subordinate party is first admonished, but then the superior party is reminded of his obligations to those who have been entrusted to his care. This means that the directive to the subordinate party to submit must not be misunderstood or misused. If the one party is called to obedience, the other party is called to place himself in the situation of the subordinate, and to be guided by the commandment of love.

The command to women to be subordinate to men (cf. also Eph. 5:22; 1 Pet. 3:1; 1 Tim. 2:11) corresponds to the general rule. The basis that makes such conduct obligatory is not provided by the general rule, however, but by the added words "in the Lord." To be sure, in some cases—as in the corresponding directions in the Pastoral Letters—the subordination of women can be given particular emphasis (2 Tim. 2:11–15; cf. also 1 Cor. 14:34–35, apparently a later addition to Paul's original letter; cf. p. 66 above). With all this, the simultaneous appeal to "the Lord" is a reminder that in Christ Jesus there is neither male nor female, but all are one in him (Gal. 3:28; Col. 3:11). The Ephesian letter takes this into account by prefacing the *Haustafel* with this command that applies to all members of the congregation: "Be subject to one another out of reverence for Christ" (5:21). The men are commanded to love their wives. They are thereby forbidden to behave in an overbearing manner or to fancy themselves to be superior beings. On the contrary, the command directs them toward a life of loving partnership, which is to determine the relationship of husband and wife from the ground up. In Ephesians 5 the appeal to the love commandment, the decisive factor in all Christian ethics, is provided with an emphatic christological grounding, underscored by the commanding authority of the Lord: "Husbands, love your wives, just as Christ loved the church and gave himself up for her" (5:25).

Children are to be obedient to their parents, simply because it is the "right thing to do." But here also the appeal to the insight of common sense is strengthened by the reference "in the Lord." He is the one who commands; it is his command that is to be followed without contradiction. Ephesians 6:2 adds the Old Testament command to honor father and mother. Even though children are to honor both parents, the fathers are given special responsibility. They are to take care not to provoke their children nor be too demanding, so that they do not become listless or unsociable. The admonition is then given a positive reinforcement in 6:4, where fathers are commanded to bring their children up "in the discipline and instruction of the Lord."

The most extensive instructions are given to the Christian slaves. The question that demanded an answer was how the freedom given in Christ is related to the continuing fact of slavery, a situation in which slaves must continue to serve their earthly masters (cf. 1 Cor. 7:21–24). The admonition directed to slaves could thus not merely fall back on traditional statements of moral instruction, but had to be reformulated as specifically Christian teaching. Slaves who had become Christians were told to acknowledge earthly slavery as the station in life assigned to them and to obey their earthly masters in all things. By carrying out their duties conscientiously, they perform them to the honor of the Lord, who will require an accounting from all. If they have to endure suffering in this service, they are pointed to the suffering Christ as their model (cf. 1 Pet. 2:18–25; see below, pp. 182–83).

Only a brief word is addressed to the masters. At that time there would only have been a few Christians who were wealthy enough to own slaves. In the Letter to Philemon Paul appeals to the master of a runaway slave, asking him to receive him back in the love of Christ. The *Haustafel* says nothing about love at this point, but the master is commanded to treat his slaves justly and fairly, thus appealing to the generally accepted norms of moral conduct. For Christians, however, the issues of "justice" and "fairness" attained a new significance, for they are responsible to the Lord. If both slaves and masters know that they belong to Christ and that the one as much as the other owes obedience to the Lord, then the right standard for their relationship with each other has been given.

All Christians—this is what the directions for household and family are concerned to teach—have the responsibility of following the command of the Lord in the situation in which they stand. There is no call for a revolutionary reformation of society, neither the legal equality of men and women nor the freeing of slaves. But powerful expression of the concept of partnership is given by the appeal to the love commandment. The present social structures remain valid, but the conduct required within them is now subjected to the authority of the Lord. It thereby becomes clear that what is given here is neither timelessly valid instruction nor is any particular social structure legitimized forever. The rules that are generally accepted are recognized, but their regulations are limited to the sphere of secular activity. But transforming power is unleashed by the confession of the Lord and by service done in love, power that can become a factor in the transformation of the social structures by which people live together.

The passage of time brings changes in the general judgment as to what is proper and fitting. But Christian admonition is unvarying in its insistence on obedience to the Lord. How this obedience is to be realized concretely in any given situation must constantly be thought out anew. By acting in love, it is the Christian's responsibility to walk worthy of the Lord in the realities of their everyday lives, and to do all that they do in the name of the Lord Jesus—to the praise and honor of God.

The idea of the community grounded in love, as it is set forth in the *Haustafel*, and the consciousness that in Christ there is neither Jew nor Greek, neither slave nor free, neither male nor female, but all are one in Christ Jesus (Gal. 3:28), provides the fundamental orientation for a Christian social ethic. Contemporary relationships are no longer determined by the legal superiority of men to women, just as they no longer know the contrast of slaves and masters. And yet, in view of the fact that discrimination and injustice continue to exist, there is still a need for applying the determining motifs of love, mutual respect, and partnership provided by the early Christian kerygma to our present situations. From this critical and constructive principle the relation of husband and wife, children and parents, management and labor, as well as the relations of peoples of different races and ethnic backgrounds can be thought through and reformed. In such discussions the fundamental question of what can be considered appropriate and right is raised, and a response grounded in biblical faith can contribute to the discussion of the social, educational, and economic issues of the present.

Suggestions for Further Reading

Aune, D. "Codes of Household Ethics." In *The New Testament in its Literary Environment,* p. 196. Philadelphia: Westminster Press, 1987.

Balch, D. "Household Codes." In *Greco-Roman Literature and the New Testament,* pp. 25–50. D. Aune, ed. Atlanta: Scholars Press, 1988.

———. *Let Wives Be Submissive: The Domestic Code in 1 Peter.* Chico: Scholars Press, 1981.

Barth, M. *Ephesians.* Anchor Bible 34, 34A. Garden City, N.Y.: Doubleday, 1974.

Crouch, J. E. *The Origin and Intention of the Colossian Haustafel.* Göttingen: Vandenhoeck & Ruprecht, 1972.

Hartmann, L. "Some Unorthodox Thoughts on the Household-Code Form." In *The Social World of Formative Christianity and Judaism,* pp. 219–32. J. Neusner et al., eds. Philadelphia: Fortress Press, 1988.

Lohse, E. "The Rules for the Household." In *Colossians and Philemon,* pp. 154–57. Philadelphia: Fortress Press, 1971.

Petersen, N. R. *Rediscovering Paul.* Philadelphia: Fortress Press, 1985.

Sanders, J. T. *Ethics in the New Testament,* pp. 68–81. Philadelphia: Fortress Press, 1975.

Schroeder, D. "Lists, Ethical." In *Interpreter's Dictionary of the Bible, Supplementary Volume,* pp. 546–47. Nashville: Abingdon, 1976.

Ethical Instruction
in the Pauline School Tradition

The common stock of early Christian tradition appears often in the letters of Paul, who adopts it, expounds upon it, and applies it to the particular situation of the church or churches he addresses. In the Christian community with which he made contact after his conversion, Paul found that the process of formulating directions for living the Christian life had already begun. While in his correspondence with the Corinthian congregation the apostle was primarily engaged in debates concerning concrete issues disputed in the current life of the congregation, in other letters he takes up more comprehensive ethical traditions and delivers them to his churches. Thus in the parenetic section of 1 Thessalonians 4:1–12 and 5:12–25 we find a collection of traditional material. Galatians 5:26–6:10 presents a collection of instructions derived from the church's tradition. Both collections illuminate the nature of the Christian life by giving a list of directions for ethical conduct.

The structure of Paul's Letter to the Romans has been formed with extreme care, producing a document in which the apostle, as in a last will and testament that he wishes to hand on to Christianity, summarizes the content of his preaching and teaching. Once more we see parenesis developed as the consequence of the proclamation and promise of salvation, elaborated in the last major section, which is provided with a solemn introduction (12:1–2). Then 12:3–8 treats the specific Christian theme of the unity of the body of Christ, which is constituted by the variety of its members. The following section, 12:9–21, incorporates a series of ethical maxims taken from tradition. This general Christian instruction is intended to make clear what it means to live out an affirmative response to the responsibilities imposed by everyday life by drawing on the resources of faith.

The apostle had obviously addressed this task repeatedly in the churches and had illustrated it to his disciples and colleagues. The parenetic sections of Paul's letters have a firm, consistent pattern, which indicates that they were not first formulated at the time of the composition of the letter, but must have been intensively used in the instructions that the apostle had given his churches and especially his co-workers. His disciples appropriated such materials from his letters as well as from the oral apostolic tradition, reformulated it for new situations, and passed it on. As his co-workers and followers adopted, adapted, and elaborated his theology, Paul had an influence on the postapostolic tradition unlike any other teacher of the first Christian generation.

The Deutero-Pauline writings can be distinguished from the authentic letters of Paul by their linguistic and stylistic features as well as by their contents. These writings want to extend the apostolic word into a changed situation. They thus place their interpretations explicitly under the authority of the apostle to the gentiles, to whose name and words they appeal, and maintain the letter form in order to communicate their message to the churches after the model of Paul himself. Thus one can notice many passages that not only presuppose the oral apostolic tradition, but also allude indirectly to authentic Pauline texts, which were read, interpreted, and commented upon in the context of the developing Christian school tradition.

Just as the Letter to the Romans makes clear by its carefully thought out structure that the promise and announcement of salvation is the call and basis for an authentic Christian life, so the letters to the Colossians and Ephesians are so structured that the initial section of theological instruction (Col. 1–2; Eph. 1–3) is followed by a section on Christian ethics (Col. 3–4; Eph. 4–6). By this means parenesis is explicitly shown to be based on the promise and announcement of salvation presented in the didactic material in the first part (Col. 3:1; Eph. 4:1), and therefore as the necessary consequence that Christians must draw for their lives and conduct from the gospel. To have "died with Christ" (cf. Col. 3:3) must have as its conclusion "put to death therefore whatever in you is earthly" (Col. 3:5). "If then you have been raised with Christ, seek the things that are above, where Christ is, seated at the right hand of God" (Col. 3:1). Whoever has accepted Jesus Christ is now exhorted also to live in him, to be rooted and grounded in him, established in the faith (Col. 2:6–7). Christians are called to forgive each other, as God has forgiven them in Christ Jesus (Eph. 4:32), and to walk in love, as Christ has loved them (Eph. 5:2).

The Pauline character of their ethical instruction can also be seen in the juxtaposition of the "putting off" of the old nature and the "putting on" of the new self (Col. 3:9–10; Eph. 4:24). That means "but now you must get rid of all such things: anger, wrath, malice, slander, and abusive language from your mouth" (Col. 3:8); or "so then, putting away falsehood, let all of us speak the truth to our neighbors, for we are members of one another" (Eph. 4:25). What is to be "put off" is set forth in cataloguelike lists of vices that are strictly to be avoided (Col. 3:5, 8; Eph. 4:25–32). The positive counterpart is represented by compact series of characteristics that portray what the life of the believer should look like: "As God's chosen ones, holy and beloved, clothe yourselves with compassion, kindness, humility, meekness, patience" (Col. 3:12). The experience "in Christ" of having been liberated from darkness to light will in this way attain visible form by a life lived "in the Lord."

Although the moral instruction developed in Colossians and Ephesians is determined in its essential points by Pauline elements taken over from the tradition, on the other hand it must not be overlooked that the ethic set forth in them presupposes a different situation in the churches, and therefore has been reformulated in terms of its content. The eschatological expectation that is at the heart of the Pauline train of thought has receded, only vague echoes of which are now heard from time to time (Col. 3:3). In Paul there is a clear distinction between statements that affirm that Christians have already died with Christ and statements that affirm their future resurrection (Rom. 6:3–4), but in Colossians and Ephesians it can now be said that they are already risen with him (Col. 2:12; 3:1). Christ is already enthroned at the right hand of God; the Christian's view is directed upward to him. A different perspective replaces the expectation of the approaching day of the Lord in the imminent future, a perspective no longer directed forward, but upward. The foundation of the believer's confidence is no longer the eschatological hope, which is aware of the shortness of the available time, but the confession of Christ who already rules as Lord of the cosmos (Col. 1:15–20).

The address to the community that follows is based on this confession of the lordship of Christ, which announces their reconciliation to God as something that has already occurred and in which they already participate, and which obligates them henceforth to live their lives as holy, blameless, and without reproach (Col. 1:22). They must therefore hold fast to the hope in the gospel and remain firm in the faith (1:23). They will be enabled thereby to avoid false teaching and be loyal to the true confession of faith. Teachers had appeared who claimed that the cosmic powers that shape our destinies must be venerated, ascetic rules must be carefully followed, and certain days must be observed as especially holy times (Col. 2:8–23). The author of Colossians opposes this by appealing to the common Christian confession of faith that Christ had already triumphed over the principalities and powers, and robbed them of their power to threaten human beings. Whoever therefore has placed trust in Christ as Lord is thereby freed from any coercion based on law and shares in the triumph of Christ. By their faith and deeds, believers have committed themselves to him as their Lord, the one who has let his universal triumph already be experienced as a present reality in the life of the church.

The Letter to the Ephesians deals with the ecclesiological significance of the theme of the lordship of Christ: the exalted Christ is the head of the cosmic body that spans the world, the one church. Thus the parenetic section of the letter is prefaced by an elaborate doctrine of the church (Eph. 4:1–16). As members of the body of Christ, Christians are bound to one another, and they grow toward the maturity of the one who is the head, Christ. The triumphant song of exultation that sounds forth from believers can thus be expressed in the words that God "even when we were dead through our trespasses, made us alive together with Christ . . . and raised us up with him and made us sit with him in the heavenly places in Christ Jesus." The fundamental affirmation of the Pauline doctrine of justification is taken up with the statement "for by grace you have been saved through faith; and this is not your own doing, it is the gift of God—not the result of works, so that no one may boast"

(Eph. 2:8–9). But then it is immediately added: "For we are what he has made us, created in Christ Jesus for good works" (2:10). Accordingly, in God's plan the kind of life that Christians are to live has already been determined in heaven, and when Christians do good works it is this divine determination that is coming to expression.

The conviction that Christians are already enthroned with Christ in heaven is not intended to make room for any kind of fanatical enthusiasm, but to name the goal toward which the life of the believer is directed. The Christian is not yet in that blessed state untouched by attacks of doubt and temptation. Believers must rather endure in the constant struggle and defend themselves against the deceitful attacks of the devil. In order to endure in this fight, Christians are urged to take on the whole armor of God and resist the attacks of the evil one (Eph. 6:10–17). Just as is the case in the Qumran texts, where the community is called to fight on the side of the "sons of light" against the threat of the powers of darkness, and with God's armor to stand their ground against the assaults of Belial and his hordes, so also the ethical struggle is pictured as the battle between light and darkness in which the "children of light" are called to serve. Whoever belongs to Christ has been called out of darkness, henceforth to live as a "child of light" (Eph. 5:8). The "fruit of light," however, is found in all that is good and right and true (Eph. 5:9). Wherever love as the bond of perfect harmony binds the members of the community together (Col. 3:14), there life is lived that is worthy of the calling to which Christians have been called (Eph. 4:1).

Solemn admonitions to be applied to human responsibility in the world are also presented by the Pastoral Letters. As in the case of Colossians and Ephesians, so also the writings addressed to Timothy and Titus reject both fanatical utopian enthusiasm, on the one side, and ascetic legalism on the other. With words of hymnic creedal confession, praise is given to the saving grace of God that has appeared for all people (Titus 2:11). Christ has given "himself for us that he might redeem us from all iniquity and purify for himself a people of his own who are zealous for good deeds" (2:14). The demonstration of God's grace in Christ should result in believers' renouncing worldly passions and all that is ungodly and the living of sober, upright, and holy lives in this world (2:12).

The "sound doctrine" handed on and interpreted as apostolic tradition has for its content not only the message that affirms the good news of the gospel, but also has obligatory moral directions for a life that is righteous and pleasing to God (1 Tim. 1:10; 2 Tim. 4:3; Titus 1:9; 2:1). In all this the doctrine of justification is held fast—that is, that people are not justified before God on the basis of worthiness or human achievement, but only by God's gracious decree (2 Tim. 1:9; Titus 3:5-6). However, the intense debate in which the apostle once had to engage in order to make clear that the justification of human beings before God could never rest on works of the law (Gal. 3; Rom. 4) already lies so far in the past that now the life of the Christian can be called rich in "good works" without giving it a second thought (1 Tim. 5:10, 25; Titus 2:7, 14; 3:8, 14). What these works consist of can be described with the goals commonly accepted for a good life—namely, that it be pious and upright. Thus to a large extent the concepts and terminology of typical Hellenistic ethics are taken over, so that εὐσέβεια ("godliness," "religion"), φιλανθρωπία ("kindness"), and καλὰ ἔργα ("good works") are repeatedly named as the characteristics of a righteous life. Whoever orders their life by these guidelines will not be misled by legalistic demands for abstinence to disdain the world or to withdraw from it. But neither will they surrender to libertine arrogance and immoral excess. Sensible, level-headed moderation and a circumspect manner of acting will guard the Christians' life in the world.

Christians are expected to live "a quiet and peaceable life, in all godliness and dignity" (1 Tim. 2:2). It is to this task that the challenge is directed: "Train yourself in godliness; for while physical training is of some value, godliness is of value in every way" (1 Tim. 4:7-8). The Christian is not called to the observance of ascetic prescriptions that lead to world denial, but to the grateful use of all good gifts that God has created, for "nothing is to be rejected, provided it is received with thanksgiving" (1 Tim. 4:3-4).

Exemplary conduct is especially the responsibility of those who hold office. Thus the obligations that are placed on a bishop are itemized in dependence on the catalogues of virtues in general circulation. It is expected that the bishop will be "above reproach, married only once, temperate, sensible, respectable, hospitable, an apt teacher, not a drunkard, not violent but gentle, not quarrelsome, and not a lover of money" (1 Tim. 3:2–3). In this list of the necessary qualifications for a holder of church office, competence in teaching is noteworthy as a requirement that is especially necessary for the leadership of a congregation. In view of the task of leading the congregation, the traditional catalogue is expanded by two prerequisites that have to do specifically with the ministry of one who serves in a church: "He must not be a recent convert, or he may be puffed up with conceit and fall into the condemnation of the devil," and he "must be well thought of by outsiders, or he may fall into reproach and the snare of the devil" (3:6–7).

Similar standards are presented for deacons, who must be respectable, "not double-tongued, not indulging in much wine, not greedy for gain" and so on (1 Tim. 3:8, 9–13). By their exemplary conduct they should exhibit what a Christian, pious life is supposed to look like. At the same time, all Christians should be mindful that the sum total of all Christian instruction is "love that comes from a pure heart, a good conscience, and sincere faith" (1 Tim. 1:5). By orienting their way of life to the content of the Christian confession and the voice of a good conscience, they fight the good fight of faith to which they have been called (1 Tim. 1:19; 3:9; 2 Tim. 1:3; Titus 1:15). A life lived according to God's commands, which at the same time knows it is obligated to measure up to the standards of the prevailing moral philosophy, has earned the right to be considered religious and respectable, and can count on general approval. Piety is of great advantage to those who wish to live stable, moderate lives, people who are inclined neither toward sensuous over-indulgence nor to otherworldly disdain of the good gifts of God. Such conduct always knows how to find the golden mean between the extremes of gluttony and ascetic legalism. One knows that one brought nothing into the world, and can take nothing out, and can thus be satisfied with food and clothing (1 Tim. 6:7–8). The rich, however, are warned not to be proud and to place their hope in uncertain riches. They should rather do something useful with the goods at their disposal, be rich in good works, liberal and generous in their help to others, "thus storing up for themselves the treasure of a good foundation for the future, so that they may take hold of the life that really is life" (1 Tim. 6:17-19).

The ethic developed in the Pastoral Letters is characterized by a prudent reflection on the obligations imposed upon one by life in this world. Considered judgment and pious conduct are to a large extent portrayed in terms borrowed from the current teaching on morality in the surrounding culture, with the result that it could appear as if the content of ethical instruction by which the church is to direct its life is practically identical with the standards generally acceptable in society. The ethic of the Pastoral Letters has therefore sometimes been described as the expression of a Christian bourgeois mentality by which Christians attempted to adjust to the world and find their place in it. This description is correct to the extent that it perceives that the churches of the Pastoral Letters no longer expect an imminent end of the world, but rather—as can already be seen in the Colossian and Ephesian letters—are concerned to preserve the faith energized by love in the context of a new situation. This risky undertaking could not be achieved easily, and so should not be too easily criticized, although it should not be denied that the extensive reliance on the cultural standards of conduct already present could involve such an accommodation to the social conditions already present that the specific contours of Christian existence could become blurred.

The idea of a "Christian bourgeois mentality" could easily be perceived in a pejorative sense and thus lead to an evaluation based on a misunderstanding. The task that the second and third Christian generations saw themselves as facing could more appropriately be designated as the "worldliness of faith." On the one hand, it was necessary for Christians to find their place in the continuing world, but on the other side, they had to take care that they did not simply lose themselves in the world in the process. They had to remain aware of the dangers to which they were exposed as they attempted to live their lives out of the power of their confession of faith. The author of the Pastoral Letters was thoroughly aware of this responsibility. With a specific appeal to the authority of the apostle Paul, whose word was available not only in traditional expressions in the apostolic tradition, but especially in his own letters, he made clear that he too has no other concern than to set forth the truth of the gospel so that it could be lived out in the lives of believers. In this respect the Pastoral Letters are concerned not only to take up and extend Pauline theology, at the same time they present it as the critical norm by which they themselves intend to be measured. The Pastoral Letters too leave no doubt about the firm conviction that believers are saved not by their own deeds but only through "Christ Jesus, himself human, who gave himself a ransom for all" (1 Tim. 2:5-6), and that in their life and work they are to fight the good fight of faith in order to give fitting expression to the "good confession" (1 Tim. 6:12).

The churches of the second and third Christian generations were aware of being borne along by the conviction that the gospel had brought Jews and gentiles together through faith in the crucified and risen Lord into one people of God. By confessing Christ as their peace (Eph. 2:14), who had brought Jews and gentiles into the fellowship of the one body, they knew themselves at one and the same time to be both obligated and enabled to keep the unity of the Spirit in the bond of peace (Eph. 4:3), and thereby to make room for the peace of Christ, so that it could rule and unfold its saving power in them (Col. 3:15). Christians thus became servants of a peace that surpasses all understanding (Phil. 4:7) in the midst of a world oriented to a different faith, and sought through their daily behavior in love to fulfill their assigned task of serving as peacemakers.

Suggestions for Further Reading

Cannon, G. E. *The Use of Traditional Material in Colossians.* Macon, Ga.: Mercer University Press, 1983.

Collins, R. F. *Letters That Paul Did Not Write.* Wilmington, Del.: Michael Glazier, 1988.

Culpepper, A. "Ethical Dualism and Church Discipline, Eph. 4:25-5:20." *Review and Expositor* 76 (1978): 529-39.

Donelson, L. R. *Pseudepigraphy and Ethical Argument in the Pastoral Epistles.* Tübingen: J. C. B. Mohr, 1986.

MacDonald, M. Y. *The Pauline Churches: A Socio-historical Study of Institutionalization in the Pauline and Deutero-Pauline Writings.* Cambridge: Cambridge University Press, 1988.

Sampley, J. P. *"And the Two shall Become one Flesh." A Study of Traditions in Ephesians 5:21–33.* Cambridge: Cambridge University Press, 1971.

Schweizer, E. *The Letter to the Colossians.* Minneapolis: Augsburg, 1982.

Towner, P. H. *The Goal of Our Instruction. The Structure of Theology and Ethics in the Pastoral Epistles.* Sheffield: Sheffield Academic Press, 1990.

Verner, D. *The Household of God: The Social World of the Pastoral Epistles.* Atlanta: Scholars Press, 1983.

Wild, R. A. "The Warrior and the Prisoner: Some Reflections on Ephesians 6:10–20." *Catholic Biblical Quarterly* 46 (1984): 284–98.

Chapter Eight

LAW AND COMMANDMENT

The Law of Christ

God's will is made known through his law; its command is holy, just, and good (Rom. 7:12). Its instruction is valid—as explained by the apostle Paul—for Jews, gentiles, and Christians—for everyone. Although the Torah was given to Israel alone at Sinai (Rom. 9:4), the gentiles too know God's requirement, for the work of the law is written in their hearts (Rom. 2:14–15). The will of God is therefore not concealed from humanity, but may be discerned by the gentiles in the works of creation and is explicitly revealed to the Jews in the law of Moses.

A cardinal aspect of the law's nature, however, first became clear for Christian faith—namely, that the law was incapable of opening the way of life to humanity—but became for them a "written code" that "kills" (2 Cor. 3:6), since when they encounter the law they are always and already dominated by sin. Through the disobedience of Adam, sin as an enslaving power found an entrance into the world, with the result that since then all have become disobedient and violate the good and gracious will of God (Rom. 5:12). Sin makes use of the law, in order with its help to increase its compelling power and to exert its power all the more inescapably.

The apostle Paul describes the perverse alliance between sin and law, in his first-person description of the situation of humanity enslaved to sin: "If it had not been for the law, I would not have known sin. I would not have known what it is to covet if the law had not said, 'You shall not covet.' But sin, seizing an opportunity in the commandment, produced in me all kinds of covetousness. Apart from the law sin lies dead. I was once alive apart from the law, but when the commandment came, sin revived and I died; and the very commandment that promised life proved to be death to me. For sin, seizing an opportunity in the commandment, deceived me and through it killed me" (Rom. 7:7–11).

In these statements Paul is not speaking psychologically of his own life experiences, but discloses the despairing situation of the unredeemed person, as it is first recognized through faith within the perspective of the one who has already been freed through Christ. Through this new vision it becomes clear that one's first impression of the law—that it is a means for holding sin in check—is entirely wrong. Rather, it is the law that first provokes sin to register its full force, in that it actually incites sinful desires. But this was in fact God's will. The intent of the law is to bring to light that human beings are sinners whose fate is death. Human beings are not able to free themselves from this lostness, and are thus not capable of standing justified before God from their own resources.

Then why did God give the law at all? In the Letter to the Galatians Paul provides his provocative answer: "for the sake of transgressions" (Gal. 3:19 [NRSV "because of transgressions"]). This means that the law was intended to give rise to transgressions "until the offspring would come to whom the promise had been made" (Gal. 3:19). The law was not there at the beginning. On the contrary, it "came in between" (namely, between Adam and Christ) "in order to make the transgression all the greater" (Rom. 5:20 [NRSV "with the result that the trespass multiplied"]). Nevertheless, in contrast to Marcion's fundamental rejection of the law advocated a century later, Paul holds fast to the conviction that the law comes from God's own hand, even if it was mediated through angels (Gal. 3:19). If Judaism regarded this angelic mediation as a mark of the law's distinction, Paul gives a different evaluation to the matter: God speaks promises directly, but gives the law through intermediaries. All the same, it is of divine origin and remains God's command and God's will. But since sin has pressed the law into its own service, the result is that sin's power is increased and the law functions to expose the fact that humanity is alienated from God and under the power of sin. When the law is named "our custodian until Christ came" (Gal. 3:24; παιδαγωγὸς εἰς Χριστόν, often translated "our schoolmaster to bring us to Christ" [as KJV]), this does not mean that it exercises a pedagogical function in the life of the individual. Rather, it describes the intended function of the law in the period prior to the coming of Christ. For God confined all under sin, in order to have mercy on all (Gal. 3:22; Rom. 11:32). The law functions to charge every human being with sin and to lock them all in a prison from which there is no escape (Gal. 3:22).

This role of the law as presented by Paul stands in sharp contrast to the Jewish evaluation of the Torah. In Judaism the law is a demonstration of God's grace bestowed upon Israel, so that they could live and act according to God's will. Paul comes to an opposite understanding of the law on the basis of conclusions he infers from his interpretation of the early Christian kerygma: "God sent his Son, born of a woman, born under the law, in order to redeem those who were under the law" (Gal. 4:4–5). Christ has opened the prison and broken the coercive power of sin. He thereby made it clear once and for all that the law was incapable of granting life and that human beings by their own resources were incapable of attaining that righteousness by which they could stand before God. The death and resurrection of Christ revealed that God's righteousness is given to believers entirely by God's gracious act in Christ, without any demonstration of works required by the law (Rom. 3:28). Thus Christ is the end of the law (Rom. 10:4), for by taking upon himself the curse of the law (Gal. 3:13) he brought about the end of the domination of law and sin, and triumphed over them. This was the advent of the decisive turning point. No one can satisfy God by presenting achievements required by the law, but only through a faith that puts its trust in God — that is, by letting Christ be one's righteousness.

If the apostle is to establish this challenging thesis that human beings are justified entirely through faith apart from works of the law, then he must be prepared for severe resistance. Do not these words in fact destroy the law (Rom. 3:31), the law that contains the "holy and just and good" will of God (Rom. 7:12)?

Paul has no illusions concerning the weightiness of this objection. He takes it seriously, in that he claims to restore the law to its true purpose (Rom. 3:31). The form of the argument is that of living, dialogical speech. At first the objection is formulated that Paul's appeal to faith would simply nullify the law. Then the objection is rejected with indignation — "by no means" — and the opposite thesis is affirmed: "we establish the law." This thesis had of course to be supported from the Scripture. This is the purpose of the following extensive appeal to the story of Abraham, which one can read in the very first book of the law. The story is interpreted to support Paul's claim that not only is the law not destroyed by the preaching of the gospel, but on the contrary is brought to its true significance. With this formulation Paul intentionally makes use of current rabbinic expressions, according to which "establishing the law" means to lift up its original meaning and put it into operation. But how does that happen?

_____

Over against the law that requires works, the apostle Paul places the "law of faith" (Rom. 3:27). The Pentateuch contains the story of Abraham, of which it is said "Abraham believed the LORD, and the LORD reckoned it to him as righteousness" (Gen. 15:6; Rom. 4:3; Gal. 3:6). Paul does not understand this faith of Abraham as a past event from a far distant time. Rather, just as the promise once given to him corresponds to the gospel that is declared to the church, so Abraham's faith appears as the paradigm of faith as such, as it is now alive in the Christian community that places its trust in the gospel of the crucified and resurrected Christ. Thus those who believe are children of Abraham (Gal. 3:29), and Christians describe Abraham as their father (Rom. 4:1).

How is this faith described in the Scriptures related to the requirements posed by the law? Paul points out that at that time, when Abraham trusted God by accepting his declaration in faith, the commandments of the Torah received by Israel at Sinai did not yet exist. While in the current Jewish understanding of the story of Abraham, the patriarch observed all the commandments even though they were not present to him in written form, and thus proved himself to be a pious man of God, Paul emphasizes that Abraham lived long before the giving of the law at Sinai. Abraham acted by the power of faith that places its trust in the promise of God. From that, the apostle infers that circumcision was only given to him later, like a seal impressed on the righteousness he already had by faith, and which it therefore did not cause. When Abraham initially relied upon the word of God, he had not yet received circumcision, the sign of the covenant, but was uncircumcised like the gentiles (Rom. 4:10–11). The promise was there before the requirements of the law, and the grace of God precedes the demand for righteousness. Thus Abraham remains the father of all who believe, to whom also faith will be reckoned as righteousness, so that they walk in the footsteps of the father of all believers (Rom. 4:12).

Thus "establishing the law" means for Paul that the original significance of the Torah, covered over by later tradition, is again revealed, so that it becomes a witness for righteousness by faith against the later developments of righteousness by law. With this understanding—so goes the claim made by the apostle—it is not as though the law were robbed of its honor; rather, it is for the first time understood in its true significance. Wherever the grace of God is grasped in undivided trust, there at the same time freedom is established, a freedom that realizes itself in loving service. Since the necessity of demonstrating one's own righteousness has been done away with, love now becomes the fulfillment of the law (Rom. 13:10).

———

If the law is depicted in accordance with this exposition as the law of faith, then from this understanding derive corresponding consequences for the determination of ethics. The law, which had been commandeered by sin, is named by the apostle a "law of sin and of death" (Rom. 8:2). For, since humanity had been misled by the false hope that they could attain life by works of the law, they were in fact not led to life, but inescapably delivered over to death. Christ, however, has triumphed over the principalities and powers and through his victory over sin, death, and the law has dissolved that unholy alliance, so that the law can once again serve its original purpose of testifying to the "holy, just, and good" will of God (Rom. 7:12). The lives of believers, who belong to the Christ and are led by the power of the Spirit, are lived under the direction and command of the Lord. Thus also the new life to which Christ has freed his own stands under a law, for the freedom of believers is realized in obedience to their Lord. Thus Paul can describe the contrast between "once" and "now" by placing the law of sin and death over against the law of the Spirit, the Spirit that gives life in Christ Jesus (Rom. 8:2).

Whoever reads the law to say that one can find the way to salvation by works of achievement perceives it in such a way that it can be only the law of sin and death. Not until the law is heard as a testimony to the message of Christ is the law "established," because now it begins to speak as promise, which truly opens the way to life. Thus the same writing, the same words, the same letters, can be read in one way or the other. But whoever now reads the law as testimony to Christ is not "outside the law" (ἄνομος), but rather "under Christ's law" (ἔννομος Χριστοῦ, 1 Cor. 9:21). Such people stand under the sovereignty of the Lord, whose word is instruction for their lives that cannot be ignored.

———

"Bear one another's burdens and in this way you will fulfill the law of Christ." With these words the apostle summarizes his instruction for the conduct of Christians (Gal. 6:2). It is clear that this statement was presupposed as already familiar to the churches, for it receives no further elaboration. When it is applied concretely, it means on the one hand that in the congregation some who had allowed themselves to be overtaken by sin should be helped back to the right path (6:1); on the other hand, the reminder is given that when someone thinks oneself to be something, when in fact one is nothing, such a one is self-deceived (6:3). To take the burdens of the other on oneself is an expression of the love with which people are to interact and stand by each other. For "the whole law is summed up in a single commandment, 'You shall love your neighbor as yourself'" (Gal. 5:14). It is thus made unmistakably clear that for the Christian the command of Scripture has not lost its significance, but now for the first time can be grasped and followed in its true meaning.

Under the domination exercised by the alliance of sin and the law, it was impossible to measure up to the just requirement of the law, to overcome sin and death, and attain to life. Sin commandeered the law and exercised its power by ruling over "the flesh"—that is, the human being understood in its self-determination by which persons by their striving and action sought self-realization. The law must necessarily therefore be "weak" (Rom. 8:3). That one could be blameless according to the law was just as undisputed among contemporary Jews as it was for Paul the Jew (Phil. 3:6). But even if one could keep all the commandments, the power of sin could not be broken, for "the flesh's" striving can never be subject to the law of God (Rom. 8:7). But now the bondage within which sin and the law hold all human beings captive has been brought to an end, for God has sent his Son, the only one who has been truly obedient, "in the form of sinful flesh" (Rom. 8:3), and thereby defeated the power of sin once for all on its own turf. What was never possible under the law has now become possible: among those who belong to Christ, "who walk not according to the flesh but according to the Spirit," "the just requirement of the law" is fulfilled (Rom. 8:4). Where the Spirit that creates life is at work, there God's will and command are recognized and done.

The gate to freedom has been opened through the sending of the son of God. However, this freedom means at the same time constraint—not the slavery that prevailed in the past, however, but the obedience of those who pursue the "holy, just, and good will of God" in their life and behavior. Through the death and resurrection of Christ the law has been delivered from its envelopment by sin and has now been given back to its rightful Lord. Its word, therefore, is for Christians by no means optional. Rather, it presents the elaboration and unfolding of God's will, an orientation determinative for the shape of the

Christian life. What stands written in Scripture applies to Christians too as a guide for how to live their lives: "You shall not commit adultery, you shall not murder, you shall not steal, you shall not covet" (Rom. 13:8). These are binding directives that cannot be disregarded. These commands of the Decalogue, "and any other commandment, are summed up in this word, love your neighbor as yourself" (Rom. 13:8). But this means that "love is the fulfilling of the law" (Rom. 13:10).

The life of the Christian is therefore governed by love, the love made real to them in Christ, which they must demonstrate to their neighbors in the way they live their lives. This love surpasses all the gifts of the Spirit and the variety of charisms. While these will one day come to an end, love always endures. Its incredible potency, its unfaltering patience and stability, its steadiness that never grows weary, as well as its capacity to take on the day's tasks, is described by Paul as a number of links that together make up one chain "Love is patient, love is kind; love is not envious or boastful or arrogant or rude. It does not insist on its own way; it is not irritable or resentful; it does not rejoice in wrongdoing, but rejoices in the truth. It bears all things, believes all things, hopes all things, endures all things" (1 Cor. 13:4-7).

Love attains concrete form as it is guided by the will of God expressed in the individual commandments, with the result that the law is fulfilled. All Christians are called to live a life corresponding to their call in that situation where they were encountered by the message of the gospel. Whether one was grasped by this word as Jew or gentile, as free or slave, is not decisive for the shaping of one's life as a Christian. The only determining factor is the call, which points in the direction that life is to be henceforth lived. Even slaves are advised not to worry about whether they could obtain freedom in the external, secular sense. Slaves were to be aware that "whoever was called in the Lord as a slave is a freed person belonging to the Lord" (1 Cor. 7:22). This was not commending some sort of Stoic doctrine to disdain external circumstances and to be concerned only with inner independence and inner tranquility; it is rather a pointer to Christ as the only founder of true freedom. Whoever belongs to Christ is truly free. Whoever has disclaimed their calling is indeed a tyrannized slave, even if externally and superficially "free." For transforming power goes forth from the love of Christ, power that changes the relationship of slaves and masters from the ground up.

The rule of life by which Christians are to live can also be formulated in the instruction to accept one another, as Christ has accepted his own—for the glory of God (Rom. 15:7). Living in a manner "in accord with Christ Jesus" (Rom. 15:5) means nothing else than "living in accord with love" (Rom. 14:15 [NRSV: "walking in love"]). Wherever one person regards another more highly than self and is concerned to be of service to the other person, there God's will is done and the law of Christ is fulfilled.

Suggestions for Further Reading

Belleville, L. L. "'Under Law': Structural Analysis and the Pauline Concept of Law in Galatians 3.21–4.11." *Journal for the Study of the New Testament* 26 (1986): 53–78.

Hays, R. B. "Christology and Ethics in Galatians: The Law of Christ." *Catholic Biblical Quarterly* 49 (1987): 268–90.

Hübner, H. *Law in Paul's Thought.* Edinburgh: T. & T. Clark, 1984.

Lull, D. J. "'The Law Was Our Pedagogue': A Study in Galatians 3:19–25." *Journal of Biblical Literature* 105 (1986): 481–98.

Matera, F. J. "The Culmination of Paul's Argument to the Galatians: Gal 5.1–6.17." *Journal for the Study of the New Testament* 32 (1989): 79–91.

Räisänen, H. *Paul and the Law.* Philadelphia: Fortress Press, 1986.

Sanders, E. P. *Paul, the Law, and the Jewish People.* Philadelphia: Fortress Press, 1983.

Schreiner, T. R. "The Abolition and Fulfillment of the Law in Paul." *Journal for the Study of the New Testament* 35 (1989): 47–74.

Snodgrass, K. R. "Justification by Grace—To the Doers: An Analysis of the Place of Romans 2 in the Theology of Paul." *New Testament Studies* 32 (1986): 72–93.

Williams, S. K. "The 'Righteousness of God' in Romans." *Journal of Biblical Literature* 99 (1980): 241–90.

The New
Commandment

In the farewell discourses of the Fourth Gospel, the
disciples of Jesus are charged with keeping the new
commandment given to them by the departing lord: to love each
other as he has loved them. This is the mark by which everyone
is to recognize that they are his disciples, that they love one
another (John 13:34–35). These words do not represent the statement of an ethical principle according to which they are henceforth to order their lives. If they were understood in this sense,
then they could be separated from the person of the one who
speaks them, and could be described as a general truth. But the
new commandment is grounded by pointing to the love that
binds Jesus to his own. Those who are committed to him experience the love of their Lord who has come down among his
own and humbled himself as a servant. In response to this, the
disciples' love is triggered, the love that sets them free from self-
concern and opens them up to concern for others.

The commandment of familial love virtually represents
the last will and testament that Jesus leaves behind to his own.
Even though he himself will no longer be among them, still the
power of love that he has bestowed upon them will continue at
work within and among them. Then when they stand together
in this love they have experienced, all the world can recognize
that they belong to him. As his disciples, they are to continue
in his word and witness to its truth by their faith and their very
lives. Jesus' instruction to his own is grounded in the Father's
own love to the Son, and directs them: "Abide in my love. If you
keep my commandments, you will abide in my love, just as I
have kept my Father's commandments and abide in his love."
(15:9–10).

The command of familial love receives its specific character through its christological grounding. Only in the unity that
binds them fast to their Lord can the disciples preserve the love
that has met them in Christ and demonstrate the reality of the
love that binds them to each other. Thus the commission with
which they are charged is prescribed neither as love for the

neighbor in general nor as a challenge to do good works in the world at large, but exclusively as love for sisters and brothers that binds together the community of faith.

If in the farewell discourses of the Gospel of John the directive concerning familial love is described as the "new commandment," so 1 John can speak of the "old commandment" that has been in effect from the beginning, the command that the community is to obey as *the* word they have received (1 John 2:7; cf. 2 John 5). This means that it was presupposed that the command of brotherly love had a firm place in the tradition of early Christian instruction, so that there can be no doubt that it represented a fundamental obligation of the Christian life. Although the Gospel speaks of the "new" commandment and the Epistles of the "old" commandment, they agree in emphasizing that it imposed a valid obligation on every Christian. Except for a different emphasis here and there, they all have the same view of this command as ethical instruction.

Familial love receives both its power and its direction from the experienced love which the Lord has shown to his own. The gracious God has so loved the lost world that he gave his only Son, so that all who believe on him will not be lost, but have eternal life (John 3:16; cf. also 1 John 4:9). Wherever this message is accepted in faith, there death is robbed of its power and eternal life is given, life that cannot be destroyed even by physical death (John 11:25–27). The central affirmation concerning God's love shown in the giving of his Son receives no ethical application in the immediate context, but is referred exclusively to the salvation received by faith. Nonetheless, Jesus' love, which he has granted to his own, carries with it the assignment he gives to them—as is repeatedly explained in the Johannine theology. They are directed to Jesus' own conduct as the model, so that they will love one another as he has loved his own (John 13:34). By serving his disciples as a slave, washing their feet, he gave them an example, so that they would serve each other as he had served them (13:15). Only the one who has received the love of Jesus is able to practice true familial love. Since the content of this love is determined by Jesus' own deed, it needs no further elaboration in order to describe their assignment in detail. Jesus' command is simply that the disciples love one another as he loves them (John 15:12).

Just as a branch can bear no fruit unless it remains on the vine, so the disciples of Jesus can do nothing apart from him (John 15:1–8). Only the one who abides in him—and that means, in his word—knows how to fulfill his will. Only by the faith that trusts in Jesus' word and holds fast to it will recognize his command and render him obedience. Those who belong to Jesus will bear much fruit, as the love command becomes the point of orientation of all they do. Whoever loves Jesus will also keep his commandments (John 14:15), for—as the farewell discourses teach—it is the one who has Jesus' commandments and keeps them who loves him. Those who love Jesus, however, are also the ones loved by the Father (John 14:21). Believers can tell that they know God by the fact that they keep his commandments (1 John 2:3). There can be no authentic knowledge of God if his commands are not followed (2:4). The plural "commandments" are in fact summed up in the one command of love, which has been given to them. The divine command has one goal, that people believe on the name of the Son of God, Jesus Christ, and that those who believe love one another as Jesus Christ has loved them (1 John 3:23). Since faith and love are seen together in an indissoluble unity, it can be boldly said that "his commandments are not burdensome" (1 John 5:3). For where the power of love experienced in Christ is at work, there life triumphs over death.

————

Believers who follow the command of familial love therefore no longer belong to the world alienated from God, which in hostility stands over against him as the cosmos (John 8:23; 1 John 2:16; 4:5), but lead their lives as those who are born of the Spirit (John 3:8). To be sure, they continue to live in this world and must therefore endure hatred and persecution, but they already participate in the victory of Christ over the cosmos (1 John 5:5). Through his suffering, death, and resurrection, Christ has overcome the world. Wherever this message is accepted in faith and God is honored as the creator, there the lost world is saved and again subjected to its Lord as God's creation.

To be sure, Jesus' disciples must experience anxiety and grief; but they can live in the secure confidence that Christ is the victor over the world (John 15:13). They participate in the victory he has attained, in that he has already presented the greatest proof of his love by the giving of his own life: "No one has greater love than this, to lay down one's life for one's friends" (John 15:13). When it is immediately added that "you are my friends" (15:14), it becomes clear that the preceding statement was not a generalization, but speaks directly of Jesus' act for his own. He gives his life for them and thereby bestows upon them the love of a friend who intervenes for the sake of his own. At the same time, his love gives the ground and direction for their ethical conduct: "You are my friends if you do what I command you" (John 15:14). Whenever "love" is spoken of in the Johannine writings, without further indication of to whom the love applies, it always means the inseparable unity of love to God and love to the brothers and sisters of the Christian community.

As the world is overcome by faith, so also by love. Thus it is said: "Do not love the world or the things in the world. The love of the Father is not in those who love the world" (1 John 2:15). The world passes away, with all its charm and allurements. Only the one who does the will of God abides forever. With this repeated emphasis on the love commandment, the First Letter of John directs its attack against heretical teachers whose false christology and warped view of ethics share the same interdependent conceptual basis. They clearly place their exclusive emphasis on the spiritual appearance of Christ and advocate the view that the son of God did not really appear in the flesh. Against this docetic christology, according to which Christ only appeared to become a truly human being, it is emphatically declared that the Christ is the son of God who has come in the flesh (1 John 4:2-3); he is the one who truly died as an expiation for sins (1:7; 2:2; 4:10) and is the savior of the cosmos (4:14). What the opponents say and do is evidence of their origin: from this cosmos, so that only those become their followers who are likewise oriented to this world hostile to God (4:5-6).

The way the false teachers live their lives is related to their christology. Since they do not take seriously the reality of bodily life in the world, they do not grasp the reality of redemption (4:2-3). This is also the reason they pay no attention to the commandments (2:3-4; 5:2-3) and show no concern for their brothers and sisters (2:9-11; 3:10, 14-15; 4:8, 20; 5:2). But to neglect the brother or sister is the same as murder (3:12). "How does God's love abide in anyone who has the world's goods and sees a brother or sister in need, and yet refuses to help?" (3:17). This question exposes the absurdity of such an attitude, for whoever claims to love God while hating his brother or sister is a liar (1 John 4:20).

On the one hand, 1 John can affirm that the believer does not sin (3:9; 5:18), but on the other hand, "if we say that we have no sin, we deceive ourselves, and the truth is not in us" (1:8). These statements present a paradoxical state of affairs: we do not sin and yet we sin. Believers are free from sin in that they participate in Christ's victory over the cosmos. Therefore they are called to walk in the light and to manifest the reality of their faith in deeds of love. By being warned not to have any illusions about the continuing power of sin, while at the same time being pointed to Christ's triumph over sin, the ethical instruction receives its grounding and its urgency at one and the same time. Preaching and exhortation make visible the great separation in process: while on the one side it is declared that those who do not love remain in the world of death, on the other side the joyful certainty is proclaimed, "we know that we have passed from death to life because we love one another" (1 John 3:14).

The Johannine ethic of love is strictly oriented to its christology. Only the one who looks to Christ, believes his word, and abides in it can experience what love means. And only by holding fast to his word will someone be enabled to fulfill the new command of familial love, which is at the same time the old commandment, because it has brought the truth to light. "In this is love, not that we loved God but that he loved us and sent his Son to be the atoning sacrifice for our sins" (1 John 4:10). From that it necessarily follows that we ought to love one another, because God has loved us (4:11).

Suggestions for Further Reading

Brown, R. *The Community of the Beloved Disciple.* New York: Paulist Press, 1979.

———. *The Epistles of John.* Garden City, N.Y.: Doubleday, 1982.

Collins, R. F. "'A New Commandment I Give to You, that You Love One Another. . . .' (Jn 13.34)." *Laval Théologique et Philosophique* 35 (1979): 235–61.

Fortna, R. *The Fourth Gospel and Its Predecessor.* Philadelphia: Fortress Press, 1988.

Käsemann, E. *The Testament of Jesus.* Philadelphia: Fortress Press, 1968.

Kysar, R. *The Fourth Evangelist and His Gospel.* Minneapolis: Augsburg, 1975.

Lieu, J. M. "Authority to Become Children of God: A Study of 1 John." *Novum Testamentum* 23 (1981): 210–28.

Rensberger, D. *Johannine Faith and Liberating Community.* Philadelphia: Westminster/John Knox, 1989.

Segovia, F. *Love Relationships in the Johannine Tradition: Agape/Agapan in 1 John and the Fourth Gospel.* Chico: Scholars Press, 1982.

Smith, D. M. *Johannine Christianity: Essays on its Setting, Sources, and Theology.* Columbia: University of South Carolina Press, 1984.

The Law of Liberty

When properly understood, the law is a royal law (Jas. 2:8), the law of liberty (1:25; 2:12). This is the way the author of the Letter of James, who describes himself as a teacher (3:1), wants to characterize the ethic he presents. He understands the commands contained in the Old Testament and those that occur in Christian instruction under the one heading of "law." The law is called "perfect," because it contains the undiluted will of God, the fulfillment of which leads to the righteousness that can stand before God. It is called "royal," because it is promulgated by God, the King of kings. All its prescriptions are to be carefully followed, especially the obligatory command to love one's neighbor as oneself (2:8). "For whoever keeps the whole law but fails in one point, has become accountable of all of it. For the one who said, 'You shall not commit adultery,' also said 'You shall not murder.' Now if [so his explanation goes] you do not commit adultery but if you murder, you have become a transgressor of the law" (2:10–11).

The law thus forms a unit, which includes not only the commands of the Old Testament, but also all ethical directions. Stoic rules based on experience, of the kind that had found a place in the instruction of the Hellenistic synagogue, are included within this understanding of the law, just as much as didactic materials from the Old Testament and Jewish tradition, or even sayings of Jesus that are taken up into the Letter of James as ethical rules (see above, pp. 26–27). Obvious echoes of a series of sayings of Jesus found in written form in the Sermon on the Mount can be noted especially in James's material that seems to have been transmitted in catechetical contexts due to its parenetic content (see above, pp. 61–62). Examples are the prohibition against swearing and the demand that one say a simple "yes" or "no" (Jas. 5:12; Matt. 5:34–37), the statement about God's hearing prayer (Jas. 1:5; Matt. 7:7), and the urgent appeal to be doers of the word and not hearers only (Jas. 1:22; Matt. 7:24–27). These sayings are never cited as "words of the Lord" or identified as such. They are inserted into a structure of ethical statements woven together from different elements into a single wreath. This somewhat catechetical collection of moral instruction as a whole is called the "law of liberty."

The Letter of James understands the law as a unity, that sets one free rather than leading into slavery. It offers a clear point of orientation for the lives of Christians. They are exhorted not to be forgetful hearers, but to serve God with their actions (1:25–26); they are to speak and act as people who are guided by the law of liberty (2:12). "For" — so goes the explanation — "judgment will be without mercy to anyone who has shown no mercy; mercy triumphs over judgment" (2:13). Although the love commandment is listed as one among others and is not singled out as the highest or greatest, special significance is still ascribed to the quality of mercy, for this is God's guide in judgment.

With this understanding of the law of liberty, James stands in the tradition of diaspora Judaism, which he has taken up and extended further in a Christian form. The cultic and ceremonial laws, which in the Hellenistic synagogue had already receded in importance behind the ethical exposition of the law, does not come in view at all. On the contrary, true worship is understood in terms of moral and ethical conduct, prime examples of which are visiting widows and orphans in their affliction and keeping oneself unstained from the world's defilements (1:27). The seriousness of this obligation is grounded by reference to the law. For whoever speaks evil or judges a brother or sister, speaks evil or judges the law itself (4:11). But one must not become guilty of this, for if one becomes a critic of the law, one is no longer a doer of the law, but its judge. But this is a violation of God's own majesty, for God alone is the lawgiver and judge who "is able to save and destroy" (4:11–12).

The law of liberty, as it is developed in James as the summary of Christian ethics, shows to Christians how they may attain that perfection that will allow them to stand before God's judgment. By this unadorned and unpretentious doctrine, intended to provide illumination by the directness of its statements, James would like to prevent the churches from becoming weary and neglecting to carry out their mission. Genuine freedom, in the conviction of James, is only present where the directives of the law as understood from the point of view of Christian faith are affirmed with the whole heart, and faith is expressed in corresponding conduct.

The sentences of ethical instruction brought together in the letter of James include no theological arguments as their foundation, because as the commands of God they speak a language that makes its own self-evident claim. They still require an explanation, however, to defend against misunderstandings that easily arise. In the form of a didactic discourse in which argument and objections are balanced against each other and a valid conclusion is formulated at the end, the author of James engages in debate with skeptical reflections that could be introduced against the binding force of the doctrine of the law he presents (2:14–26).

He begins by announcing the theme of the disputed topic—namely, that when one stands before God, faith without works cannot save (2:14). Then he shows by example that faith must be matched by action, since a person in need cannot be helped with good wishes, but only by loving deeds that actually help. Thus the statement proves true, that faith without works is dead (2:17). In a second line of argument he begins afresh to evoke the insight that faith without works is dead in a way that cannot be contradicted (2:26). Thereby the protest of an anonymous objector is introduced, in the manner of the Cynic-Stoic diatribe (see above, pp. 19–20), who advocates the separation of faith and works: one has faith, the other has works. But this objection is considered a theological short circuit and waved aside as irresponsible. Salvation is by no means mediated merely by the belief that there is one God. This refers to the common Jewish creedal statement that the oneness of God gives the content of the faith one has in mind, without specifically characterizing the faith in any way that is recognizably Christian. Monotheistic orthodoxy, however, is not adequate. The demons too believe that there is one God, and tremble before God, but that does not mean they are saved. So faith without works is useless.

After eliminating the false understandings, he shows positively that faith must necessarily bring forth works. The example of Abraham serves as an illuminating and confirming scriptural proof. Abraham was justified on the basis of his works, for he offered his son to God. With the help of Genesis 22, the story of the sacrifice of Isaac, an exposition of the statement in Genesis 15:6 is presented. Abraham "believed the Lord, and the Lord reckoned it to him as righteousness" (2:23). The story of Abraham accordingly shows how works bring faith to completion, so that from faith and works together that perfection is attained which is the goal of God's will and command. Thus "a person is justified by works and not by faith alone" (2:24). "For just as the body without the spirit is dead, so faith without works is also dead" (2:26).

In this line of argument one can recognize clear echoes of Pauline expressions. There are no direct quotations from Pauline letters, but obviously they refer to key words and expressions that had been used in coarse interpretations that appealed to Paul for support, thereby showing that the apostle had been grossly misunderstood. Paul too had never doubted that faith must be active in love (Gal. 5:6). Still, he had emphasized as forcibly as possible that the person who stands before God cannot be saved by doing the works required by the law, but by faith alone (Rom. 3:28; Rom. 4:3 and Gal. 3:6, which likewise use the quote from Gen. 15:6). While Paul deals with works required by the law, James speaks in general of "works," without qualifying them as "works of the law." The law is understood by him exclusively as a collection of ethical instruction. According to James, the moral demand of the law corresponds to deeds that manifest righteous conduct. The apostle Paul understands the content of faith as the confession of the crucified and risen Christ. In James, on the other hand, faith is understood to be acknowledgment of the oneness of God.

Thus the two lines of thought do not really meet; the two authors are fighting on different fronts. For while Paul directs his attack against a self-righteousness that boasts in its own achievement and would like to base the status of justification on it, a generation later James's polemic is directed against the inertia of Christians who think that "faith" is enough and feel no obligation to express this faith in their daily lives. Nevertheless, the line of theological argument developed in the letter of James cannot hold its own in a comparison with Pauline theology. It knows neither the profound lostness of the human condition nor the power of Christ's redemption that alone is able to save. But it does set forth in a few crisp sentences the inadequacy of a faith that is only a matter of words, and shows that true faith must always lead to corresponding deeds.

———

Through the catechetical-like arrangement of admonitions and rules for daily living set forth under the authority of James, the Lord's brother, the Letter of James has the intention of explaining to Christians the law of liberty, according to which their everyday lives should be directed. In this little booklet of Christian ethics, on the one hand arguments taken over from the Stoic tradition are used, so that laws of proper human conduct are derived from careful observation of nature. Just as a tiny spark can set a whole forest in flames, so the small bodily organ, the tongue, can initiate things both great and dangerous

(3:5-6). And just as the small rudder can turn the course of a great ship, so the tongue is a small member that can have big effects (3:4-5). Therefore its potential must be utilized in the right way, in praise of the Lord and Father, but not for the cursing of one's fellow human beings, because they are made in the image of God (3:9).

On the other hand, James takes up Old Testament traditions in which he renders the rules and insights of wisdom, commending patience as the appropriate conduct in life's difficult situations (1:2-8). There is also a renewal of the prophetic preaching of repentance, which warns against losing oneself amid the allurements of the world and the dangers of riches. Whenever one extends a lavish greeting to a rich man who comes to worship, but makes poor people feel unwelcome, there the good name that is pronounced "over" the Christians is blasphemed (2:1-13.) This expression probably alludes inconspicuously to the act of baptism, in which the name of the Lord is invoked over the one being baptized, so that it now belongs to the baptized. For the sake of the Lord invoked in baptism, Christians are obligated to live their lives with grace toward all, the grace that makes no distinctions between people. Those who are rich should boast only about the lowliness of their new estate in the Christian community, for their riches are only temporary. Just as the flower of the field has only a fleeting glory, so the rich will fade away amid their success (1:10-11). Their riches will become rotten, and their fine clothes will become food for moths (5:1-6). All those who presently have earthly possessions over which they have authority should reflect on this, and not casually think they can make plans, carry on business, and rake in profits, instead of carrying out all their planning and doing under the appropriate rubric, "if the Lord wishes we will live and do this or that" (4:15).

Finally, the compelling power of the divine command is sharpened by the inclusion of words of the Lord in the series of directions. For God's word must not only be heard, it must be done; otherwise one has simply deceived oneself (1:22). Wherever this admonition, which calls at once to reflection and repentance, is taken seriously, there it will be understood that it is a matter of having patience until the coming of the Lord

(5:7). The Old Testament example of Job, a man of great patience, can show what a good outcome true tenacity can have, "for the Lord is compassionate and merciful" (5:11). Maintaining persistence and steadfastness of heart—that is the task with which Christians have been charged. God's will is violated not only by the commission of transgressions against God's command, but also by neglecting positive right conduct. "Anyone, then, who knows the right thing to do and fails to do it, commits sin" (4:17). By a godly life and deeds of love, Christians are to fulfill the law of liberty and so strive for the goal of perfection (1:4; 3:2).

With this as the rule for Christian ethics, James wants to guide Christians to the right kind of Christian life. His explanations proceed from the naive perspective that the combination of faith and works produces righteousness (2:22; see above, pp. 173–74). Luther's analytical criticism based on the subject matter itself, especially as expressed in the Preface to James in the September Bible of 1522, is directed precisely to this point: directly against Paul and the rest of Scripture, the Letter of James attributes justification to human achievement; it lacks any essential evangelical character and advocates works. The authentic touchstone for the evaluation of all books must be whether or not they proclaim Christ. Thus no apostolic character can be attributed to the Letter of James.

Luther's criticism notwithstanding, James cannot be evaluated as a real antithesis to Paul. Still, it is true that it contains no elaboration of the Christian kerygma, but a bundle of ethical admonitions. Despite his negative theological judgment, Luther conceded that James contains many good sayings. As a little handbook for the issues of everyday Christian living, it is not without reason that James was included in the canon—albeit on the edge. Its goal is restricted and modest: to offer direction for a life well-pleasing to God.

Suggestions for Further Reading

Adamson, J. B. *The Epistle of James*. Grand Rapids: Wm. B. Eerdmans, 1976.

Davids, P. H. *The Epistle of James.* Grand Rapids: Wm. B. Eerdmans, 1982.

Dibelius, M. *James: A Commentary on the Epistle of James.* Hermeneia. Philadelphia: Fortress Press, 1982.

Johnson, L. T. "The Use of Leviticus 19 in the Letter of James." *Journal of Biblical Literature* 101 (1982): 391–401.

Laws, S. *A Commentary on the Epistle of James.* San Francisco: Harper & Row, 1980.

Lorenzen, T. "Faith without Works Does Not Count before God! James 2:14–16." *Expository Times* 89 (1978): 231–35.

Martin, R. P. *James.* Waco: Word, 1988.

Nicol, W. "Faith and Works in the Letter of James." *Neotestamentica* 9 (1975): 7–24.

Perdue, L. G. "Paraenesis and the Epistle of James." *Zeitschrift für die Neutestamentliche Wissenschaft* 72 (1975): 241–56.

Via, D. O. "The Right Strawy Epistle Reconsidered: A Study in Biblical Ethics and Hermeneutics." *Journal of Religion* 49 (1969): 253–67.

Chapter Nine

ENDURANCE
IN SUFFERING

The Ground of Hope

The everyday lives of Christians were burdened
with many difficulties, which they experienced as
imposed upon them by the surrounding world. The First Letter
of Peter, directed to Christian congregations in Asia Minor
toward the end of the first century, does not have a major
persecution in view, in which matters of life and death are at
stake, but deals with those difficulties that constantly emerged.
These arose from widespread lack of understanding of the
Christians' faith and manner of life, on the one hand, and inten-
tional acts of discrimination and injustice, on the other. The
churches were called to endure amid these experiences of
suffering by holding fast to their confidence in Christian hope,
thereby giving outsiders powerful testimony to the reality of its
substance.

The Christian faith is repeatedly characterized by 1 Peter
as "hope." Thus in the doxology that prefaces the letter, God is
praised because of having "given us a new birth into a living
hope through the resurrection of Jesus Christ from the dead"
(1:3). Hope is not only directed to the future, but in baptism
grounds the new life, a life that stands under the sign of hope

by virtue of the resurrection of Christ from the dead. What the prophets announced, but did not experience themselves, has now been revealed (1:10–12). Therefore Christians should set their hope entirely on the grace that is offered in Jesus Christ (1:13). The present power of hope is shown in the temperate life-style of Christians, in that as obedient children they no longer give themselves over to the passions they formerly served during their ignorance. Just as the one who called them is holy, so they too are to be holy in all their conduct (1:14–15). The example of holy women such as Sarah, who live by their hope in God, is followed by Christian women when they do right and let nothing discourage them (3:5). She is held up as an example so Christians could be encouraged to follow. The Christian life is accordingly borne along by the hope that will not allow itself to be disconcerted either by suffering that must be endured or the allurements of the surrounding world, but which places its trust in God.

Since in this manner hope as the content of faith and the ethical assignment of living a holy life are firmly bound to one another, word and deed must also agree with each other. If Christians have to put up with all sorts of evil slander from outsiders, along with accusations falsely lodged against them, they must nonetheless be always ready to give a response to everyone who asks them concerning the hope that is in them (3:15) — and that with gentleness, good conscience, and the fear of God, so that those who revile them will be put to shame when they speak disparagingly about their good life in Christ (3:16). The Christian hope is the enabling power for both the sanctification of the Christian's own lives, and for testimony to those who demand an accounting for the ground of their faith and the reason for their way of life. The persecution and suffering that burden the Christian life again and again will not fail to appear in the future as well. But if they are zealous for doing good, then finally no one will be able to do them harm (3:13). They must only be careful that they do not receive deserved punishment for false or substandard conduct, but that whatever suffering comes their way is because they have done what is right (3:16–17).

The ethical materials contained in 1 Peter are composed of different elements. Quotations from the Old Testament, particularly from Proverbs and the wisdom Psalms, both Palestinian and Hellenistic traditions, along with materials from early Christianity, stand alongside each other and are called up in turn as they are needed to respond to particular issues. The different catechetical items have been formed in the oral tradition that preceded their written fixation and their being inserted into the framework of the present writing directed to Christians in Asia Minor. The author knows that he and his readers are united in the conviction that they live in this world as aliens and exiles, who need not settle down here permanently (1:1; 2:11). They find themselves on the way that leads to fulfillment in heaven, and need not be held up by enticements or hardships en route. In the awareness that their whole life is a pilgrimage, they must live a righteous life among the "gentiles," so that their ill will or slanderous judgments will be proven false, and they will see the good works of Christians and glorify God on the great day of visitation (2:12).

Even though the individual items of the exhortations were to a considerable extent already given in the tradition taken over by 1 Peter, they still receive a specifically Christian grounding that communicates the perspective from which the traditional materials are to be appropriated and how they can be understood as directions for living a Christian life. Differently than in the Pauline theology, where the moral claim is derived from the proclamation of salvation already announced, in 1 Peter the imperative is not based on the previous declaration of the indicative, but in the reverse order: ethical exhortation stands first, and is then provided with a more specific grounding. Thus the charge directed to the elders to "tend the flock of God" (5:2) is followed by a saying about the "chief shepherd," Jesus Christ (5:4), who as the true shepherd represents the model of all true pastoral ministry. In 1:15–16 the charge to lead a holy life is followed by the rationale from Leviticus 19:2: "You shall be holy, for I am holy." Again in 5:5 there appears first the saying directed to all, to conduct themselves in humility toward each other, to which is then added the quotation from Proverbs 3:34, "God opposes the proud, but gives grace to the humble." In other places the exhortation is supported by a short statement such as "since love covers a multitude of sins" (4:8) or a reference to the will of God (2:15; 3:9). For the manner in which 1 Peter makes use of Old Testament quotations, it is typical that the verses from Psalms 34:13-17 are introduced with a "for" [γάρ] in 3:10-12 and then quoted with minor alterations from the LXX, with an additional grounding "for" [ὅτι] added in v. 12. This places an emphasis on the theological basis for the exhortation, which in the Psalm follows the preceding imperative without any connective: "For the eyes of the Lord are on the righteous, and his ears are open to their prayer. But the face of the Lord is against those who do evil."

The ultimate motivation offered by 1 Peter for ethical conduct, however, is of a christological nature. As in the Pauline Letters the traditional parenetic material is incidentally christianized by the addition of "in Christ" or "in the Lord," thereby giving a new way of appropriating traditional content (see above, pp. 33-34). So also 1 Peter inserts a small theological comment such as "for the Lord's sake" [διὰ τὸν κύριον, 2:13] or "for conscience' sake" [διὰ τὴν συνείδεσιν (θεοῦ); (NRSV "aware of God," 2:19)], and characterizes the Christian course of life as "good conduct in Christ" (3:16). Several times, however, an extensive grounding of the parenesis is given by joining creedal and hymnic material to parenetic elements. Thus it is explained in 1:17-21 that Christians should live their lives in the fear of God, since they know that they have not been redeemed with corruptible things such as silver and gold, "but with the precious blood of Christ, like that of a lamb without defect or blemish." The whole community is challenged to suffer on account of doing right, if God so wills, rather than to receive deserved punishment for doing wrong. "For Christ also suffered for sins once for all, the righteous for the unrighteous, in order to bring you to God" (3:17-18). To this saying, which echoes Isaiah 53, a hymn to Christ is added that portrays the saving work of Christ from his death through the journey to Hades, the resurrection, ascension, and enthronement at the right hand of God to his universal rule. This is the way 1 Peter sets forth the compelling necessity of living in accord with the letter's parenetic instruction.

Slaves who must suffer hardship under their earthly masters are pointed to the suffering of Christ, who bore it obediently and with patience (2:21–25). Here too, the point is not supported by excerpting stories from the narrative of Jesus' passion, but with traditional parenetic material that pictures Jesus' suffering and death in dependence on Isaiah 53. Since the traditional hymn to Christ was not originally directed to the distress of slaves, but was sung by the whole community, 2:24 speaks of "our sins." We may also suppose that in 2:21 the hymn originally spoke of Christ suffering "for us" [ὑπὲρ ὑμῶν]. But by the fact that the author of 1 Peter now applies the hymn to the situation of his readers, the confessional statement in the address has been altered to read "Christ also suffered for you."

"Christ also suffered for you" (or "for us")—the hymn opens with this affirmation. In this brief declaration the theme of the song is given, which however in v. 21b is modified by the author of the letter in that he holds up Christ as an example for the slaves. It is to them that the charge to follow in the footsteps of Christ is directed. Thus the substitutionary death of Christ is no longer the subject, but Christ's suffering is understood as an example. The kerygmatic accent of the hymn is set aside in favor of parenesis, so that v. 21b will not have originally been a part of the traditional early Christian hymn.

The following verses, 2:22–23, portray the patient endurance of Jesus in four statements. The first alludes to Isaiah 53:9. The central ones show in two antithetical statements that Jesus suffered in silence: "When he was abused, he did not return abuse; when he suffered, he did not threaten." The fourth is a counterstatement showing the effective meaning of Jesus' silence, that he rested his case with the one who judges fairly. Verse 24 returns to the allusion to Isaiah 53 and concludes the portrayal of Christ's suffering with a reference to the reconciliation he accomplished. This brief section formed on the basis of Isaiah 53 is thus framed with two statements about Jesus' atoning death and thus emphasizes for whose sake all this was done. In 2:25 too, no notice is taken of the context in which the previous ethical exhortation stands. Rather, the hymn comes to an end with the reminder that it is on the basis of the forgiveness accomplished by the suffering and death of Jesus that they who were once straying sheep have now been gathered into a community under the shepherd and guardian of their souls. So these words too seem to be an adaptation of previous tradition, and not sayings composed for this particular occasion.

In their suffering the Christians are pointed to their Lord for consolation and encouragement. The eschatological event that has broken into history in his death and resurrection also includes the suffering of Christians. Christ has suffered; and those who belong to Christ are called to follow him on his path of suffering. As strangers and resident aliens in this world they travel toward their heavenly homeland in joyful hope.

———

The concrete ethical directions are held together throughout by the motif of showing one's true character by enduring the test of suffering, which permeates the whole letter. Because Christians have no permanent homeland in this world, but are on a pilgrimage toward heavenly fulfillment, they must remain aware that by baptism they have been called out of darkness into his marvelous light (2:9). Belonging to the Christian community means above all renunciation and rejection of the old life (1:14; 2:1) and a new beginning "like obedient children" (1:14). The joy that fills them gives them the power to deal with the trials and tribulations with which they must deal as members of the community (1:6). Malice, guile, insincerity, envy, and slander must no longer find any place in their lives (2:1). Instead, they are to allow themselves to be built as living stones into a spiritual house and holy priesthood (2:5).

The admonition is directed to the whole community to abstain from fleshly passions and to live a life oriented to doing what is right (2:11-12). This challenge stands like a title over the household code (*Haustafel*) that follows. The first item on this code calls to obedience to governmental authorities, after which the mutual duties of men and women and slaves and masters is addressed (2:13-3:7). As in the other household codes in the New Testament (see above, pp. 138-45), the admonition to "be subject" is based on the order established by God's creation. On the other hand, from the perspective of the Christian confession the idea of partnership is developed, which calls men and women, slaves and masters to be responsible for each other for the sake of Christian love. By their good deeds suffering Christians should put to silence the comments of foolish outsiders made in ignorance (2:15). By thus offering testimony for the truth of their faith (2:12), they make the proper response to criticisms of their way of life and acts of malicious mistreatment. Just as individual Christians are reminded to fulfill God's will in their particular station in life, so the exhortation applies to the community as a whole: "have unity of spirit, sympathy, love for one another, a tender heart, and a humble mind. Do not repay evil for evil or abuse for abuse; but on the contrary repay with a blessing. It is for this that you were called, that you might inherit a blessing" (3:8–9).

"For Christ also suffered"—this basis for ethical instruction derived from the kerygma is held fast throughout the letter to the very end (3:18–22; 4:1). As sin was overcome through the suffering of Christ, so the break with sin has occurred for all who belong to this Lord (4:1–2). To be sure, Christians too, like "the gentiles," once lived their lives in "licentiousness, passions, drunkenness, revels, carousing, and lawless idolatry" (4:3). But what once was the rule no longer applies. The past has been abolished, so that Christians need not fall back into the old pagan way of life. Unbelievers, who stand outside the community and consider the way it lives its life, are surprised that Christians no longer participate in the same wild life-style as before (4:4). Misunderstanding and suspicious ill-humor influences the way people perceive Christians and leads to their creating difficulties for them in matters of everyday life. But believers should not allow themselves to be surprised at this. Whoever among them does not suffer as a murderer, thief, or evil-doer, but as a Christian, must not be ashamed, "but glorify God because you bear this name" (4:16)—that is, with the name "Christian," named after their suffering Lord.

The ground of their hope, for which they are called to give account even when they are suffering (3:15), binds all members of the community together. Several times 1 Peter calls for maintaining "brotherly love" (φιλαδελφία). By being responsible for each other, Christians realize that they are strengthened by being bound together in the solidarity of faith, and that they are united with all their brothers and sisters in this world who bear the same sufferings as do they (5:9).

Suggestions for Further Reading

Balch, D. *Let Wives Be Submissive: The Domestic Code in 1 Peter.* Chico: Scholars Press, 1981.

Beare, F. W. *The First Epistle of Peter,* 3rd ed. Oxford: Basil Blackwell, 1970.

Best, E. *1 Peter.* New Century Bible. Grand Rapids: Wm. B. Eerdmans, 1971.

Elliott, J. H. "Backward and Forward in His Steps." In *Discipleship in the New Testament,* pp. 184–209. F. Segovia, ed. Philadelphia: Fortress Press, 1985.

———. *A Home for the Homeless.* Philadelphia: Fortress Press, 1981.

Hill, D. "'To Offer Spiritual Sacrifices . . .' (1 Peter 2:5); Liturgical Formulations and Christian Paraenesis in 1 Peter 4." *Journal for the Study of the New Testament* 16 (1982): 212–31.

Michaels, J. R. *1 Peter.* Waco: Word, 1989.

Piper, J. "Hope as the Motivation of Love: 1 Peter 3:9–12." *New Testament Studies* 26 (1979–80): 212–31.

Talbert, C. H., ed. *Perspectives on First Peter.* Macon, Ga.: Mercer University Press, 1986.

van Unnik, W. C. "The Teaching of Good Works in 1 Peter." *New Testament Studies* 1 (1954–55): 92–110.

Holding Fast to the Confession

During periods of pressure from outside the community and temptations from within it, Christians were called to hold fast to the confession of faith, even if it resulted in their enduring severe sufferings or possibly even death. This responsibility is explicitly urged on its readers by the Letter to the Hebrews. Its discussions revolve around selected Old Testament texts from the Psalms and the Prophets, which are interpreted in lengthy homiletical expositions. This sermonic tone of address peaks in concrete parenetical applications

(2:1–4; 3:7–4, 13; 5:11–6:20; 10:19–39; 12:1–13:17). The "word of exhortation" (λόγος τῆς παρακλήσεως, 13:22) launched into the community includes both encouraging words of comfort and challenging calls to action. For in view of threats already experienced and persecution anticipated in the future, faith can be endangered and the temptation to fall away and withdraw from the Christian community become real. But where the resolve to hold fast to the Christian confession is present (4:14; 10:23), there the Christian life is on the right path.

The confession, the binding nature of which the readers are reminded, is determined by its christological content. What it means to confess Jesus Christ as son of God and as high priest is set forth in Hebrews in full detail. The author thus seeks to show to those beset with doubts and temptations that eternal salvation has been obtained and absolutely guaranteed through Christ. By pointing the community to the surpassing greatness of the salvation attained for his own by Christ, they are to be filled with confidence and given the courage to hold out in times of distress. The uniqueness of the gifts granted by Christ to his own is emphasized by contrasting them with the salvation achieved by the old covenant and its sacrificial cult. Just as Christ has attained a much higher status than the angels, so too he is incomparably superior to Moses and Aaron. Beside his death and resurrection, the temple cultus of the old covenant, the sacrifices made by earthly priests, and the acts that mediate forgiveness on the great day of atonement fade away into mere shadows that must pass away, once the priest after the order of Melchizedek has been installed. Against the background of what once was done by priests in order to effect reconciliation between humanity and God, the work of Christ stands out in its absolute superiority. In terms of its power to give hope, there is simply nothing that can be compared with the atonement and the salvation accomplished by Christ. The Letter to the Hebrews thus wants to set forth that the matter of being a Christian, steadfastly remaining a member of the Christian community, living in hope of the future fulfillment, really is not an empty hope.

Holding fast to the confession shows its true colors in discipleship to Christ. His is held up as an example to the community as the "pioneer of our salvation" (ἀρχηγὸς τῆς σωτηρίας, 2:10). This phrase expresses the twin conviction that he is both the deliverer who instituted salvation and the leader who guides us in the right path. On the one hand Christ is named the "source of eternal salvation" (5:9); on the other hand he is described as the pathfinder and scout who goes on ahead of believers. He is both the community's redeemer and its forerunner to prepare its way. God has made him perfect through suffering, so that his intention of bringing many sons and daughters to glory would be realized (2:10). Because Christ has already attained the goal, he now draws his own after him as the "pioneer and perfecter" of their faith (12:2), so that as the wandering people of God they might proceed toward the heavenly goal and attain the rest promised by God.

The development of the christological confession is bound most closely to the corresponding hortatory section. For as Christ learned obedience and was exalted by God, so he has become the source of eternal salvation for all who obey him (5:9). Therefore Christians must attend to his word and follow it, in order not to miss the salvation Christ has won for them. The heavenly inheritance is already prepared, but is still hidden until the day of redemption (9:15). Christ is already exalted, but the time when everything is to be subject to him has not yet come (2:8). He is seated at the right hand of God and awaits the time when his enemies will become the footstool under his feet (10:13). But the subjection of the enemy is—as is explained in view of the threatened situation of the community—already underway. It can not be much longer (10:37) and then the victory of Christ will be manifest. Thus the urgency of not falling away, so that the coming salvation will not be forfeited.

The admonition repeatedly emphasized in the parenetical sections of Hebrews is attuned to this one keynote: hold fast to the confession, stick by the church, do not allow yourself to be misled under the pressure of various threats and distress. For the goal toward which the people of God makes its pilgrimage through time stands unshakably secure. Thus when those who belong to Christ look to the one who has already gone on ahead of them, a clear direction for their lives is given. All the individual elements of ethical instruction are subordinated to or recede behind this one guideline that serves as the point of orientation for everything else. At the same time, reminders are given of how the life of Christians should look in concrete instances. For to make the confession of faith in Christ as the son of God and high priest includes the commitment to doing what his will commands.

Traditional words of instruction are found particularly in the concluding parenesis (chap. 13). First appears the reminder of familial love (13:1). Then follows the command to show hospitality, since in doing so some have entertained angels without being aware of it (13:2). Those in prison should be remembered, and marriage is to be held in respect, for God will judge the immoral and adulterous (13:3–4). The love of money is rejected (13:5). Strange doctrines are to be avoided (13:9). They should not neglect to do good and to share what they have, for such sacrifices are pleasing to God (13:16). These and other statements introduced in this context represent traditional catechetical material that is to be called back to mind. The current relevance of these admonitions is brought home when it is pointed out that it is precisely in the time of suffering that following them means the most. In the struggle against sin they have not yet offered the ultimate resistance—shedding their blood (12:4). And the Scripture teaches that whom the Lord loves, he disciplines (12:6). God's "educational policy" is experienced precisely in the reality that God deals strictly with his children in order to keep them on the right way. If such discipline is hardly a happy occasion in the moment it is being experienced, but rather a painful one, still God's guiding hand cannot be experienced apart from it. That is why it must not be rejected, but find a place in their lives. Drooping hands and weak knees are to be strengthened (12:12), firm steps are to be taken, peace is to be pursued, and they are to see to it that no one lets the grace of God slip by unappropriated (12:14–15).

———

The repeated admonition to remain faithful in times of distress is given special emphasis in Hebrews by developing one idea not found elsewhere in the New Testament documents: the impossibility of a second repentance. No one should be deceived

by the notion that for those who fall away from Christ, withdraw from the community, and surrender their faith in the
Christian confession, will have another chance. This is not the
case; it is an illusion. This warning is expressed several times,
so that there is no way it can be missed. It must in fact, be considered impossible that those who were once enlightened, who
have tasted the heavenly gift and have become participants in
the Holy Spirit, and have tasted the good word of God and the
power of the future world and have committed apostasy anyway,
can be brought to repentance again. On their own account they
have crucified the son of God afresh and hold him up to public
contempt (6:4–6). Whoever maliciously and with full awareness
of the fact goes ahead and sins, after having received the
knowledge of the truth, has despised Christ's atoning death,
and can therefore henceforth have no other sacrifice for sins. For
this person there remains nothing but a fearful expectation of
judgment (10:26–27). The warning example narrated by the
Scripture tells of Esau, who sold his birthright as firstborn for
a single meal, and later found no room for repentance, although
he sought it with tears (12:17).

The seriousness of these repeated warnings is christologically grounded. Purification from sins is accomplished through
Christ's high-priestly sacrifice. After the death of Christ, no
other atonement for sins will be given. For Christ died once for
all on the cross – and this event will not be repeated. What that
means is shown by a comparison (9:27–28). Just as people die
once and after that comes the judgment, so Christ was offered
once as a sacrifice to take away sins. But when he is revealed the
second time, it will not be to deal with sins, but he will appear
for the salvation of those who await him as their savior. Again,
behind this christological discussion the parenetic application is
visible. Christ has already made the final and all-sufficient
atoning sacrifice, the saving effect of which has been conferred
on Christians by baptism. Thereby the old guilt is wiped out
and the way to God is opened up. That is why one must hold
fast to the confession and remain faithful until the dawn of the
day of salvation.

For Hebrews, apostasy is simply identified with sin as
such (3:12–13). Whoever commits apostasy has simply undone

what Christ accomplished by his death: the putting away of sin. Such persons restore to power the sin that had already been demolished. For them there can no longer be an atoning sacrifice (10:26). Gaining or losing eternal salvation is therefore a matter of present decision. One must therefore take advantage of the salvation accomplished in Christ's death and appropriated in baptism, and in faithful obedience enter into the sanctuary opened by Christ, in order to receive mercy and grace (4:16; 10:19). But for the one who has no trust in the forgiveness effected by Christ's death, there is no possibility of some new and different act of reconciliation.

The denial of a second repentance, as expressed in Hebrews in view of the impending persecution facing the community, was not affirmed by later church doctrine. Luther already rejects this denial in the "Preface to Hebrews" in his September Bible of 1522, and reprimands this New Testament document because it offers no repentance for the Christian who sins after baptism. That would be against all the Gospels and all the Letters of Paul. Nor can its clear statements be explained away by any interpretation. Luther's critique based on the essence of the gospel itself is rightly directed against every attempt to claim Hebrews in support of a legalistic doctrine of repentance and penance. But it must be noticed that Hebrews' statements are conditioned by the special situation addressed by the letter. By urgently warning the community against apostasy from the living God as the most dangerous form of sin (3:12), Hebrews wants at the same time to strengthen faith by pointing out that through Christ's death sin has become ineffective in God's sight and its power has been broken. Thus there is no excuse for those who surrender their confession of faith and withdraw from the community.

Suggestions for Further Reading

Attridge, H. W. *Hebrews*. Hermeneia. Philadelphia: Fortress Press, 1989.

Brown, R. E. "The Epistle to the Hebrews." In *Antioch and Rome: New Testament Cradles of Catholic Christianity*, pp. 139–58. New York: Paulist Press, 1983.

Childs, B. "Hebrews." In *The New Testament as Canon*, pp. 400–418. Philadelphia: Fortress Press, 1984.

Hagner, D. A. *Hebrews.* San Francisco: Harper & Row, 1983.

Fuller, R. H. "The Letter to the Hebrews." In *Hebrews-James-1 and 2 Peter-Jude-Revelation,* pp. 1–27. G. Krodel, ed. Proclamation Commentaries. Philadelphia: Fortress Press, 1977.

Jewett, R. *Letter to Pilgrims: A Commentary on the Epistle to the Hebrews.* New York: Pilgrim Press, 1981.

Johnson, W. "The Pilgrimage Motif in the Book of Hebrews." *Journal of Biblical Literature* 97 (1978): 239–51.

Käsemann, E. *The Wandering People of God.* Minneapolis: Augsburg, 1984.

Peterson, D. *Hebrews and Perfection.* Cambridge: Cambridge University Press, 1982.

Thompson, J. *The Beginnings of Christian Philosophy.* Washington, D.C.: Catholic Biblical Association, 1982.

Steadfastness and Loyalty

In view of a severe persecution of which early Christianity was in dread, the Revelation to John wants to strengthen the confidence of the churches and to encourage them to faithfulness. The book is composed as the message of the exalted Christ, which he has charged his servant John to deliver. As the King of kings and Lord of lords (17:14; 19:16) he holds all authority in his hands, and has by the forgiveness of sins called his own to participation in his own royal and priestly office (1:5–6). They can therefore be certain that the powers of this world do not have the last word, but the triumph of their Lord already stands secure. In the hymns of praise, which again and again sound through the pictures of the terrors of the last times (4:8, 11; 5:9–13; 7:10–12; 11:15–18; 12:10–12; 15:3–4; 19:1–10), this conviction comes to expression: "The kingdom of the world has become the kingdom of our Lord and of his Messiah, and he will reign forever and ever" (11:15). The members of his people have been sealed with his seal, and belong to him as his own (7:1–8). They are therefore secure in his custody during the hour of greatest danger.

The churches of Asia Minor are named as the book's recipients and directly addressed in the seven messages (chap. 2–3). Each of these letters is formulated as both call to repentance and encouragement from the exalted Lord, to whom nothing remains hidden, but who sees both their faithfulness and their lack of it. The situation of each church is seen without any sentimentality. Each is matter-of-factly praised when there is faithful endurance, love, and loyalty, and blamed and warned wherever the Christian life has become lukewarm and sluggish. No ideal picture of early Christian churches is painted, but denial, lovelessness, and failure to stand their ground against heretical teachers are openly exposed.

The most dangerous internal temptation comes from those groups who advocate the view that Christians could without reflection go ahead and accommodate themselves to the syncretistic environment, eat meat sacrificed to idols, follow a libertinistic ethic, and participate in sexual immorality (2:6, 14–16, 20). The community should resolutely turn away from such conduct and follow the command of their Lord (2:5, 16, 21–22; 3:3, 19, and often). When the command to repent is not obeyed, the coming judgment is the inevitable consequence. For how can disobedient, lukewarm, or sleeping churches be in shape to endure the coming trials, if they do not abandon their deplorable conduct, return to practicing the love they had at first, and prepare themselves for the coming day of the Lord? (2:4–5; 3:3, 20, and often). Just as all members of the community who dawdle, neglect, or are unaware of their situation, are urgently warned, so those who remain faithful are promised as "those who conqueror" that they will participate in the future glory. Each of the seven messages contains as its conclusion a specific encouraging promise that "conquerors" will find their place at the side of the exalted Lord (2:7, 11, 17, 26–28; 3:5, 12, 21). A variety of apocalyptic pictures describe the blessedness into which they shall enter. These promises are intended to offer encouragement to hold out faithfully even to the point of death, in order at the end to receive the crown of life (2:10; cf. also 3:11).

The urgent admonitions to faithfulness found in the messages to the seven churches also permeate the portrayal of the eschatological events given in a dramatically colorful series of alternating pictures. The external ordeals of famine, plague, and cosmic catastrophes, the terror of which becomes increasingly intense, raise the anxious question of who, then, can endure through these last times? The harassed and distressed churches are to be strengthened by the message that the eschatological plan of God for history is held in the hand of the slaughtered lamb who has become Lord of the world. He is the one who breaks its seals and determines its events. Nothing can happen without his will. Even if it appears that the powers of this world have become almighty, they can after all exercise their destructive powers for a limited interval. Then the day will come when their nothingness will be revealed.

In the distress and persecution of the last time, many will waver and fall away from the faith. In the last judgment it will be exposed that the moral decline that pervades all realms of life has brought to ruin the great city of Babylon (17:4–5; 18:5–8, and often). Before the judgment throne, people will be asked about their works (20:12). Judgment will be pronounced on all according to their deeds (20:13). Only those whose names are in the book of life will be saved (3:5; 13:8; 17:8; 20:12, 15; 21:27). But all those not found written there will be cast into the lake of fire (20:14). Those who have remained faithful will enter into salvation (21:7). "But as for the cowardly, the faithless, the polluted, the murderers, the fornicators, the sorcerers, the idolaters, and all liars," they will be excluded from the New Jerusalem (21:8). In this catalogue, which lists a number of vices taken over as a traditional list (see above, pp. 83–84), "cowards" and "faithless" are placed emphatically at the beginning of the list. The list represents those who will be condemned to the second—eternal—death. This urgent warning is to be understood by the community as a call to that endurance by which they can hold fast to the commandments of God and the faith of Jesus (14:12), until the near day of redemption arrives and God makes everything new (21:5).

The call to patient endurance is directed to Christians during a time of particular danger, which threatened them near the end of the rule of the emperor Domitian (81–96 C.E.). He required all the subjects of his empire to honor him as "Lord and God." The eschatological oppressing power had received its power from the antigod dragon, whose wrath was directed against all "who keep the commandments of God and hold the testimony to Jesus" (12:17). They are now to be exposed to a storm of incomparable fury. But they should know that Satan has already been defeated and that the wrath of the dragon is only a sign of his impotence. The beast who enters the scene as a tool of the dragon represents the feared appearance of the antigod ruler, who emerges in the end times as the counterpart and parody to Christ, the true King of kings. One of its seven heads had received a mortal wound, but its wound had been healed, so that all the world was astonished with awe (13:3–4). This was a mimicking of the death and resurrection of Christ. It appeared that no one would be able to resist the beast. Its true character as adversary to Christ is revealed by the fact that it utters terrible blasphemies against God—but for only 42 months (=the 3½ years of Daniel 7:25; 12:7); then its time will expire. For what the beast does is "given" it to do. That means that God permits—but does not cause—what happens. God's rule, even when it does not appear so at the time, is incomparably superior to the fury of the dragon and the beast, for God has set limits to their power. But within these limits, they take advantage of their opportunity not only to speak blasphemous words but also to take actions against the saints, beginning a war with them and "conquering" them (13:6–7). The success attained by the beast impresses all the inhabitants of the earth, so that all those whose names do not stand in the book of life kneel in submissive worship to the beast (13:8). Only those listed in the Lamb's book of life see through the charade, recognize what is really happening, and refuse to join in the general wonder and praise of the beast.

The great deeds achieved by the adversary appear to make any resistance foolish. Thus the portrayal of the events that produce such anxiety is interrupted by the cry, "Here is a call for the endurance and faith of the saints" (13:10). In the difficult test that comes upon the people of God, steadfastness that keeps true to the faith is required. For it is only by obedience to the will of God that the community can hold out to the end, so that they can finally behold the victory and triumph of the Lamb.

The pressure is increased by additional measures directed against the holy community of God. All who refuse to worship the image of the beast—and thereby refuse to participate in acknowledging the divinity of the emperor—are to be killed (13:15). A law is put into effect that everyone must bear a sign on the right hand and forehead, "so that no one can buy or sell who does not have the mark, that is, the name of the beast or the number of its name" (13:17). The mysterious number 666, which is specified as the number of a name, is apparently to be resolved as "Nero Caesar," and refers to the violent ruler expected to appear in the near future who would bear the traits of Nero returned from the grave.

By the marks on their hands and foreheads people are designated as belonging to the beast, who represents the oppressive emperor of the last days, and are obligated to obey him unconditionally. The Greek word used for "mark" (χάραγμα) was the official expression for the seal and stamp of the emperor. This clearly indicates that the mark of the beast had to do with the worship of the emperor in the Caesar cult in which everyone was expected to participate. Those who would dare to withdraw from participation in the cult and not bear the mark of the beast would bring economic ruin upon themselves. No one would be permitted to conduct business with anyone who had refused to be subject to the state's demand that its imperial power be worshiped as divine.

The picture sketched in Revelation 13 reflects the situation in which the Christians of Asia Minor found themselves at the end of the first century C.E. But even there, the ordering of society that is the responsibility of the state is not simply rejected as satanic. What is resisted here is the state that not only requires obedience from its citizens to the valid laws established by its authorities (Rom. 13:1–7, see above, pp. 133–35), but beyond that requires worship of its leadership as divine. By making this kind of religious claim that Christians along with everyone else must pay this kind of respect to the government, the state has become a rival church, has shattered the order it is charged to establish, and has been perverted into a demonic menace. In this situation there can be only one binding obligation—namely, to remain true to its Lord and not be shaken from its steadfast commitment to him.

Suggestions for Further Reading

Boring, M. E. *Revelation. Interpretation: A Commentary for Preaching and Teaching.* Louisville: Westminster/John Knox Press, 1989.

——. "The Theology of Revelation." *Interpretation* 40 (1986): 257–69.

Collins, A. Y. *Crisis & Catharsis: The Power of the Apocalypse.* Philadelphia: Westminster Press, 1984.

——. "The Political Perspective of the Revelation to John." *Journal of Biblical Literature* 96 (1977): 241–56.

Fiorenza, E. S. *The Book of Revelation: Justice and Judgment.* Philadelphia: Fortress Press, 1985.

——. *Revelation: Vision of a Just World.* Proclamation Commentaries. Minneapolis: Fortress, 1991.

Krodel, G. *Revelation.* Minneapolis: Augsburg, 1989.

Minear, P. S. *I Saw a New Earth: An Introduction to the Vision of the Apocalypse.* Washington/Cleveland: Corpus Books, 1968.

Rissi, M. "The Kerygma of Revelation." *Interpretation* 22 (1968): 3–17.

Chapter Ten

EARLY CHRISTIAN
ETHICS IN
LATE ANTIQUITY

Ethical Conflicts and
Their Resolution

Early Christianity included within itself different groups, with different opinions and schools of thought. In many places contrasting understandings of the Christian life emerged, which gave disparate answers to the problems of Christian ethics, and consequently resulted in varying patterns of conduct. How should Christians shape their lives in order to live in accordance with the gospel and so as not to hinder people's coming to accept it in faith? This question was raised again and again, and had to be resolved over and over in view of the conflicts it evoked.

The influence of libertine conduct, widely regarded as acceptable in the Hellenistic world, precipitated debates in the gentile Christian churches as to what was permitted and what would not be condoned. Paul's correspondence with the Corinthian church presents an especially clear picture of such differences of opinion that could result in severe conflicts. Obviously in Corinth the view was widely advocated, both outside the church and within it, that Christians were free from constraints to do as they pleased. Thus some members of the congregation continued their relations with prostitutes without giving it a thought. Indulging the body's sexual appetites could—so the argument ran—affect only the body, not the spirit, so that in any case the real "I" of the Christian remained untouched (see above, pp. 116–17). Everything that is transitory will pass away; so one need not deny the body what it desires (1 Cor. 6:12–20). Even when a particularly scandalous incident of sexual mis-behavior occurred in the Corinthian congregation, no one seemed to notice. A member of the congregation had been "living with his father's wife" for some time, without being called to account by the others (1 Cor. 5:1–5). To marry one's stepmother was prohibited by both Jewish and Roman law, but presented no problems for the Greek-Hellenistic perspective that prevailed in Corinth. But in the case addressed by the apostle Paul, it was hardly a matter of marriage. Rather, a member of the church was living with his stepmother, and without raising an eyebrow in the congregation. Paul reacts to this incident with sharp criticism, directed primarily not against the offending individual but against the church as a whole. They were so puffed up with their own sense of superiority that they could overlook such conduct. Caught up in the exalted feel-ing of having experienced redemption by receiving the gifts of the Spirit and its limitless freedom, they imagined themselves to be already transported into the realm of blessedness (1 Cor. 4:8). So how could one be bothered with the troublesome matter of thinking through the heavy issues of commitment to the binding obligations of a Christian life?

In Paul's judgment, anyone who behaves like this irre-sponsible member of the congregation can no longer belong to the community but must be excluded. The apostle chooses a harsh way of expressing this: the man is to be delivered to Satan for the destruction of the flesh, so that his spirit can be saved in the day of the Lord Jesus (1 Cor. 5:5). Exclusion from the com-munity pushes the guilty party back into the world of Satan's power, so that he lapses back into the state of judgment. But these severe measures of church discipline finally serve not to deliver the sinners to eternal damnation, but to lead to their salvation on the day of the Lord.

The Corinthians responded to the apostolic admonition not to associate with immoral people by asking how it could be possible to live one's life in a cosmopolitan harbor city where at every turn one met people who assumed a permissive attitude toward sexual activities without giving it a second thought. The apostle acknowledges the validity in their objection, while conceding that he was not proposing that Christians completely withdraw from the world in which permissive attitudes and corresponding conduct are widely considered to be the usual thing. But Christians must think about what it means to live in such a world as members of a community that lives out its authentic existence in tension with the surrounding culture. God will pronounce judgment on the conduct of the outside world—it is not the Christians' business to do that. But they must be clear that there is no place in the community for sexual immorality and indulgence in vice (1 Cor. 5:9–13). This means that the community should not have anything to do with members of the congregation, so-called brothers and sisters, who practice immorality or who are greedy, idolators, revilers, drunkards, or robbers (5:11). And even though the congregation has members who once engaged in such practices, the past has been washed away in baptism. The only thing that counts now is the reality of the new life in Christ, and one's present conduct must correspond to this new reality (1 Cor. 6:9–11).

Where there is doubt about how Christians should shape their lives, an answer is sought from the message of the gospel itself, the gospel that calls for a corresponding life, a gospel that sets boundaries to guard against the misuse of Christian freedom. To be sure, no one can gain acceptance with God by one's own conduct, however correct it may be; but it would be dangerous to put God's patience to the test. By a casual manner of life that thoughtlessly shrugs off the command of God and adopts the seductive view that once the gift of salvation is received it can never be lost, salvation can be gambled away and lost, with the condemning judgment of God the only result (1 Cor. 10:1–13).

Disputed questions emerged not only within the gentile Christian congregations, but also especially in those meetings where Jewish and gentile Christians lived together. They had to make clear how they should come to terms with the instructions of the Torah. No one ever doubted that the commandments of the Decalogue remained in force. But the question still remained how the actual law of the Old Testament should be evaluated. While these laws continued to be observed in the strict Jewish-Christian circles, in the large Christian community of Antioch a different attitude obviously became dominant. Here Jewish and gentile Christians found themselves participating in the same table fellowship. Peter too joined in this fellowship during his stay in Antioch—obviously on the basis that in Christ Jews and gentiles are all one (Gal. 2:12). But then a delegation arrived in Antioch from James, the Lord's brother in Jerusalem. They objected to the new practice in Antioch and apparently claimed that it endangered the continuing relationship between Jewish Christians and the Jewish community in Antioch, since ignoring the ritual laws made association with other Jews at least difficult, if not impossible. This argument must have made such a strong impression that along with others, Peter too backed away from his previous practice and withdrew from the table fellowship with gentile Christians. Paul called this an act of hypocrisy. In fact this attitude leads to the inevitable result that gentile Christians could only be admitted to table fellowship with Jews when they had made the adjustment from their side and yielded to the commands of Torah—that is, they must become Jews before they could become Christians. Perhaps Peter had not really seen this conclusion clearly. But Paul pointed out to him the effect of his vacillating conduct—namely, that he was compelling gentile Christians to adopt the Jewish ritual laws as their own as the condition for the unity of the church (Gal. 2:11–14).

The critical standard of judgment proclaimed by Paul in the conflict at Antioch is "the truth of the gospel" (Gal. 2:5, 14): the only reasonable conclusion that can be drawn from the liberating message of the cross and resurrection of Jesus. The truth of the gospel permits no other condition for membership in the Christian community than accepting the gospel in faith and incorporation into the body of Christ through baptism. With this criterion as the standard, the question of the shape of the Christian life must be decided. No legal prescriptions are to be fulfilled as a condition of salvation. Rather, the justification declared and accepted on the basis of Christ's saving act is appropriated by faith alone (Gal. 2:15–21). For the sake of the love of Christ, one can become a Jew to Jews and a gentile to gentiles, in order to win as many as possible. But neither the one manner of life nor the other may be required as an indispensable condition of salvation or admission to the Christian community (1 Cor. 9:19–23). Both the Christian attitude toward the law of Israel received in the Bible and the assignment given by the Christian's own ethical code are to be clarified only in the light of the truth of the gospel. Included with this answer is the decision that the Christian churches could not be understood as Jewish sects — even if in many places in the diaspora more liberal attitudes were advocated than in the home territory of Judaism, attitudes that Christians could have adopted as their own. Christianity understood itself as the new people of God, a people that lived in the conviction that the promises of the Scripture were fulfilled in Christ. The conduct of Christians would therefore be determined neither by consideration for what was written in the law nor by tactical considerations; they must rather be guided by the truth of the gospel alone, by which Jews and gentiles are bound together as members of the one community of Jesus Christ.

Although finally the Pauline decision was of pioneering significance for the way the early Christian mission developed, it was still the case that mediating and compromising solutions were attempted, according to which the fulfilling of a minimal list of ritual laws was required, as was done in a comparable manner in the Jewish diaspora. According to the "Apostolic Decree," the gentile Christian communities were supposed to be willing to observe certain regulations in order to make possible table fellowship with Jewish Christians: no meat sacrificed to idols was to be eaten, no marriage with a close relative was to be contracted, no meat was to be eaten not slaughtered in accord with the ritual rules acknowledged in the Jewish community, and no food was to be eaten that contained blood (Acts 15:20, 29). These prescriptions were originally in force only in a particular region, in order to facilitate Jewish and gentile Christians living together in Antioch, Syria, and Cilicia. The impression that the "Apostolic Decree" was a fundamental principle binding on the whole church was first given by the Lukan editorial work.

After a while this regulation became meaningless in any case, because the life-style of the gentile Christian congregation came to differ so radically from that of the Jewish Christian congregation. The decisive change of attitude brought about by the Pauline theology had the result that it was no longer a matter of observing certain prescriptions of the ritual law in order to make possible fellowship between Jewish and gentile Christians. They recognized each other as united in Christ by faith. The "Western Text" takes account of the changed situation by transforming the content of the "Apostolic Decree" from ritual regulations into a list of ethical instructions. Now the requirements to which gentile Christians must conform read "keep yourselves from the defilements of idols, immorality, and blood," understood as prohibition of idolatry, sexual immorality, and murder. The problem of whether the observance of ritual prescriptions is to be required of all members of the community has receded into the background, so that the later tradition was aware only of ethical principles that were universally applicable.

In congregations in which weighty problems of Christian life-style became controversial, groups of "strong" and "weak" stood over against each other. Thus in Corinth opposite answers were given to the question of whether Christians could eat meat from animals that had been slaughtered in the pagan temples and that had therefore at least indirectly been associated with the worship of idols (1 Cor. 8–10; cf. above, pp. 91–92). The apostle agrees in principle with the point of view of the "strong." Because the Christian knows that the whole earth belongs to the Lord and there can be no other gods beside God, there need be no anxious questioning about the source of food and drink set forth on the table, for there is no need to worry about having to distinguish between "clean" and "unclean."

The adoption of this fundamental position, however, does not mean that the issue under consideration had been resolved. For it was clear to the apostle that not all members of the community saw themselves in the position to make decisions and live by them in such a liberated, uninhibited manner. There were people who continued to feel themselves bound by the Jewish dietary laws. Others had not been able completely to lay aside the idea held over from their pagan past that the "gods" had demonic powers at their disposal that could continue to pose a dangerous threat. They were afraid that making too free a use of Christian freedom might land them back in the realm where demonic powers were still effective.

The apostle takes these considerations seriously and thus addresses himself to the "strong." Since love is a higher value than knowledge, it constitutes the primary criterion by which a difference of opinion such as the one upsetting the Corinthian church is to be resolved. Not the independent value of one's own opinion, however good the grounds for it may be, but one consideration alone is the decisive factor in providing a real resolution for disputed issues: what truly serves the edification of the community.

What the apostle Paul discussed in 1 Corinthians in debate with concrete questions that had arisen is presented in his letter to the church in Rome as a matter of principle. There too "weak" and "strong" stand over against each other. The one side feels obligated to observe ascetic regulations and to abstain from eating flesh. The other side does not share these convictions. Paul permits neither a disdaining dismissal of those who refuse to eat meat, nor may their scruples be elevated to a rule that all must obey. Rather, "those who eat must not despise those who abstain, and those who abstain must not pass judgment on those who eat; for God has welcomed them" (Rom. 14:3). That means that all must have due regard for the others and not selfishly assert only their own view. For however the one or the other decides, one must proceed on the assumption that each has resolved on a certain course of conduct as a way of expressing thanks to God. The decisive criterion is again given through the christological confession: "We do not live to ourselves, and we do not die to ourselves" (Rom. 14:7). For after all—the pointed conclusion is drawn—Christ both died and lived again, that he might be Lord of both the dead and the living (14:9).

This christologically oriented argumentation means no relativizing of ethical decisions by leaving them to the discretion of a person's arbitrary judgment. On the contrary, it intends to set boundaries both to legalistic concerns and to an understanding of Christian freedom that has not yet been thought through, so that the way Christians decide to live their lives on such issues will be guided by the one consideration of how it affects the brother or sister "for whom Christ died (Rom. 14:15). Thus the appropriate rule to help in the resolution of concrete problems is, "Welcome one another, therefore, just as Christ has welcomed you, for the glory of God" (Rom. 15:7).

Paul seeks to make clear to the church that being a Christian is dependent neither on attention to dietary laws nor on the opposite attitude of "freedom," but exclusively on the grace of Christ by which he has accepted us. Confessing faith in him sets the conscience free from scruples at the same time it binds it in love. A disputed ethical point cannot then be decided by the triumph of the so-called strong over those regarded as weak. Rather, only the awareness that Christ died and rose for us all will help one to give attention to feelings and thoughts of others as one charts one's own course of action. This is what enables them to remain together in one fellowship guided by love, even though differences of opinion and practice on disputed issues continue to prevail. Uniform practice on such issues is not the goal to be sought after, but mutual respect must determine the fellowship in which each defends the other's rights. For the one Spirit is manifest in a fullness of gifts and possibilities and at the same time holds all members of the church together in the one body of Christ. All must listen to each other and attempt to be of the same mind and to show the same kind of love to each other (Phil. 2:2).

Not all ethical problems that were discussed in the early Christian congregations arrived at clear solutions. In the broad range of ethical issues that had to be responsibly thought through, there were many areas in which a variety of answers could appear as possibilities, or where finally only a discretionary decision could be made, the validity of which of course had to be tested later. The New Testament documents contain several examples of such consideration, which carefully weigh the different aspects of the issue in order by careful testing of arguments and counter-arguments to find viable answers.

Thus, to name one example, it was a firm conviction of early Christian ethics that no one can be subject to two masters, and therefore one cannot serve both God and mammon (Matt. 6:24; Luke 16:13). But this did not mean that as a matter of principle all Christians must renounce claim to ownership of all personal property. To be sure, particular individuals can be challenged to leave everything and follow Christ (see above, pp. 47–49); but there is no general rule and no binding law put into effect. Rather, one must reflect on what the right use of goods and property would be from case to case, in order to enjoy the gifts of God with thanksgiving and to help others.

Another disputed problem concerned the question of whether Christians may get entangled in legal disputes. To be sure, early Christianity realized the value of the law in establishing and maintaining order (Rom. 13:1-7). But how should Christians conduct themselves when members of the church are involved with each other in a legal dispute? As a matter of principle – so the apostle Paul decided – Christians should be careful not to bring the disputes they have with each other before the secular courts (1 Cor. 6:1–8). For what a disgrace it is when fellow Christians bring a disputed case to court to be settled by unbelievers (1 Cor. 6:6)! With all due respect for the law, Christians must be asked to consider it better to suffer injustice than to do injustice (1 Cor. 6:7–8). Thereby a question is raised which must be decided from case to case by a careful weighing of various points of view. Even when in emergencies disputes between Christians must be settled by an arbitration board established in the church, this must not be only a court of last resort. Both parties should rather consider whether they are able to renounce the pursuit of their own rights and to accept the experience of injustice for the sake of love.

A third realm in which ethical decisions can be a matter of one's own discretion pertains to the choice between marriage and remaining single. The apostle Paul asks them to consider whether it would not be more right, in the stressful situation in which they lived (the distress of the eschatological woes, in Paul's view) to be bound by as few earthly responsibilities as possible, but to live exclusively for the Lord (1 Cor. 7). To this extent, and from his own point of view, he can agree with the thesis advocated in Corinth that it would be good for a man not to touch a woman (1 Cor. 7:1; see above, p. 118). Still, this statement functions only as advice, not as a binding rule. For whoever goes ahead and marries his fiancée does well; but the one who refrains from marriage does better (1 Cor. 7:38). The "better" conduct here described is not thereby designated as belonging to a higher level of ethics; nor is any devaluation placed on the positive valuation of the "good" marriage. But Christians concerned to make the right decision must take into consideration that the time is short and the form of this world is already passing away (1 Cor. 7:29–31). It is neither an ascetic tendency nor a disdaining of the goodness of creation that determines the apostle's judgment on marriage matters, but the one consideration of how to live one's life in this time of special distress, so that before all else it is a matter of doing the will of the Lord. In all this Paul is clear that not all Christians have received the same gifts, and he acknowledges that to him the gift of celibacy has been given, without having to understand this life-style as a matter of legal constraint. Even if he might wish that all were like himself, still he knows very well that all have their own gift from God, one of one kind and one of another (1 Cor. 7:7). It can thus happen that different Christian people, each with well-thought out reasons, can come to different conclusions, without having to question the sincerity of each other's faith.

This kind of discretionary decision, such as the choice between being married or single presented as a legitimate example by Paul, is of course not intended to open the door to all conceivable answers to ethical problems. However one responds to the choice between getting married or remaining unmarried, still all Christians must be clear that they may not use their bodies in just any way, for they belong to the Lord (1 Cor. 6:13). When Paul concludes his comment with the complementary pair that just as the body is for the Lord, so the Lord is for the body, he is explicitly emphasizing that it is precisely in the bodily existence of Christians that Christ wants to see his lordship realized. Christians must constantly manifest the way in which their lives are strictly determined in this regard, whether they are single or married. Where it is acknowledged that a variety of life-styles is accepted, no one may be absolutized. Rather, each person must respect the other's decision and the reason for it, and in this light reflect critically on their own conduct.

Even when individual members of the congregation have thought through the various possibilities and come to different decisions, all are urged to have the same mind (τὸ αὐτὸ φρονεῖν Rom. 15:5 [NRSV "live . . . in harmony"]), so that with one voice they may glorify God. The variety of discretionary decisions can thus never claim a timeless validity for "the" Christian way of life, but remain related to the particular situations in and for which they were made. They make clear that Christian ethics represent neither a rigid set of norms nor a network of casuistic deductions, but that the meaning of God's holy and just command is to be thought through from case to case in the light of the gospel, in order to do justice to its truth in concrete decisions and acts.

Right ethical conduct and right confession of faith are necessarily interdependent; neither may be separated from the other nor played off against the other. The mistaken concept of an "ethical heresy" could suggest the equally incorrect idea that it would be possible to conduct oneself in a heretical manner by what one did or left undone, while continuing to preserve an orthodox confession of faith. But right conduct is always oriented to the truth of the gospel. Lack of interest in the theological truth of the confession of faith reveals a misunderstanding of the obligatory character of such truth for fashioning life. Heretical teaching and heretical conduct have this common root in the denial of the grace of God, so that in an "ethical heresy" a lapse from authentic faith is always visible. Where the command of God is disdained, it is not only a matter of the deviations from the right path that is visible in the foreground, as though they were unrelated to faith. Rather, the truth of the gospel must be emphatically recalled to memory. This is the truth recognized by the Reformation, which declares that the Christian is a free human being in all respects, subject to no one—through faith—and at the same time a ministering servant in all respects, subject to everyone—through love.

Suggestions for Further Reading

Achtemeier, P. *The Quest for Unity in the New Testament Church.* Philadelphia: Fortress Press, 1987.

Catchpole, D. R. "Paul, James and the Apostolic Decree." *New Testament Studies* 23 (1976–77): 428–44.

Farmer, W. R. "Peter and Paul." In *Jesus and the Gospels,* pp. 50–62. Philadelphia: Fortress Press, 1982.

Karris, R. J. "Romans 14:1–15:43 and the Occasion of Romans." In *The Romans Debate,* pp. 75–99. Karl P. Donfried, ed. Minneapolis: Augsburg, 1977.

Lambrecht, J. "The Line of Thought in Gal. 2.14b–21." *New Testament Studies* 24 (1977–78): 484–95.

Luedemann, G. *Opposition to Paul in Jewish Christianity.* Minneapolis: Fortress Press, 1989.

Meeks, W. A. *The First Urban Christians: The Social World of the Apostle Paul,* pp. 111–13, 117–25. New Haven and London: Yale University Press, 1983.

Munro, W. *Authority in Paul and Peter. The Identification of a Pastoral Stratum in the Pauline Corpus and 1 Peter.* Cambridge: Cambridge University Press, 1983.

Schmithals, W. *Gnosticism in Corinth.* Nashville: Abingdon, 1971.

Tyson, J. B. "The Emerging Church and the Problem of Authority in Acts." *Interpretation* 42 (1988): 132–45.

Catechesis and Catechism

C atechetical instruction, in which rules of ethical conduct were transmitted and explained, existed in early Christianity from the very beginning (see above, pp. 1–3). There is no basis in the clear statements of New Testament texts for the idea that the formation of a Christian ethic did not occur during the earliest period that still expected the soon coming of the parousia, but only after this expectation had receded and it was clear that Christians would have to find their way in a world that was not going to go away. Eschatology and ethics are by no means mutually exclusive—as already Jesus' call to repentance shows (see above, pp. 39–42)—neither do they merely stand beside each other as unrelated items. It is rather the case that the eschatological proclamation that witnesses to Christ as the coming Lord at the same time calls us to live as children of light in the dawning new age. The eschatological hope thus does not make ethical instruction superfluous, but rather makes it the more urgent. The enthusiastic movements that repeatedly appeared represented a temptation to deny the ethical seriousness of Christianity or to pass it by in the name of a presumed Christian freedom: such arguments represented a false understanding of the nature of Christian existence. For those who confess Christ as Lord cannot live their lives according to their own whims, but must harken to the word of this Lord.

In early Christian teaching, moral conduct was neither required in order to come nearer the ideal of the self-sufficient, well-developed personality, nor in order to satisfy legal requirements that would be able to stand before God's penetrating eyes in the judgment. It is thus not the intention of catechetical instruction to give direction and motivation to human striving and ambition. The ethical conduct of Christians is rather to be thought of as the living out of discipleship that gives honor to the Lord and by its own weak deeds seeks to offer the testimony of praise to him.

Since the moral instruction of the churches could rely on a rich treasure of traditions, which it had to view in a new perspective and reformulate in the light of the gospel, the developing early Christian ethic soon took on a more fixed form. Its contents, which are described in the individual chapters of this book, may be drawn together in a relatively compact summary that expresses the common Christian convictions. The absolute validity of the love commandment as that which determines everything else is impressed on all forms of early Christian catechesis. To love the neighbor as oneself—this instruction is no longer limited to those who are fellow citizens of the same nation or to members of a special group distinct from the world in general. To be sure, love can also be defined as "familial love" (see above, pp. 166–68), but this does not designate any program of separation from others or exclusion of them, but rather points to the concretizing of the love command in the immediate sphere of one's life. Since love is to be shown even to the enemy regardless of consequences, it respects none of the barriers that have been erected to separate people from each other.

God created humanity as man and woman—not so that one would dominate the other, but so that they would turn to each other in partnership, complement each other, help, and stand by each other. This orientation of human existence, already given in creation, is fully revealed in the Christian confession of Christ. Just as men and women respond in the same way to Jesus' word and find themselves united in discipleship to him, so male and female are one in Christ (see above, pp. 97–100). Neither has a head start on the other that would confer priority or a position of higher rank. Men and women receive the salvation given in Christ in the same way, only by faith that trusts in God's mercy. Since they are enabled to perceive their participation in the new creation that has come in Christ, they relate to one another in love and know how to form a community characterized by partnership.

It could be the case, of course, that the instructions specifically directed to the mutual relations and responsibilities of men and women are comprised entirely of traditional statements taken over from the social customs of the ancient world. Their adoption by early Christianity would not mean that absolute validity or permanent character would be attributed to them. They were accepted as tried and true guides to right conduct in that situation, but the authority finally to determine one's life belongs to the Lord alone, with all the social relations of any particular cultural situation to be placed in his service (see above, pp. 141–42).

The discussion concerning the renewing power that derives from love also includes instructions on the relation of masters and slaves. Under the prevailing law slaves were considered not persons but property over which the master had unlimited authority. Early Christian ethics acknowledged the existing social order, but transformed the manner in which masters and slaves lived together by teaching that both masters and slaves were bound by the commandment of love that allowed them to relate to each other as brothers and sisters in the one family of God (see above, pp. 143–45). In this regard also, early Christianity manifested none of the characteristic features of a political revolution. But by their confidence that love was capable of transforming social and interpersonal human relationships from the ground up, they pointed to the way that would in fact eventuate in a revolutionary change in the social order.

The statements of early Christian moral instruction on work and vocation correspond to those that were generally prevalent at the time. Each one is called to fulfill the assignment designated by the role in which society has cast them. In order to earn a living all should give themselves to the work of this appointed slot. The role model provided by the example of the apostle himself, who does not work for pay from the churches, but earns his living as a tent maker or carpet weaver, makes clear that no member of the community is permitted to sit with hands in lap and be unwilling to work. The day's duties are to be accepted and done with matter-of-fact realism, so that everyone can make a decent living. Every Christian has an assigned job to do in the place where the call of the gospel has encountered them, and in that set of circumstances is to live worthily of the calling (see above, pp. 164–65).

Possessions and property were not subjected to any fundamentally critical judgment in early Christianity, but were rather regarded as a matter of their relative value. There was no general demand that Christians must renounce their property. Yet money and goods were only rightly used when they serve to manifest deeds of love. Christians are therefore expected to stand by the poor, to ameliorate social distress according to their ability, and in those who need their help to recognize the face of Christ himself.

In early Christianity the opinion was repeatedly expressed that true Christians should turn away from the world and divest themselves of all their possessions. But these ascetic tendencies were decisively rejected, for renunciation of one's property must not be done as though one could thereby achieve salvation.

Early Christian ethical instruction shared the high value Judaism had already placed on the giving of alms and a willingness to help the poor. On the other hand, in many Christian communities a tendency soon emerged to pay special attention to the rich and people of high rank, and to give them a special place in the congregation's seating arrangements. In opposition to such views not only were alarms sounded against the danger of riches, but warnings were issued against an attitude that surreptitiously casts longing looks at human prestige and external success.

Christians must give due regard to governmental authority, and respect its work in the preservation of law and order. In this regard too, early Christian catechesis follows the teaching that had already been developed in the synagogue (see above, pp. 131–33). Civil order is established by God's will, so that people can live together in a context of justice, where good is rewarded and evil is punished. Christians are called to fulfill their civil responsibilities like everyone else, to pay taxes and tolls, and to follow government regulations—so long as these do not violate God's own command. Should the civil power claim divine status for itself and demand the corresponding worship from its subjects, then Christians must remember that there is only one who is king of kings and lord of lords, and that they belong to him and not to any earthly sovereign. But even this threatened danger, as anticipated in the Apocalypse (see above, pp. 194–95), changes nothing with regard to the generally positive evaluation of civil government advocated throughout the ethical instruction of the early Christian communities.

Wherever Christians are subject to suffering, there they are encouraged by being pointed to their suffering Lord. The external troubles and distress to which they are subject, the misunderstanding and ridicule they received from outsiders, must not cause them to go astray in their faith or even bring them into the temptation to abandon the church altogether. In their suffering they can rather experience the loving hand of God, who guides the community and will not let them fall (see above, pp. 188–89). It is precisely in hard times that the truth of faith can be held fast in the confident hope that it is God who sets both a limit and a goal to the suffering.

While in the Hellenistic world a determining significance for ethics is attributed to the concept of virtue or "excellence" (NRSV) (ἀρετή), which had also had found a place in the moral instruction of the synagogue, the word and concept plays almost no role in the New Testament writings. The apostle Paul speaks once, and then almost incidentally, of "virtue" (ἀρετή) as he introduces it as one of several items on a list: "Whatever is true, whatever is honorable, whatever is just, whatever is pure, whatever is pleasing, whatever is commendable, if there is any excellence (ἀρετή), and if there is anything worthy of praise, think about these things" (Phil. 4:8). "Excellence" does not here head the list, but is one item among others chosen to describe how Christians should focus their critical gaze on the surrounding world as they attempt to sort out what in it could be a factor in the shaping of their own lives.

Only in the latest writing of the New Testament, 2 Peter, is "virtue" (ἀρετή ["goodness" NRSV]) named, in the context of admonitions directed to the church, as they are instructed to supplement their faith with virtue, and their virtue with knowledge (2 Pet. 1:5). Two verses earlier it had been said that God has called us through [NRSV "by"] God's own glory and excellence (ἀρετή). This Hellenistic manner of expression is used to speak of God's power, by which God makes the divine glory known and by which God deals with humanity (cf. 1 Pet. 2:9). To this extent the concept of "virtue" or "excellence" is used in this context in a sense determined by the presuppositions of the Old Testament. But the specific reference to virtue as something that is to be preserved by faith indicates that in this passage Christian ethical exhortation is dependent on current Hellenistic ideas in a way not found elsewhere in early Christian catechesis.

Even when early Christian exhortation makes regular use of the "virtue catalogues" and "vice catalogues" (see above, pp. 83–84), these lists are never organized under the heading of "virtue" (ἀρετή). The designation of these catalogues as "virtue catalogues," as has become common in recent exegetical discussion, must not therefore encourage the misunderstanding that these lists are used in the New Testament to advocate a doctrine of "virtue." Their purpose is rather to show, on the one side, the kind of conduct that is to be avoided at all costs, and on the other hand to illustrate some of the characteristics of Christian life in the Spirit as it fulfills the love commandment. Early Christian ethical instruction has no interest in encouraging a view of ethics as the development of one's self-understanding or the unfolding of one's own self-realization, but wants to show how

Christians can live and act in a way that brings praise and honor to God.

If Christians have received the wonderful gift of God's peace, then the whole of their lives must stand under the sign of this experience. They know that those who make peace have been blessed by their Lord (Matt. 5:9), and are thus intent on living in peace with all other human beings, to the extent that it is in their power (Rom. 12:18). Although the members of the early Christian congregations could hardly have had any influence on the political events of their times, still the way they confessed their faith and lived it out in their daily lives made a testimony to the value and importance of peace—a testimony that had an increasing effect on their environment.

When the New Testament writings sometimes refer incidentally to the "ways in Christ" (1 Cor. 4:17; see above, p. 82) or to a few "basic teachings" (Heb. 6:1–2; see above, p. 126), one should not draw the conclusion that already in the time of Paul there was an early Christian catechism, the didactic content of which could be presupposed by the New Testament letters. The development was rather in the other direction: in the first and second Christian generations, traditional ethical instruction that was already available in the environment was often adopted and given a new form. Thus statements from the Old Testament were combined with Hellenistic popular philosophy, and Jewish proverbs were combined with words of Jesus, to make series of affirmations portraying the manifold nature of the Christians' job of expressing their faith in everyday life. Both the Letter of James (see above, pp. 171–78) and the Sermon on the Mount (see above, pp. 61–73) show, each in its own way, how catechetical instruction took on the traits of the later Christian catechisms, in order to impress Christian moral teaching on the mind and make it easily memorable.

From this catechetical tradition there gradually emerged the outline of a catechism that is not yet documented in the New Testament, but is already present in the writings of the apostolic fathers (Did. 1–6; Barn. 18–20; see above, pp. 87–88). Thus the Ten Commandments are bound together with the love commandment, the normative validity of the Golden Rule is combined with other sayings of Jesus, with an eschatological section at the end to underscore the obligation to live the Christian life. But moral instruction as communicated in the early Christian congregations had not yet taken on the form of a catechism with a fixed outline. Its goal was not to develop a new law, but to carry out the mission with which Christians were charged: to live worthy of the Lord and appropriate to the gospel.

Suggestions for Further Reading

Bauckham, R. J. *Jude, 2 Peter*. Waco: Word, 1983.

Brown, R. E., and J. P. Meier. "The Didache." In *Antioch and Rome*, pp. 81–84. New York/Ramsey: Paulist Press, 1983.

Daniélou, J. *The Theology of Jewish Christianity*. London: Darton, Longman, & Todd, 1964.

Daube, D., and E. G. Selwyn. *The First Epistle of St. Peter*. Grand Rapids: Baker, 1981, reprint.

Davies, W. D. *Paul and Rabbinic Judaism*, pp. 132–36. 4th ed. Philadelphia: Fortress Press, 1980.

Dodd, C. H. *Gospel and Law*. Cambridge: Cambridge University Press, 1951.

Grant, R. M. *Greek Apologists of the Second Century*. Philadelphia: Westminster, 1988.

McDonald, J. I. H. *Kerygma and Didache*. Cambridge: Cambridge University Press, 1980.

Martin, R. A., and J. Elliott. *James, I Peter, II Peter, Jude*. Minneapolis: Augsburg, 1982.

Neyrey, J. H. "The Form and Background of the Polemic in 2 Peter." *Journal of Biblical Literature* 99 (1980): 407–31.

Faith and Action

Faith in the crucified and risen Christ will come to expression in deeds of love (Gal. 5:6). Faith is therefore fulfilled in action, and action derives its motivation and orientation from the power of the confessed faith. The freedom of faith, which proves itself in loving service, is the basis for that reasonable judgment that is capable of avoiding both skeptical resignation and overconfidence, since it knows how to make an objective evaluation as to which of the many insights provided by traditional moral regulations and experience are helpful and worthy of attention.

According to the common testimony of all New Testament documents, the essence of Christian ethics is to be found neither in an ethical program nor in a plan for Christian transformation of the world, but in the modeling before the world of the meaning of following Christ as it finds its distinctive form within the conditions of this world – guided by being alert to the constant question of what is to be regarded as the will of God here and now, in each individual situation. The Ten Commandments and the love commandment are considered of unquestionable validity – not as a way that one could follow for the sake of finding salvation, but as an expression of what God's will requires in order to glorify God in thankful praise. Alongside the positive declaration of the love commandment, which places no limitation on the act of human self-giving, the primarily negative restrictions of the Decalogue continue to be important. For it is often easier to say what absolutely must not be done, on the basis of a clear "thou shalt not," than to determine unambiguously what is the right thing to do in this or that case. When trying to distinguish what must be done and what must be avoided, the love commandment offers a clarifying point of orientation – not only as the keynote of moral instruction in the early Christian communities, but in the answering of current problems.

To have experienced the love of God in Christ means to know that one has been accepted for Christ's sake. He has turned toward us in grace, without our being worthy or without having fulfilled conditions laid down in advance. That does not mean, however, that everything continues just as it has been, for henceforth the life of the Christian stands under the determining orders of discipleship to Christ, who commands us to resist sin and calls us to loving service. Christians must therefore live their lives in the faith that Christ is their righteousness and their sanctification, but also in the awareness that the gift [*die Gabe*] of new life given them contrary to all expectation also represents an assignment [*die Aufgabe*] that alone determines their future path. Through Christ they have experienced the joyous liberation from the godless claims of this world, to a free and thankful service to his creatures (Thesis 2 of the Barmen Declaration of 1934). Early Christian ethics attained its unchangeable character from the conviction that discipleship to Christ is to be lived out in ethical action—namely, in confession of the crucified and risen Lord, in the certainty that the essential character of this world is passing away, but that believers have their citizenship in heaven, and in the service of compassionate love put into effect amid life in the everyday world.

From the writings of the New Testament no "early Christian ethic" can be derived in the sense of a system of universally valid general truths, for ethics had its place in the context of preaching and teaching within the churches. That Christians had to do what is good and right was a matter of instruction given along the way. But the question of just what this "good and right" in fact was, had to be raised and decided time and again in careful searching for the will of God and in circumspect probing of traditional teaching.

Maxims of ethical instruction were minted before, alongside, and after the beginning of Christianity in a variety of forms, and were always couched in such a way as to find the broadest possible endorsement. They obtained this endorsement on the basis of their inherent power of persuasion addressed to the common human sense of rational judgment. They therefore had to be so formulated that they not only provided illumination to those who belonged to a specific group or shared a certain perspective, but had to be seen as logically persuasive in and of themselves. A theological ethic of the New Testament must therefore also be concerned to present such evidence of its own validity, for theological reflection on ethics shares this general concern for identifying the good and bringing it to realization.

Ethical concern is a general phenomenon of human experience, but this concern for ethics experiences an essential deepening in the context of Christian proclamation. Nevertheless, the Christian message addresses human beings as sinners embraced by the mercy of God, who receive the meaning of their life not by their own attainment, but by God's grace alone. Not by their works, but by the acceptance announced in the gospel that grants them freedom for Christ's sake, do they receive the grounding of their being, the true support for living their lives. It therefore follows that the specifically Christian character of ethical instruction does not mean an increase in the number or intensity of commands or prohibitions, but in a concentration on the one fundamental commandment of love, which receives its motive power from the experience of having received God's own love. That love that does not seek its own advantage, but the good of the other, places itself as the critical orientation point for evaluating the variety of traditional ethical maxims in circulation. In so doing it in no way feels excused from the general requirement of making the validity of ethical statements understandable to people in general by means of rational evidence, with the goal of having them accepted as widely as possible. The good reputation that the early Christians enjoyed among outsiders is documented by the persuasive impression that the ethical instruction of the churches and the way Christians have conducted themselves in their relations with each other made on the world around them.

The early Christian ethic, as both taught by the churches and practiced by early Christians, was noted by the surrounding world with increasing respect. The early Christian apologists, who wanted to make clear in the critical forum of their contemporaries both the truth of the Christian faith and the sincerity of Christian lives, pointed to their straightforward and natural conduct as a testimony to the validity of their way of life that spoke for itself.

About the middle of the second century C.E., Aristides, a Christian philosopher from Athens, dedicated an apology to the emperor Antoninus Pius (possibly already written in the time of Hadrian), in which the life of Christians is described as follows:

> They have impressed the commandments of their Lord Jesus Christ on their hearts, and they live by them, just as they live in the hope of the resurrection of the dead and the life of the world to come. They do not commit adultery or visit prostitutes, nor do they bear false witness. They do not covet the possessions of others, they honor their parents, they love their neighbors. They judge by the standards of justice. What they

do not want others to do to them, they do not do to others. When they are mistreated, they respond with good words and win their opponents over to become friends. They are even eager to do good to their enemies. They are gentle and kind. They will have nothing to do with anything illegal or impure. They do not neglect widows, nor are they harsh with orphans. Those who have help those who have not, with no reproach to those in need. When they meet a foreigner, they take him into their own home, as glad to see him as if he were a real brother. They call each other brother and sister, not as a matter of flesh and blood, but to express their relationship in the Spirit [15:3-7].

This list presupposes a catalogue of ethical instruction that is acknowledged in the churches as prescribed conduct, the validity of which is self-evident. The Decalogue, the Golden Rule, the love commandment, and sentences from the Sermon on the Mount are all combined. By sketching the common life of the churches and the basic moral ground rules by which they live, in such an unpretentious manner that must impress anyone who observes them, the apologist seeks to strengthen the statement made by the faith and life of the Christian community.

Similar words were used in the Letter to Diognetus, a pamphlet from the pen of an unknown author toward the end of the second century C.E. who presents an impressive testimony of early Christian apologetic by describing the life of the small Christian communities who find themselves in the midst of a world that does not share their faith:

For Christians cannot be distinguished from the rest of the human race by country or language or customs. . . . Yet, although they live in Greek and barbarian cities alike, as each man's lot has been cast, and follow the customs of the country in clothing and food and other matters of daily living, at the same time they give proof of the remarkable and admittedly extraordinary constitution of their own commonwealth. They live in their own countries, but only as aliens. They have a share in everything as citizens, and endure everything as foreigners. Every foreign land is their fatherland, and yet for them every fatherland is a foreign land. They marry, like everyone else, and they beget children, but they do not cast out their offspring. They share their board with each other, but not their marriage bed. It is true that they are "in the flesh," but they do not live "according to the flesh." They busy themselves on earth, but their citizenship is in heaven. They obey the established laws, but in their own lives they go far beyond what the laws require. They love all men, and by all men are persecuted. They are unknown, and still they are condemned; they are put to death, and yet they are brought to life. They are poor, and yet they make many rich; they are completely destitute, and yet they enjoy complete abundance. They are dishonored, and in their very dishonor are glorified; they are defamed, and are vindicated. They are reviled, and yet they bless; when they are affronted, they still pay due respect. When they do good, they are punished as evildoers; undergoing punishment, they rejoice because they are brought to life ([5:1, 4–16]; translation by Cyril C. Richardson, *Early Christian Fathers*. Library of Christian Classics. Philadelphia: Westminster Press, 1953).

Just as Hellenistic-Jewish authors, with a barely restained pride, could point out that in practically every city of the Roman Empire small Jewish communities were present whose members conducted themselves as loyal Roman subjects on the one hand, but lived their lives according to God's law on the other, so also the unknown author of the Letter to Diognetus speaks of the early Christian communities that were to be found in many different places. They fulfill their civic responsibilities, but at the same time are aware of their heavenly citizenship. The influence of Paul's phraseology is already seen in this description (Phil. 3:20), especially in the juxtaposition of glory that is experienced precisely in suffering (1 Cor. 6:9–10).

The Jewish example is followed by the Christians, in that they take God's commandment seriously, respect the gift of life, and do not expose their newborn infants (see above, p. 23), think of purity as a moral obligation, and seek to style their lives in an exemplary fashion. A specifically Christian understanding is expressed in the fact that the members of the community, in an awareness that their true citizenship is in heaven, know how to bear up under discrimination and even persecution, doing good with a love that never gets tired and quits, without being disconcerted by the injustice they have to endure. The adoption of current ethical maxims that had already been developed in the Hellenistic synagogue, and the Christian reinterpretation of traditional material are bound together in a harmonious description of the Christian life as sketched in the Letter to Diognetus.

Even if this presentation of early Christian ethics is to some extent an idealized picture, it still reflects the effect that was produced by the way the early Christians lived out their ethics. Because they had experienced in faith the liberation from legalism of whatever and had received the overpowering gift of divine grace, they could reflect soberly on the demands of the day, and put into practice their concern for the neighbor and their readiness for active help and pragmatic decision for the task at hand. If misunderstanding, discrimination, or even persecution did not have the power to extinguish love's perseverance, believers remained convinced that God's grace could not be won by a show of human strength, but experienced the amazing power of God precisely in its own weakness. Thus the ground was taken out from under every tendency to boast of one's own moral attainment. The common Christian understanding was that whoever would boast, could only boast in the Lord. From this conviction of faith, which served as the guideline for the way early Christians actually conducted their lives, there went forth a strong attractive power into the world of late antiquity, which learned more and more to recognize and then to adopt for themselves the unity of faith and life as it had been developed in the early Christian ethic.

Suggestions for Further Reading

Benko, S. *Pagan Rome and the Early Christians.* Bloomington: Indiana University Press, 1984.

Davies, W. D. "The Moral Teaching of the Early Church." In *Jewish and Pauline Studies,* pp. 278–88. Philadelphia: Fortress Press, 1984.

———. "The Relevance of the Moral Teaching of the Early Church." In *Jewish and Pauline Studies,* pp. 289–302. Philadelphia: Fortress Press, 1984.

Grant, R. *Greek Apologists of the Second Century,* pp. 36–39, 178–79. Philadelphia: Westminster Press, 1988.

Meeks, W. A. *The Moral World of the First Christians.* Philadelphia: Westminster Press, 1986.

Quasten, J. *Patrology,* Vol. I, pp. 191-95, 248-53. Westminster, Md.: Christian Classics, 1983 (reprint).

Verhey, A. *The Great Reversal: Ethics and the New Testament.* Grand Rapids: Wm. B. Eerdmans, 1984.

SCRIPTURE AND ANCIENT SOURCES

OLD TESTAMENT

APOCRYPHA AND PSEUDEPIGRAPHA

NEW TESTAMENT

Index

233

OTHER SCRIPTURE AND ANCIENT WRITINGS

Index

C—Classical Literature